GOD IN AFRICA

GOD
IN AFRICA

*Conceptions of God in African
Traditional Religion and Christianity*

by Malcolm J. McVeigh

CLAUDE STARK
Cape Cod, Massachusetts 02670 and Hartford, Vermont 05047

Library of Congress Catalog Card Number: 74–76005
International Standard Book Number: 0–89007–003–2

PRINTED IN THE UNITED STATES OF AMERICA

To my wife
MARION BOYD MCVEIGH

Acknowledgments

It is not possible to name personally all those who have contributed to the preparation of this book. A few, however, are deserving of particular mention.

I am deeply grateful to the Board of Global Ministries of the United Methodist Church for their financial support of my studies at Boston University School of Theology.

To Professors Per Hassing and Leroy Rouner goes a special vote of appreciation. Their advice and encouragement during my early research and at the later writing stage were a constant source of help and stimulation.

My thanks also extend to Dr. Claude Alan Stark, who urged me to publish this study and indeed has personally made this edition possible.

I offer my tribute to my African friends, to the Bantu people and their communities, from whom I learned of their culture and their conceptions of God.

Lastly, I would like to thank my wife and children for their forbearance, inspiration and assistance, without which this work would never have seen the light of day.

Appreciation is expressed to authors and publishers whose works have been quoted from or cited in this book. All such materials are indicated in the bibliography and notes.

Contents

Foreword

by *CLAUDE ALAN STARK*

God in Africa is conceived as dynamic, not static. As the Bible speaks of the living God (Matt. 16:16), the African speaks of God as a living Force, the ultimate Power in a universal hierarchy of power.[A] These two concepts of God, Being and Force, do not contradict but rather supplement each other, as do the world-views from which they arose.[B]

We have much of great value to learn from the African. For example, only recently in the post-modern scientific era have we become aware of the matter-energy-life-mind-spirit continuum as a proposition of empirical science,[C] while to the Bantu this has long been a part of his life experience. For him, all reality—animate, inanimate, and post-animate—represents different states of the same energy, with God the transcendent-immanent, all-powerful One who creates, regulates, permeates, harmonizes and supports all other forces in the universe, and yet as absolute Power is beyond them. God as Power is accorded personality and the whole universe is personal by analogy: a universe alive with personal forces. God is the ultimate Person, but people, like God, are forces that interact rather than beings that coexist. From this view springs the sense of Bantu community, a community of interrelationship of forces of persons and thoughts, animals and things, God and forefathers: a sense of community which we in ignorance call "tribalism."

Such a world-view was once incorrectly labeled "animism" by

hasty observers, and the term is still commonly used in describing African traditional religious experience. Now we must modify our attitude from one of condescension to appreciation for the Bantu's early perception of that which we are just now ourselves apprehending.

In recognizing that as Christians our own world-view must presently correspond with the findings of science yet maintain the biblical perspective, we may discover in the Bantu philosophy a treasury of insights that could, when assimilated, enable Christianity and science to converge more closely on fundamental issues.

Dr. McVeigh is among those Christian scholars from the Western world who approach the God of Africa with humility and reverence, and the Bantu people with an open spirit of respect and fellowship. Regretfully, such scholars have been few indeed, but the Bantu are patient with us, and this patience (Gal. 5:22) is itself now bearing fruit. Dr. McVeigh's work can thus be characterized as among the "first fruit" of both the emergence of our humility and the persistence of African patience.

Some important questions arising in response to such a study are as follows: How should traditional African religion be regarded by Christians? Should it be viewed only as a prelude to African Christianity (cf. Acts 14:17), or can it be approached as a religious force co-determinant of man's destiny with the other world religions, Islam, Judaism, Buddhism, Taoism and Brahmanical Hinduism, as well as the Christian faith? Otherwise stated, can the persuasive dialogue into which we as Christians must enter with non-Christian African communities generate a richer total religious experience for us as well as for them, as it is now doing and has done through history with the Muslim, Judaic, Buddhist, Taoist and Hindu communities?

Religious history shows that a persuasive interaction of the Christian with the non-Christian world has produced for Christianity not only its share of un-Christian accomplishments and more than its share of missionary accomplishments (with nearly one billion confessed Christians recorded in 1970), but also a wealth of insights into religion and life itself.

In this context, then, is African Traditional Religion a viable world religion on a par with the others, or is it an unwanted appendix in the right side of the Body of Christ, the Church universal, which should at all pains and costs be surgically removed?

Should the African really be treated on his own terms with respect, and his God too, or should he be regarded as in process of growing up to becoming a Christian?

These questions, it is submitted, are broader than the ground on which the Christian-Traditional African meeting takes place. They are questions which, like petulant boys, pull at our very coat-sleeves and beg us to look first within as Christians for greater self-understanding, and only then with clearer eyes without. Are we strong enough in our personal commitment to Christ, individually and collectively, to risk a prolonged look—even a glance—at the God of Africa? of India? of China? of the Islamic world?

Dr. McVeigh's best witness as a Christian and a missionary in Africa is that he has taken such a look, first through the eyes of Edwin W. Smith and then through his own. In the following pages he shares his vision with us, deserving for it a serious and grateful readership.

Preface
by *PER HASSING*

The author of the present volume, Malcolm J. McVeigh, brings a number of excellent if not unique qualities to the study of religion in Africa. As a missionary he lived and worked intimately with African people on the village level in several parts of the continent. He studied their religion and learned their way of thinking at first hand through the medium of their own language. This has been supplemented by an extensive and intensive academic study of the relevant literature available from several parts of the African continent, so that he is at home with all the major writers, their presuppositions and theories. The present volume testifies to his extensive knowledge.

He also brings to his task certain personal qualities which are not frequently met with in the scholarly world. His academic record testifies to his brilliance of mind, but one has to know him personally to become aware of the true humility found in him; and those who want to learn from the people in an African village have to be humble enough to bow the head in order to enter through the door of the kitchen. This Dr. McVeigh has done; and thereby he has learned to love Africa and its people, and to say, with the great Danish thinker and founder of the "people's high schools" in Denmark, N. F. S. Grundtvig, "That person has not yet lived who has understood what he has not first loved." The author of the present volume has that love.

The study of African religion in the now somewhat remote past suffered partly because of lack of real knowledge and factual information, and also because of the preconceived, often inadequate, notions of the earlier writers. The result was sometimes an inadequate, negative, or even false picture which saw little that was good in African religious life and thinking. But in recent years the pendulum has swung back and the descriptions given of the traditional religious life of Africans have sometimes consciously or unconsciously refused to deal with difficult or negative aspects of the subject. Dr. McVeigh's love for his subject and his objectivity help him to strike a balance between the two extremes. He does not hide what he considers to be defective or inadequate ideas in the African religious life. In the study of any religion, and in scholarly discussions about religious phenomena and their meanings, honesty and open-mindedness are required. Difficult areas must not be removed from serious discussion, and no good cause is served by pretending that difficult areas do not exist.

Dr. McVeigh has chosen to approach his subject through the mind of Edwin William Smith, who in his day was one of the greatest authorities on Africa. E. W. Smith was at home in African religion, general African history, African church history, African anthropology and languages. It is very fitting that Dr. McVeigh pays great tribute to that grand interpreter of Africa by examining one area of his thinking, namely, how Smith understood the African idea of God. It is to be hoped that Smith's other contributions to African studies will be subjected to similar scrutiny, perhaps in the framework of a biography.

In paying this tribute to his great predecessor, Dr. McVeigh does not overlook the weaknesses in Smith's thinking, one of the major ones being the philosophical framework in which he worked, namely, the idea of evolution in religion which he inherited mainly from late nineteenth and early twentieth century theoreticians in the study of religions. As we now know, a scholar like Smith would have been better off by not knowing their ivory-tower theories, which too frequently had little to do with the facts of religious life and thought. But this weakness, inherent in Smith's philosophical framework, should warn present-day students of the danger which may be hidden in the historical and philosophical biases of our own time. Some of the most dangerous scholars in the field are those who think they have no biases, or no theological or philosophical presuppositions.

This study is meritorious in yet another aspect. It takes seriously the idea of interpenetration of traditional African and Christian ideas of God. Africanists have been all too slow to recognize the fact that not only is Christianity now an African religion, but it is the most widely spread religion on the continent and will probably be the dominant one before the year 2000 A.D. This means at least two things: that the original African ideas of God will be changed or transformed by the power of the Christian influence, and that the Christian religious heritage will be interpreted in and through the African mind and the African religious experience. There is, however, an important factor in this interpenetration which sometimes is overlooked. The traditional African religion is an essentially oral tradition with no scriptural canon or credal forms against which it may be tested, while Christianity, although interpreted in and through the African mind and experience, will always be subjected to the test and correction of the Christian scriptures and the interrelationship of a now worldwide Christian community.

This last point makes it clear where the study of African religion should go in the future. There are few, if any, areas left where traditional African religious life has not been touched by the Western impact in general and the Christian impact in particular. African religion is in a stage of transition. It is this transition which must now be studied and recorded. Since Bengt Sundkler published his epochmaking work, *Bantu Prophets in South Africa* (London: Lutterworth Press, 1948), a number of studies have been made of the rich and varied African independent churches all over the continent. This is important. But at least of equal importance is the study of the religious life and thought of the millions of African Christians who belong to the more orthodox Catholic and Protestant churches. Where do these many Christians fit in the spectrum between the old African traditional religions and the thought-world of the New Testament? One interesting question here is whether one can discern a pattern of continuity or discontinuity between the past and the future. Will the old Roman saying, *"Ex Afrika semper aliquid novi,"* remain true?

Both the author and publisher of *God in Africa* are to be congratulated for bringing out this book.

Boston University School of Theology
Boston, Massachusetts
January 31, 1974.

1

Introduction

EDWIN W. SMITH: THE MAN

Christianity is growing at a faster rate in Africa than on any other continent today. The important studies of David Barrett of the Church Missionary Society in Kenya suggest the possibility that by the year 2000 A.D. Africa may boast the largest Christian population in the world.[1] This extraordinary growth prompts one to seek for reasons and specifically to ask whether the Christian conception of God may be an important factor in the acceptance of Christianity by so many Africans. One missionary statesman who shared this view was Edwin Williams Smith.

Edwin W. Smith[2] was born on September 7, 1876 at Aliwal North, Cape Colony, South Africa, where his father was a missionary and director of the Primitive Methodist work in Africa. John Smith was an able and sensitive missionary, a man with ecumenical vision and one who esteemed the African as a person of worth and dignity. He was a collector of books on Africa and had a scholarly bent which is evident in his published work, *Christ and Missions*,[3] the Hartley Lecture delivered to the Primitive Methodist Conference at Bristol in 1900. He also served for a period as president of the Primitive Methodist Church.

His son, Edwin, returned to England to pursue his studies and completed his academic work at Elmfield College, a boys' boarding school in York. Although he never attended university, he was a voracious reader and by his own efforts reached an extraordinarily high level of academic attainment. His passion for Africa was un-

1

abated in England. Forty years later he remembered that he had defended Stanley in a school debate.

In 1897 he was ordained a Methodist minister and left the following year for South Africa. The year 1898–99 was spent in Lesotho as a missionary apprentice among workers of the Paris Missionary Society. He confesses his indebtedness to the French missionary, Jacottet, who impressed on him the need to study the traditions of the African people, especially their myths, proverbs and folk tales. He was married in 1899 to Julia Fitch. Two children were born to the Smiths, a son and a daughter; the son died shortly after their arrival in Zambia.

In 1902, after a delay of more than two years at Aliwal North because of the Boer War, he moved to Zambia and began a highly significant ministry among the Ba-ila People, including the building of the mission station at Kasenga and important linguistic and ethnographical work. In 1914, a year before his departure to England, he was elected president of the first conference of Northern Rhodesian missionaries.

Smith served as a chaplain in World War I and hoped to return to Africa. Diabetes prevented him from obtaining medical clearance which was a bitter disappointment. He joined the staff of the British and Foreign Bible Society and worked successively as agent for Italy, secretary of Western Europe, literary superintendent and editorial superintendent until his retirement in 1939.[4]

During the war years 1939–42 he was a visiting professor of African history and anthropology at the Kennedy School of Missions of the Hartford Seminary Foundation and headed up the School of African Studies at Fisk University in 1943. There is a sense in which Edwin Smith never retired. He continued his scholarly endeavors until his death on December 23, 1957. His last book review was printed posthumously.

Edwin W. Smith was not accorded the world-wide acclaim that he merited. Those who have probed into the study of Africa know his work, but his reputation does not range far beyond this circle. Yet he was unquestionably a man of extraordinary accomplishments, "a leading authority on Africa"[5] to quote E. E. Evans-Pritchard. He was a founding member of the International African Institute and editor of *Africa* (1944–48) and the *Journal of the Royal African Society* (1938–40), as well as being largely responsible for the "Editorial Notes" of the latter journal for the period 1923–38. In 1944 he was awarded the Silver Medal of the Royal

African Society for his service to Africa.[6] He was closely associated with the Phelps-Stokes Foundation and the important contributions to African education which were made through its auspices. Prolific as a writer, he was equally competent as an anthropologist, linguist, historian and biographer.

Smith often referred to himself as an amateur anthropologist, but he was not so considered by others. He was a member of the Royal Anthropological Institute from 1909 until his death and served as president during 1933–35, the first and only missionary so honored. Among the many awards which came his way is included the Rivers Memorial Medal of the Royal Anthropological Institute. His great study of the Ba-ila people, written jointly with Andrew M. Dale and first published in 1920,[7] is considered a classic and has recently been republished. The well-known anthropologists E. Colson and M. Gluckman insist that his work "founded modern anthropological research in British Central Africa."[8]

Smith's linguistic ability was singular. He knew Sotho and some Xhosa when he went from South Africa to Zambia. Between 1902 and 1907 he learned Ila, reduced it to writing and wrote a grammar and dictionary of the language, *The Handbook of the Ila Language*.[9] He was largely responsible for the translation of the New Testament into Ila. He was for a period chairman of the Linguistic Advisory Committee in Great Britain and, according to D. Forde, was "a leading figure in the promotion of research, publication and teaching in African social and linguistic studies."[10] He wrote principally in English,[11] but his reviews include books written in German, Dutch, French, Italian, Spanish and Portuguese. His writings reveal also a knowledge of Arabic as well as Latin, Greek and Hebrew.

Edwin Smith's absorbing interest in African history is evidenced in such publications as *Events in African History*, *Exploration in Africa* and *The Blessed Missionaries* and in an enormous number of book reviews. Yet it is probably true to say that his greatest contribution to African history was through the medium of biography: *Aggrey of Africa: A Study in Black and White; Robert Moffat: One of God's Gardeners; The Mabilles of Basutoland; The Life and Times of Daniel Lindley* and *Great Lion of Bechuanaland: The Life and Times of Roger Price, Missionary*. Such scholars as W. Macmillan and I. Schapera make it clear that he ranks in the forefront of African historians.[12]

Religion was a subject of absorbing concern for Edwin Smith, and he was honored with a Doctor of Divinity degree from Wesley College, Winnipeg. He was deeply interested in the traditional religion of Africa. He studied it in the field and read widely the work of others. Indeed G. Parrinder, no stranger to the subject, calls him "the greatest expert on African religion."[13] Smith devoted himself especially to probing the relationship of Christianity to African culture and religion. He remained throughout a committed Christian but was never one to denigrate African life and thought. Fortes and Dieterlen credit him with playing a significant role in altering missionary attitudes toward Africa, especially through his role in the Le Zoute conference of 1926.[14] Smith's influence in this direction was exerted not only at Le Zoute but also through *The Golden Stool*, perhaps his best-known book, as well as many other publications.

Smith was especially interested in the African concept of God, and his endeavors resulted finally in the publication of the symposium *African Ideas of God*. P. Kaberry criticizes the book for failing to place the theological concepts of the various African peoples in their proper sociological context,[15] but undoubtedly the book has done much, as Parrinder perceives, to establish the view that "African peoples have had a belief in a Supreme Being as an integral part of their world view and practical religion."[16] Because of his experience and study, his commitment to the Church and interest in traditional belief, Edwin Smith is uniquely qualified to interpret the conceptions of God in Christianity and African Traditional Religion. Smith's works are worthy of extended perusal today, and it is hoped that this examination of his thought may be of use to the growing Church of Africa as it probes more deeply into the relationship of its new faith to that which went before.

THE PROBLEM

The problem of this study is to present Edwin Smith's view of the relationship of the conceptions of God in African Traditional Religion and Christianity. Specifically, attention is centered on the following points: (1) Smith's understanding of the conception of God in African Traditional Religion; (2) Smith's perception of Christianity's contribution to that view; that is, Christianity's use of African belief as a ground for its own message; (3) an analysis of Smith's position in the light of other literature on the subject. Of concern is not his view of Christianity *per se* but only his understanding of the similarities and differences between the two religions and how Christianity builds on the foundation of African Traditional Religion. Smith's identification of Christianity as the fulfillment of African Traditional Religion is examined during the course of the investigation.[17]

DEFINITIONS

In this study "African Traditional Religion" is understood as a technical term to describe the religious beliefs and practices of the Negroid Peoples of sub-Sahara Africa, prevalent before the arrival of Christianity or Islam and still adhered to by many Africans. African Traditional Religion is therefore the African equivalent of Hinduism, Buddhism, Islam and Christianity—and is always capitalized in this inquiry. "Religion" is defined as "a felt practical relationship with what is believed in as a superhuman power."[18] Smith does not use the expression African Traditional Religion, confining himself rather to the phrase "African religion"; but it is clear that there is no difference in meaning between his usage and contemporary authors when they refer to African Traditional Religion. It is important to ask whether there is a unified African Religion or whether it would be more appropriate to speak of African Traditional Religions. Smith is aware of the problem. He is conversant with the diversity of beliefs and practices among the various tribes of Africa and insists that there are also significant differences within any given tribe. However, he believes that there is an underlying identity in religion throughout sub-Sahara Africa which allows one to talk legitimately of a unified African Religion. A more thorough examination of his argument is presented at a later point in the study.[19]

Smith uses the word "Christianity" to describe the religious beliefs and practices brought to Africa by Christian missionaries and which have come to characterize the Christian Church in Africa. Obviously there has been a considerable denominational and individual diversity in Christian witness in Africa. At times Smith notes these differences in Christian approach and attitude and is not uncommonly critical of the positions assumed by Christian missionaries in Africa. Nevertheless, he also manifests an esteem for Christian missionary work. His criticisms are made from within the fellowship—a missionary and fellow Christian talking to colleagues. Sometimes Smith gives the impression that he is presenting an ideal picture of the Christian faith, especially as this may be seen in the biblical witness; but it would be unfair to assume that he compares the ideal of Christianity with the practice of African Traditional Religion. In general he does a creditable job of balancing the ideal and practical in his presentation of both Christianity and African Traditional Religion.

The word "God" is used here to designate the Creator of man and the world. Such other expressions as "High God," "Supreme Being" and "Supreme Deity" are applied interchangeably to God. Smith distinguishes carefully between "God" and the "gods" or "divinities." The latter are lesser entities in the spirit world who occupy varying positions and functions in relation to the High God. Smith employs "theism" to describe African belief and thought regarding the Creator God, while the African conception of the ancestors and divinities is defined as "spiritism." A third term is "dynamism" which refers to beliefs and practices commonly known as magic. Some scholars have questioned whether all Africans share a belief in the Supreme Deity. Their arguments must be kept in mind, but Edwin Smith insists that Africans share in common such a belief. Moreover, he identifies the Supreme God of African Traditional Religion with the Christian God.

"Sublimation" means seeking the good kernel of traditional African belief and practice and employing it as a building block in the establishment of an indigenous Christianity in Africa. The part that "sublimation" plays in "fulfillment," the word customarily used by Smith to define the relationship of Christianity to African Traditional Religion, is described at a later point in the study.[20]

The appendix contains a glossary which defines briefly the foreign words and phrases used during the course of the argument. The names and praise titles of the divinities and God are underlined when they first appear in the text. African studies present a problem in the spelling of tribal names. Smith himself is not always consistent. Apart from quotations, this study follows the spelling as adopted by J. Mbiti in his *Concepts of God in Africa*.[21] The only exception is that relating to the Ila-speaking people of Zambia, where Smith's identification of the language as Ila and the people as the Ba-ila is followed.

LIMITATIONS

Edwin Smith was a prolific writer and a man with broad interests. His competence as an anthropologist, linguist, historian and biographer has been noted. No analysis or assessment of the totality of his contribution to scholarly study is projected. Rather attention is confined to his thought regarding God. Smith's biographies and historical treatises offer at a number of points insights into various aspects of the conception of God, and are appropriated; but the greatest emphasis is placed on those books and articles which deal specifically with religion in Africa. Among the more important may be listed the following: *African Beliefs and Christian Faith; African Ideas of God; The Golden Stool; The Ila-Speaking Peoples of Northern Rhodesia; Knowing the African; The Religion of Lower Races as Illustrated by the African Bantu*[22] and *The Secret of the African.* The conception of God is the dominant motif throughout, and all other aspects of African life and religion are presented only as they are relevant to that conception.

Even in the analysis of Smith's understanding of the conception of God, it is necessary to limit the treatment of the material. In essence this investigation is centered around six questions concerning God, with Smith's answers being deduced from his writings. It is hoped that these six questions furnish scope for a significant entree into the subject and yet also provide a sufficiently limited point of reference to be dealt with adequately.

Previous Research

There has not been to date any comprehensive study of the thought of Edwin W. Smith. As indicated above, Smith has not received on the world scene the attention that his writings merit. For nearly fifty years he was an influential figure in African circles, and his books are still read with profit by those interested in African life and thought. Yet no one has set himself to the task of analyzing or systematizing his contribution. This study is an attempt to make up in some small measure for that lack.

Many books dealing with the religious thought of Africa have appeared over the past generation. One thinks particularly of the work of such Western scholars as Evans-Pritchard, Tempels, Middleton, Lienhardt, Wilson, Parrinder, and many others. African scholars are also dedicating themselves to these studies with increased vigor, as evidenced by the writings of Danquah, Busia, Baëta, Nketia, Sawyerr, Idowu and Mbiti. Furthermore, there are available now several studies which attempt to evaluate the relationship of Christianity to African Traditional Religion. Here may be mentioned especially the endeavors of Andersson, Debrunner, Welbourn, Williamson and Taylor. It is necessary to take cognizance of all in an examination of Smith's position.

PROCEDURE

The topic in question is considered by first presenting Smith's view of African Traditional Religion and Christianity's contribution to it. Smith's position is exposed in a series of six chapters which attempt to answer the following questions: Is God a Person? Is God One? Does God Love Man? Does God Reveal Himself? Does God Require Righteousness? Is God Worshipped?

In each case the first half of the chapter, entitled "Traditional View," presents Smith's conception of how African Traditional Religion has answered and continues to answer the question. The second half of each chapter, entitled "Christian Contribution," shows how Smith conceives the Christian answer in the context of Christianity's relationship to African Traditional Religion. In these chapters no attempt is made to analyze Smith's thought or to criticize it from any other perspective. The sole purpose is to present his view as concisely and accurately as possible.

These six chapters are followed by two further substantive chapters entitled "Critical Analysis: Traditional View" and "Critical Analysis: Christian Contribution," in which Smith is challenged in dialogue on the basis of other studies relevant to the discussion. The dialogue centers on what appear to be the weaknesses of Smith's argument or at least the points where further qualification seems necessary.

The brief conclusion summarizes the strengths and weaknesses of Smith's position, alluding once again to the significance of such a study for Africa at the present time.

2

Personality:
Is God a Person?

TRADITIONAL VIEW

According to Edwin Smith, behind African beliefs and actions lies
a fundamental experience, a feeling of the existence of Something
or Somebody beyond themselves, a mysterious Power which cannot be seen and is not fully understood but which is at work in
the world.[1]

Accompanying this intuition is a sense of awe and inadequacy,
of reverence and dependence.[2] Indeed, the fundamental element
not only of African but of all religion is this sense of awe in the
face of the unfathomable mystery of life. He quotes with approval
the important studies made by Rudolf Otto and finds himself in
agreement with Otto's thesis as it relates to the African situation.[3]
Although Otto calls this feeling "the holy," Smith insists with him
that the concept is devoid of ethical significance and is not to be
identified with the word "sacred."[4] The idea in its basic form is by
nature non-rational.

Like most anthropologists of his time, Smith is dominated by a
search for the origins of religion, and he naturally tends to cate-
gorize religious phenomena in terms of developmental stages. The
sense of wonder in the presence of the Unseen is for him the
simplest stage of religious life. Although he knows of no tribe, in
Africa or elsewhere, which illustrates explicitly this phenomenon,
he advances the hypothesis that all of man's religious and magical

9

views stem from this sensation of inferiority before the unknown.[5]

However, man is not satisfied to rest in the mystery. He wants to understand and explain the uncanny Power which he believes to be at work. He wants to control it and put it to use for his own benefit, or at least to render it harmless.[6] Hence, man seeks to undergird his feeling of awe with a rational basis and a practical concern. Smith says:

> The three elements enter into religion: the emotional, the intellectual, the volitional, corresponding to the three elements into which psychologists analyze the condition of mind at any moment: feeling, cognition, conation. We feel; we know, or seek to know; we do, or desire to do.[7]

Concept of Mana

Smith notes two basic facts about African life and religion which are difficult to reconcile. On the one hand, the African acts in a perfectly rational manner. In the daily activities of hunting, fishing, farming, building and smelting, he uses reliable procedures which are efficacious and often highly ingenious.[8]

No sooner has this been done, however, than the African proceeds to mix into his activities other practices which, to the Western mind, are utterly without validity. These "irrational" practices are commonly referred to as "magic," although Smith prefers the term "dynamism" to describe them.[9]

The reason for the African's action is not far to seek. In all of life's activities there are contingencies. Even with hard work and good methods success is not always attained. Disaster waits around every corner and threatens even the most capable and intelligent. A wise man is one who seeks the help of the Power or powers which, although unseen, are clearly at work in all things.[10]

Sir James Frazer, one of the early and important students of magical phenomena, had a profound influence on Edwin Smith. Nevertheless, Smith finds inadequate Frazer's explanation of magic in terms of "imitation" and "contagion." In essence Frazer's laws of association lack any reference to that special "something" which is at work in the magician's medicine.[11] What is missing in Frazer's conception is provided by the term *mana*, which was first described by Bishop Codrington in his studies of the Melanesians.[12]

In essence *mana* means "power," and the concept is by no means confined to Melanesia. In North America various Indian tribes refer to it as *orenda, manitou* or *wakonda*. In Morocco the Arabic word *baraka* is applied to it.[13] In Africa the concept is also widespread. The Ashanti call it *suman,* the Yoruba *ogun,* the Congo-Fioti *lunyensu* and other tribes *impindo, shinda* and *insambwe.*[14] A common word for this unseen power in Central Africa is *ubwanga.*[15]

The power is in itself neutral. However, it is all-pervasive and can be manipulated for good or evil purposes. The only comparable thing in Western experience is electricity,[16] although Smith also describes it as "luck."[17] As with electricity, it is dangerous. If it is misused it can effect great harm, not only to the individual but to his relatives and the community as well.[18] *Ubwanga* must be handled only by a "doctor" who knows its secrets. The doctor is called a *munganga.*[19]

Certain animals and things display an unusual form of *ubwanga* and may be designated as efficacious or dangerous for certain purposes or in specific contexts. Some may be looked upon as good signs, i.e., lucky, while others are considered unlucky. The examples are almost endless and Smith lists them in many of his writings, especially his study of the Ba-ila people. Not only is *ubwanga* basic for understanding the concept of taboo, it also explains the common African belief in the efficacy of medicines, charms and curses, as well as the reality of witchcraft.

Ubwanga is important to all aspects of life, but in crisis situations its significance is multiplied. The periods of "passage" such as birth, puberty, marriage and death are especially crucial and are therefore accompanied by proper rites and ceremonies.[20]

Drought is another crisis situation because, if the rains are withheld, the tribe will be faced with famine. Smith explains the action of the rainmaker in great detail, and thereby makes reference not only to the concept of *ubwanga* but also to that of the Supreme Being:

> The people gather together to assist the rain-doctor with their songs and prayers. He comes with an earthenware pot, the roots of a certain tree, and some water. Sitting there in the midst of the people, he puts some scrapings from the roots into the pot with water; then holding a small forked stick between the palms of his hands, he twirls it round in the liquid, producing froth. Some of this froth he throws in all directions; then he burns another drug which throws up a dense smoke. The ashes of this drug are put into a pot of water, and turn the water black. Then

the doctor twirls once again in this mixture with his stick. Meanwhile the people sing and invoke the Supreme Being, who is named Leza.[21]

The prayer to *Leza* is easily understood by Westerners, but the significance of the actions of the doctor is less obvious. The twirling movement appears to signify the action of the wind, while the black water and smoke represent the dark rain clouds which will soon make their appearance. There is obviously symbolism involved here, but it would be a serious mistake to consider this merely a symbolic act. The action is meant to influence the event in some way[22] although its exact function is not easy to determine. One would like to know, for example, what the relationship is between the "magical" practices and the prayers to Leza, whether the magic works directly causing the rain or influences Leza to make it rain. Smith states that there are no easy answers to these questions. The problem is doubly difficult because it is not fully clear whether Leza is to be conceived of as "It" or "He."[23]

Edwin Smith talks of a power, called *mana* or *ubwanga*, evident in the affairs of men, which can be manipulated for good or evil. There is also a Power working in creation and the sky. However, it is not clear whether the two are aspects of the same Power or entirely separate conceptions:

> Is the Power (working in the sky and on earth) self-conscious, having knowledge of itself and what it is doing; has it purpose, design, desire; has it heart and mind? In other words, is the Power a person—like man, only not limited as man is limited? Or is it the opposite to this—a strange, unseen force like electric-power or *ubwanga*?[24]

As the quotation makes clear, the phrase "like *ubwanga*" indicates that the two cannot be simply identified.

God and Mana

In another context Smith refers to the Power associated with creation and at work in the sky as "Cosmic Mana."[25] He believes that "Cosmic Mana" is conceived essentially in terms of a theism, a personal High God, while *ubwanga* remains impersonal:

> It would seem that in general Africans are not conscious of any direct relation between their theism and the ethic of dynamism—all that we mean by tabu . . . many Africans are aware of Some-

thing, other than themselves and other than the Supreme Being, that makes for righteousness.[26]

Nevertheless, it is difficult, if not impossible, to maintain clear distinctions. *Mulungu* is the name for the High God of the Bena people of Central Africa. Yet a Bena man may muse in talking to his charm: "This medicine is my life, it is my Mulungu," while another observes: "The evil power of the wizard is Mulungu."[27] Smith comments:

> What A. T. and G. M. Culwick say of the Bena is true of other tribes: 'The belief in Mulungu is exceedingly complicated and the ideas held about him or it are both contradictory and confused'. It is clear, they say, that among the Bena there are two entirely different conceptions of Mulungu though they are often confused. 'The first is that of a High God, the Creator: the second is impersonal, Mulungu as the summation of the supernatural, something akin to *mana* among the Melanesians and *orenda* among certain North American Indians'.[28]

In general Africans do not use images of wood and stone to represent the High God. Houses dedicated to God are rare. In some cases, where shrines are used, a man will say: "This is God," referring to the house, but it is a misrepresentation generally to picture the Africans as identifying God with buildings or images. They do not really mean that the shrine is God. Rather it is a sign of God's presence. In admonishing Western interpreters of African Religion to use care in making generalizations, Smith says: "It is a great error when men take the sign for that of which it is the representative."[29]

The same is true of the African approach to the great natural phenomena. When the African looks at life and nature, he is filled with awe and wonder, and he tends to identify that which fills him with awe as God.

The Ewe of West Africa use the same word—*Mawu*—for sky and God and seem to equate them.[30] The Thonga of Mozambique make the same association with the word *Tilo*.[31] For the Pare of Tanzania, *Ihuwa* means both sun and God, and the Luyi of Zambia also identify the sun with *Nyambe*. The Venda of the Transvaal have a double meaning for the term *Raluvimbi*, the "earth shock" as well as the "Maker of Everything."[32]

As to whether this implies an identification of God with the forces of nature, Smith replies:

> Africans take the part for the complete thing. The complete thing is outside the range of their mind, that which is seen and in touch with everyday life is enough for everyday use. They make a selection from among the greatest of the Maker's works and signs of His power—the sky, the sun, the rain, an earth-shock—and give attention to these as if they were the Maker Himself.[33]

For many Africans, clearly one makes a mistake if he identifies the seen with the unseen. It is only a way of talking. The sun is really not God even if they share the same name. The sun is rather a sign of God's presence and power. For others, these distinctions are not so clear.[34]

Smith knows the Ba-ila people of Zambia from close study and personal experience. The Ba-ila name for the High God is Leza. In their conception, Leza is intimately associated with the sky, especially the rain.[35] The Ba-ila look for the first rains in early October. If the rains are delayed, the people fear trouble and become nervous. Among the epithets of God are *Shakatabwa*, meaning "the Faller" which is a clear reference to rain, and *Mangwe*, meaning "the Flooder." The Ba-ila actually say "Leza falls" or "Leza rains."[36]

Smith calls attention to the parallelism in the use of the English prop word "it," in the sentence "it rains," and he suggests that the phrase may well go back to a much earlier stage of development when the reference was to God, meaning "God rains."[37] Once again Smith's preoccupation with the question of origins is evident:

> It is very likely that the metonymical use of "Leza" for rain is a survival from the time when the two were actually identified. We can think of them revering the elements themselves, then rising to the thought of a power behind the elements, and finally coming to think of that power as a person.[38]

Allusions to Personality

In spite of the fact that the Ba-ila say "Leza rains," they do not identify God with the rain; at least this is true of many Ba-ila. They call Leza the "Faller" and the "Flooder," but they also call Him *Kemba*, the "Rain-Giver," and *Namesi*, the "Water-Giver."[39] They sometimes call the rain "Leza's urine," but their basic view is that Leza sends the rain.[40]

The prefixes of the Ila language distinguish between references to persons and things.[41] When Leza is referred to, as for example in the expression "Leza rains" or "Leza falls," the Ba-ila invariably use personal rather than impersonal prefixes. They say for example: "Leza wawa" ("God falls"),[42] where the wa- prefix refers in essence to "He" rather than "It." Moreover, personal pronouns are used for Leza.[43]

The Ila language, as is true of Bantu languages in general, does not include in its vocabulary the abstract word "person."[44] Therefore, it is not possible to ask the Ba-ila whether they regard Leza as a Person or not. The closest they might come to answering that question is to say that Leza is a "man." Yet it is clear that neither the Ba-ila nor other African peoples would identify God as a man. He is not a man, and they insist that He never was a man.[45]

Nevertheless, God is strangely like a man in their conception. As will be seen more fully in Chapter IV, the general picture of Africa is that the High God is far away and has little intercourse with the men of the world. Yet that picture is not absolute. God does occasionally talk with men, and they in turn at rare times pray to Him. God sees, makes and does things.[46]

Generally the Africans conceive of the High God as a Great Chief; and the more highly developed any particular tribal society is from a political standpoint, the more God takes on kingly attributes. One talks to Him as one would to the chief. The further the people are separated from the earthly chief, the further they conceive themselves to be from the heavenly Chief.[47] Like the chief, God is usually pictured as having a family.[48]

The High God is like men in some things, but He is not man and never was one. Among the Zulu, for example, God is called *Unkulunkulu* which may mean either "the old, old one" or "the great, great one," and He is sometimes identified by the people as the "progenitor of the race." However, Unkulunkulu is also recognized as the Creator; so He is something more than an equivalent to Adam.[49]

Although Africans occasionally call God *muntu*, that is, "man," this is merely a way of saying that He is similar to man. In many ways God is unlike men. He has no form, for example. He talks, sees, makes and does things, but anthropomorphism is not developed extensively.[50] Smith quotes this description of God from Towegale, the reigning chief of the Bena of Central Africa:

Mulungu . . . has no face, hands, legs or body. Mulungu does not speak, but he hears and sees. Mulungu is everything at once. Mulungu does whatever he likes. There is nothing to which Mulungu can be likened. He is the lightning, and the thunder is his voice. The good are rewarded by him and the bad are punished. Mulungu is sheer mind and a very great mind.[51]

Ambiguity of African Conception

Africans believe in a great Power which they see working in the rain, thunder, sun and the events of life. They also believe in the Supreme God whom they identify with the personal names of Leza, Mulungu and Nyame.[52] However, their views of how these two conceptions are related to each other are varied and confused. Sometimes they are identified; sometimes they are separated; sometimes they are a strange mixture of the two:

Indeed many of those that use the names "Leza" and "Nyambe" and speak of God as "He" are not quite certain that He is not the natural phenomena of rain, thunder and the like, or that He is not at most the animating spirit within those phenomena. We have seen that the Bantu believe the world to be permeated by hidden mysterious energies, and it would seem that many of them do not already distinguish God from these; to them God is the power that works in and from the sky. The other facts already mentioned, especially some of the praise-titles ascribed to God, show that God is by many of the Bantu regarded as a Person.[53]

There are differences in conception between and within tribes, and most importantly within the individuals of any given tribe; so that it is not possible to arrive at a clear consistent view. Nevertheless, the weight of evidence lies on the side of a "Personal" God. Smith sums up the matter in these words:

There is room for doubt about some of the tribes; but generally it may be said that He is looked upon as a Person, though the idea of what "person" is may not be very clear in the mind of the Africans.[54]

CHRISTIAN CONTRIBUTION

In speaking of the Christian contribution it is necessary to distinguish between theory and practice. Smith is fully aware that these two do not always coincide. He is expressly critical of missionaries who are iconoclastic in their attitude and who feel that their major role is to change Africa.[55] He makes a distinction between Christianity and its presentation.[56]

Nevertheless, Smith is also convinced that Christianity has a profound contribution to make to African life and religion. There is no more noble profession than the missionary vocation, which brings Jesus Christ to Africa.[57] Moreover, the major contribution of Christianity to Africa is its conception of God, and it is precisely at this point that Christians must begin in their approach to the African.[58]

Clarification of African View

Edwin Smith is convinced that there is truth in the African conception and that this truth owes its origin to the action of the God who revealed Himself fully in Jesus Christ. The God of the Judeo-Christian tradition is the same God who has been at work on the African scene, preparing for the coming of His Son:

> Is it right to say 'he', or 'it', when we make statements about the Power? In other words, is the Power a Person or a Force? Has the Power the form of a man and the heart of a man? Or is it without feelings; something strong, but blind and without hearing, and having no purpose? Is the Power one or more than one? Is the Power the same as the Sun or Rain, or is the Power separate from these things which are made? . . .
>
> These are very great questions. We will see what answers Africans give, and we will keep in mind all the time that if there is anything true in the answers it comes from God, the Father of the Lord Jesus Christ.[59]

Although the traditional African conception of God contains truth, it does not contain the whole truth. In this sense the Christian gospel comes as the fulfillment of African Traditional Religion.[60] One way by which Christianity fulfills African Religion is in clarifying the issues of power and personality in Africa.

A familiar figure used by Smith to show Christianity's clarifying action is the image of light. He does not identify Christianity as light over against African darkness, as some Christians have done and perhaps continue to do; rather he prefers to characterize the African view as "twilight."[61] At other points he calls it the light of dawn[62] and "half-light."[63] It is real light but it is imperfect. Both the light of dawn and the light of midday owe their origin to

the sun, but they do not share the same intensity. One sees it as imperfect light only when the perfect light makes its appearance.
Jesus Christ is that perfect light. Therefore he is the measure of
all value.[64] The dimness of the past is illuminated by his presence,
since he reveals the glory of God in human form.[65] Smith says:
"The complete light which is Jesus Christ lets us see in what measure the earlier light was a true light and how far it was from being
complete."[66]

The African view of God is characterized by ambiguity. There
are Africans who make no clear distinction between God and
mana; others identify God with "Cosmic Mana"; some personify
God as "Cosmic Mana"; and still others distinguish a personal God
from "Cosmic Mana."[67] While there are differences between
tribes, often in the same tribe one can find represented all these
views. Moreover, the lines of demarcation are not always clear in
any given individual.[68]

Christianity has helped to sharpen the issues for Africa. From
the Christian context, the great celestial phenomena cannot be
identified with God. Rather God is their Creator. He is the Source
of all, and He is a Person. He is not the rain but the Giver of the
rain. This idea is not foreign to Africa. The African also knows
God as the Creator and as the Giver of the rain, but the African
witness is ambiguous in its totality. It is precisely this uncertainty
and lack of clarity which is illuminated by the Christian gospel.
The world and the universe are God's creatures and are not to be
identified with God in Himself. God is a Person and the Creator
of all things. All men owe their origin to Him, and He stands to
them as a Father does to his children. This was the essential message of Jesus' life and death, as well as his teachings. God is *Abba,*
Father.[69] Smith sums up the Christian task in these words:

> We are not surprised then that the Bantu, previous to the com-
> ing of the missionaries, had rather hazy ideas about God. It may
> be too much to suggest that the Supreme Being, as conceived by
> the Bantu, is a personification of *mana;* but we cannot wholly
> dissociate the two ideas; Leza, Mulungu, Nyambe—however they
> may name Him, He retains many of the characteristics of that
> world-energy. Leza is that 'something far more deeply inter-
> fused,' which falls in the rain, soughs in the wind, rages in the
> tempest, rolls in the thunder, flashes in the lightning. Leza is
> Power, Providence, Fate, Destiny. Yet Leza is He and not merely
> It; if not fully personal, at least Leza tends to personality. And

this magnificent, if somewhat vague conception of God it is the missionary's chief task to sublimate; Leza is to become the God and Father of our Lord Jesus Christ.[70]

Smith believes that Christianity has clarified the issues of power and personality not only for African Christians but also for those Africans who have never fully accepted the Christian faith:

> Let us keep one thing in mind. The teaching of Christianity that the Maker of all things is a Father, and so a Person, has gone widely about among Africans, even among those who have not become true Christians, and it has had the tendency to make their ideas clearer than they were before. Our desire now is to see what belief Africans had before that teaching came to them. It will not be surprising if we come to a decision that in some ways their idea was uncertain.[71]

Elimination of Fear

In clarifying the issue concerning the relationship of dynamism to theism, Christianity effects a separation between the two and sets in motion a progressive elimination of dynamism in African thought and life. In this way Christianity acts as a means to the eradication of fear in African Religion.

Smith is aware that missionaries and anthropologists have often indiscriminately stressed the element of fear in African life. He is critical of Frazer's identification of fear as a "prime source of primitive religion." He says that he did not find the Ba-ila to be "slaves of unmitigated dread," and he quotes Cullen Young to similar effect. He concludes: "There is undoubtedly some fear, a salutary fear; but the attitude is more correctly described by the Ila word *mampuba*. *Mampuba* is a complex emotion, made up of fear, reverence and affection: the specific religious emotion."[72]

However, it is clear that Edwin Smith also knows of an "unsalutary" fear in African life—the fear connected with dynamism and its stepson, witchcraft.

Smith believes that witchcraft is a reality.[73] He tells the story of a member of the Ba-ila tribe who returned home one evening to find hanging in his home a mysterious string of beads with a black object attached to one end. No one could explain how it got there; so the man concluded that he was being bewitched. He was transformed immediately from a happy, robust individual into a wretched creature who was thoroughly convinced that his death was imminent. By auto-suggestion he was literally killing himself. Smith is of the opinion that the man most certainly would have died had not he and Dale been on hand to help dispel his state of melancholy.[74]

The essence of witchcraft is its action at a distance, and this is explained by the modern scientific concepts of telepathy, telesthesia and telergy. By means of telepathy, the mind communication sets up auto-suggestion which in turn accomplishes psychologically the desired evil deed. The Africans do not explain the phenomenon in those terms. For them the medicine used has the property to manipulate *ubwanga* in order to produce the desired effect, Smith concludes: "The intuitions of the savage are the reasoned convictions of modern science."[75]

In his book *The Ila-Speaking Peoples of Northern Rhodesia* he does not differentiate between sorcery and witchcraft. Most probably the Ba-ila make no such distinction themselves. Indeed he identifies as witchcraft what is generally recognized as sorcery by later anthropologists, namely the casting of a spell by means of medicine. In later works he recognizes the difference between the two.[76] However, this does not alter his basic approach to the process, for whether the action is purely psychical (witchcraft) or by means of medicines (sorcery) the result is the same—a telepathic communication from the witch or sorcerer which sets up auto-suggestion in the victim.

Although Edwin Smith does not deny the existence of witchcraft, as many Westerners do, he does recognize it as a great evil. He calls it the darkest terror of African life.[77] When an unusual death occurs, the Africans look for a suspicious character as the cause of death. The diviners are often rascals and are not overly scrupulous in fixing the blame. Sometimes the accused is allowed to undergo an ordeal by poison to prove his innocence; death in such a case is taken as proof of guilt. In other cases where guilt has been established, the accused is dispatched with unbelievable cruelty.[78] Smith describes the results in these words:

> Myriads of innocent persons have been hurried to a shameful and cruel death. Millions of people have lived beneath the shadow of this terrible belief for centuries. It is a greater curse to Africa than ever the slave-trade was. Who can measure its baneful effect in preventing the progress of the Bantu? Men simply do not dare to be more industrious and to accumulate more wealth than their fellows; they dare not show great skill; they do not venture

out upon new paths of progress, for fear they will be condemned by public opinion of being concerned with witchcraft.[79]

Smith calls for understanding on the part of Europeans. He does not believe it sufficient merely to pass laws prohibiting the killing of witches or infants who are judged to be ill omens. Rather it is necessary to go to the root of the matter—the belief which prompts such action. Christianity thus has an important role to play.[80]

Witchcraft is but the most obvious abuse of the belief in dynamism. This is not to say, of course, that dynamism is all bad. In fact, Smith is willing to admit that from a scientific viewpoint, dynamism is not completely without basis: "Is not science telling us of the energy stored up in the very paving-stones of our streets?"[81] Moreover, in spite of the fact that it mixes up the moral and ceremonial law, calling some things bad that Christians believe have no ethical quality and passing over without censure other actions which from the Christian point of view cannot be condoned, taboo does provide an ethical standard of life.[82] In this sense again Christianity is seen as the fulfillment, not the destroyer, of African Traditional Religion.

Nevertheless, as presently structured, dynamism is a negative element in African society. It lies at the root of African conservatism and lack of progress.[83] It is "one of the things that Africans must leave behind in their onward march."[84] Edwin Smith does not believe that tribal concepts of taboo, as traditionally understood, can orient the new Africa since they are in essence based on magical conceptions rather than scientific foundations. The danger comes when, under the impact of modern science, the African throws off his tribal morality with its grounding in magic and taboo, and is left without an ethical orientation for life. Smith notes:

> Dynamism is an insecure basis for ethics. When belief in the efficacy of charms is destroyed the results may be serious. This is one reason of the disintegration that we are witnessing in Africa today. The influx of our Western civilization is destroying the roots of dynamistic morality.[85]

Smith is persuaded that African Religion cannot ultimately withstand the scientific invasion, and a new religious allegiance must of necessity be substituted for it. He says that it would be a great tragedy if the African were to receive only a secular scientific education.[86] Rather he continues to hope that Africa may become Christian. Christianity provides the African with new moral ideals to replace those of his own tradition which are increasingly called into question by the interaction of African and Western culture.[87]

At the same time Christianity liberates the African from the fears which dynamism imposes upon him. It convinces him that man can befriend the universe and use it to his own benefit, in a way which accords with modern science.[88] Dynamism is a source of fear for the people; therefore the gospel of love is also the gospel of freedom.[89]

In his introductory remarks to the book *African Ideas of God*, Edwin Smith tells of a dinner he attended in Khartoum. One of the guests was Emil Ludwig, the biographer. Upon hearing that Smith had been a missionary, he asked: "What does Christianity do for the African? Does it increase his personal happiness, and if so, how?" This was Smith's reply: "I spoke of the release from fears. 'What fears, and how release?' I pictured the fears and told how we try to induce a personal trust in a living, present, loving God who is stronger than any evil power."[90]

Elevation of Theism

The most important contribution of Christianity to Africa is its emphasis on theism. Christianity brings to Africa an assurance of the reality of a personal God who is Creator and Redeemer, King and Father. Africa was very close to this conception. Indeed Africa possessed it already: in seed in some places, in flower in others. But in the indigenous situation, there was always ambiguity, an uncertainty, a doubt, a lack of clarity.

African Traditional Religion generally pictures God as being far away and remote. This belief is seen clearly in the myths of God's departure which form part of the folklore of most tribes.[91] In the beginning God and man lived together, but due to man's foolishness or perversity God retreated and is no longer in close contact with him. This withdrawal of God from the scene of daily life has had a profound effect upon the lives of men and results in a greater emphasis on the importance of lesser beings, fetishes and charms to carry on daily existence.

The term "fetish" deserves brief comment here since it is such an equivocal word. In anthropological literature, it often refers to material objects which serve as the abode of "spirits." However, it is not always possible to distinguish between the fetish as an abode of a spirit and the fetish as a dynamistic or magical charm. In fact Smith suggests that the word "fetish" should either be abandoned altogether or restricted to charms, amulets and talismans.[92]

Some African myths picture the original state, when God was near and lived close to man, as a period free from the tyranny of fetishism or dynamism. An example is this myth told by the Ashanti of Ghana:

> It is said that long ago men were happy, for God dwelt among them and talked with them face to face. These blissful days, however, did not last for ever. One unlucky day it chanced that some women were pounding a mash with pestles in a mortar, while God stood by looking on. For some reason they were annoyed by the presence of the Deity, and told him to be off; and as he did not take himself off fast enough to please them, they beat him with their pestles. Then God retired altogether from the world, and left it to the direction of the fetishes; and still to this day people say: "Ah, if it had not been for that old woman, how happy we would be!"[93]

This story expresses the conviction that fetishes were not in the original order of creation. They have come in as a result of the Fall,[94] and life would be better without them.

There is thus in Africa a curious double movement as regards the relationship of dynamism to the Supreme God. In a real way it was man's sin which provoked God's departure and resulted in the introduction of dynamism. Yet it is also true to say that the concept of dynamism, by concentrating on things which can be seen, interferes with the development of a view of the High God as near and concerned. Smith observes:

> When we come to speak of West Africa we shall find the tangled undergrowth of fetishism (so called) almost choking the religion associated with the Supreme Being. Old priests have said again and again to Captain Rattray: "Suman (fetishes) spoil the gods." That is to say, they take the attention, and religious service, away from the gods. It is remarkable to have this great truth recognized clearly by pagan Africans. Captain Rattray thinks that if the Ashanti had been left to work out their own salvation, some African Messiah would have arisen to sweep their religion clean of all fetish, thus concentrating religious worship on the Supreme Being, whom they recognize . . . Actually, of course, it has

been left to Christian missionaries to proclaim the one God and
to sweep away the rank undergrowth of fetishism.[95]

Dynamism is both a product and a cause of the belief in a Supreme God who is far away and uninterested. But the cycle was
broken by a new action of God in the gift of His Son Jesus Christ,
which shows God to be a loving Father. The supreme contribution
of Christianity then is precisely its elevation of theism to the apex
of concern for the man of faith. Smith insists that the proper approach for Christianity in Africa is to begin where the Africans
have left off and to develop the promise which is latent in their
present vague awareness of God.[96]

The Africans were and are a deeply religious people. Smith
observes that, because Africa makes in essence no distinction between the sacred and the secular, some early missionaries came to
the erroneous conclusion that Africans were not religious.[97] He
also disagrees with the anthropologist, Marett, who believed that
dynamism was merely the raw material of religion.[98] He quotes
James Aggrey, the great African churchman of the Gold Coast
and vice-principal of Achimota College, to the effect that if the
African errs on this score it is in being, like the Athenians, too religious.[99] Christianity did not make the Africans religious; nor did
Christianity bring God to Africa. God was there before the arrival
of the gospel of Jesus Christ. Smith disputes Callaway's contention
that the Zulus had no conception of the Supreme Being apart from
the teaching of the missionaries.[100] Christianity did not even identify God for the Africans. The Africans had already identified
Him.[101] What Christianity did was to clarify the African view of
God, and this was done by making known to Africa God's own
self-revelation in Jesus Christ. This was the supreme task and the
great contribution of the Church. God is a Person, and He is the
All-Powerful. But He is also a loving Father, the One who stands
with men in all their joys and sorrows, the One who came to show
Himself to them in His Son.[102]

3

Monotheism:
Is God One?

Edwin W. Smith believes that African Religion can be divided into three essential categories:[1] (1) the belief in dynamism, the conviction that there is a mysterious impersonal power at work in the universe; (2) the belief in spiritism, the view that there are unseen personal beings, rational by nature, who influence the lives of men; and (3) the belief in theism, the conception that there is a Supreme God, who is the Creator of all things. In the last chapter an inquiry was made into the relationship between dynamism and the High God. The purpose of this chapter is to examine the conception of God in relation to the African spirit world.

Survival of Personality

There is nothing more characteristic of African life than the fact that death does not end it. Smith uses graphic expressions to make this clear, speaking of the "so-called 'living' and the so-called 'dead',"[2] "the living, and those whom we call the dead"[3] and "those who are named by foolish people 'the dead'."[4]

Although he sometimes refers to the term "soul,"[5] Smith denies that African thought is characterized by a belief in the immortality of the soul. Not only does the African view of the soul differ from the European;[6] more importantly Smith questions whether Africans consider men to be immortal in an absolute sense. While refusing to make a final determination on the matter, he suggests that the dead who are not remembered may be considered to have passed from existence.[7]

However, it is impossible to deny that African thought affirms the survival of the human personality after death.[8] In several of his books,[9] Smith describes African funerals, and these descriptions make manifest the African belief that life does not cease with death. Several actions of the mourners at the funeral rites make this clear.

Most cattle-keeping Africans do not kill their animals regularly for food. Generally they reserve them for funerals where they serve both a feasting and a ritual function. At the funeral they are slaughtered in order to accompany the dead person into the next world. The young men of the Ba-ila tribe, for example, try to accumulate as many animals as possible toward this end; and in the case of an important chief, several hundred head may be killed.[10]

In many African tribes the logic of their belief leads them to see the chief's need not only for cattle but wives, children and slaves as well; and since there is only one way to dispatch them into the invisible world, they are also killed. Smith muses: "It was a terrible custom, but nothing more indisputably proved their conviction that death does not end everything."[11]

After the corpse has been lowered into the grave, various articles may be placed beside it—beer, milk, seeds, pipe, tobacco, etc. These are also necessary on the other side, and the deceased is able to take with him their "immaterial counterparts" wherever he goes.[12] Before covering the body, the members of the family say a final farewell: "Good bye! Do not forget us! See, we have given you tobacco to smoke and food to eat! A good journey to you! Tell old friends who died before you that you left us living well!"[13]

Proof of the survival of the personality is by no means confined to funeral rites. In earlier days the Ganda refused to allow the reigning sovereign to go to the burial place of his predecessor more than once annually because such visits invariably resulted in the killing of hundreds of tribesmen to augment the deceased king's court.[14]

Recognizing that the dead live on beyond death, a question follows logically as to where they are now located. Smith indicates that the Africans are no more certain of the answer than are Europeans:

> In a similar manner the Africans will tell you, almost in the same breath, that the dead have gone to a great village under the earth, or to some far country in the east or north, where they still till the fields and reap abundant harvests; that they are in the forest surrounding their earthly home; that they are in the houses inhabited by the living; that they are wandering about in the guise of animals; that they are in their graves which are the homes of the dead. They will tell you any one or all these things; or make a more general statement that the dead are gone to God.[15]

Edwin Smith tells the story of the death of Sezongo, a Ba-ila chief, while he was serving as a missionary at Kasenga. Sezongo was buried in his own house. Some days following the funeral Smith visited his grave, arriving as several men of the village were cleaning the hut. They pointed to a tortoise walking about and indicated that the tortoise was none other than Sezongo. They removed a small layer of earth from over the grave and revealed a reed which had been planted in the corpse's ear and which had provided the avenue of escape for the tortoise. Later two lion cubs made their appearance in the house and were also identified by the villagers as Sezongo. At a still later date, a son was born to Sezongo's son, and this boy was also identified as Sezongo. Yet when the time came to make offerings to the spirit of the departed chief, the people gathered about his grave and indicated both by their words and actions that he was still there. Smith concludes: "I asked myself, as doubtless you may ask, where exactly was Sezongo—in the grave, or around the grave, or in the tortoise, or in the lions, or in the child?"[16]

This story of Sezongo presupposes one of the most common of African beliefs—reincarnation. Smith alludes to the Ba-ila view that "sooner or later, almost every person now living will return to earth."[17] The principal exceptions are spirits who are bound in service to witches and the great communal and tribal divinities.[18]

An interesting feature of African life is the attempt to discover the identity of the newborn. A diviner is often brought in, who proceeds to call out the names of the ancestors, making his decision on the basis of the reaction of the child to the various names suggested. A sudden cry or laugh or a resumption of sucking may be the tell-tale clue to the matter. The name is not merely an appellation but an integral part of the personality.[19]

The ancestor spirit thus identified is presumed to be reincarnated in the child. Yet the situation is clearly much more complicated than that, for the ancestor maintains a separate existence as well. The Ba-ila refer to the spirit in question as the individual's *muse-diakwe*, "his namesake."[20] The terms "guardian spirit" or "tutelary genius" are other epithets used by Smith to describe the phenomenon. He illustrates the belief by reference to his good friend, Mungalo, whose grandfather was also Mungalo:

> But he was named Mungalo because he actually was and is Mungalo, that is, he is his grandfather reborn! Quite so! He is Mungalo, and Mungalo is his grandfather and Mungalo is also his guardian spirit. That is to say, a man's guardian spirit, his tutelary genius, is the reincarnate spirit within him: shall we say, is himself. The genius is not only within him, but in a sense, external to himself, protecting and guiding him.[21]

The same ancestor spirit may be reincarnated in two different individuals at the same time. Sex is not involved because a woman may be reborn as a male and vice versa. Smith denies all ethical connotations in the African idea of reincarnation. He therefore insists that the African conception is different from the Hindu view of *karma* where the reincarnated state depends upon the moral quality of this present life.[22]

It is interesting to note in this context Smtih's comments on J. B. Danquah's book *The Akan Doctrine of God*.[23] Danquah is a Western-educated African, one of the first to write extensively on the subject of African Religion. Danquah also denies any African concept of *karma*, stating that individual immortality is of no significance for the Africans. However, he affirms the need of a series of incarnations for the resolution of man's imperfections and weaknesses, after which his spirit is reabsorbed into the Source, which is God.[24] God is not the wholly other but the "Great Ancestor," "the trunk of the tree of which man is a branch," so that Akan Religion is in a sense "the worship of the race."[25] In describing the African conception of reincarnation, Danquah uses the analogy of a bucket of water which must sometimes be lowered three or four times into the well before it is filled. This view seems to secure to the succeeding generations an inevitable moral progress.[26] Smith is skeptical of the argument. Danquah knows very well that degeneration is just as much a reality as progress, and yet he fails to explain the lack of progress which the accumulated merit of hundreds of generations would seem to guarantee. Especially criticized is Danquah's assertion that one may be reborn in another community or another country, with the consequent loss to the group of all previous advances.[27] While believing that Danquah must be taken seriously, Smith says: "Sometimes . . . we are prompted to ask: How much of this is Akan and how much Danquah?"[28]

Role of Ancestors

A cardinal fact of African life and thought is that the living and dead together form one community whose members are mutually dependent upon each other.[29] It is impossible to over-emphasize the attraction of the spiritual realm to the African mind. Those who have passed on are felt to be ever present. Although largely unseen, on occasion (especially in dreams and visions) they make their appearance in visual and audible form.[30]

The ancestors are dependent upon the living for their happiness. Not only do they like to be remembered; a case can be made for saying that their very existence depends upon the memory of the living.

As for the living, they need the help of the departed in their fight against the evils of life which seem to threaten them on every hand. The dead are both more knowing and more powerful than the living. Therefore they are uniquely able to provide succor in time of need.

The ancestors are subject to the same emotions as the living members of the community, and their moods are no more constant. Since they may be jealous or fickle, the living must be careful not to offend them. If the ancestors are neglected, they most assuredly will be angry and will seek to demonstrate their feelings by some vindictive action. In such a case offerings are made to placate the one offended.[31]

Some fear does enter into this aspect of the relationship between the living and the dead, although Smith tends to minimize it. The main role of the ancestors is to bless, not curse. They are concerned about the family and the community and are dedicated basically to its well-being. Even when they inflict harm on the living, it is to warn them that they are not obeying properly the taboos which are necessary to the proper functioning of society. The ancestors uniquely know the problems of life and how to resolve them. They understand evil and have the secret of avoiding it. Therefore the proper attitude toward them is one of trust and confidence. When the old men were alive, they were looked up to for guidance. Now that they are in the land of the deceased, they have become even more powerful and important.[32]

While it is true to say that the basic attitude of the living toward the dead is one of trust or reverence, there are other spirits—evil spirits—who leave the realm of the living angry and whose main preoccupation is to inflict punishment and revenge on the living. The cause of their anger is variable. They may have died by violence or taken their own lives. Perhaps their funeral ceremonies were inadequate or they were bewitched. Not uncommonly they may have been very old people who in their advanced age were neglected by their relatives and promised to haunt them after death. Smith says: "They are regarded with unmitigated dread, and many methods are adopted to appease them, to drive them off, to destroy them."[33]

Smith observes that some people seek out special drugs to make possible their transformation into animals both before and after death,[34] and he thinks that it is this belief which lies at the root of python worship in Uganda.[35]

The spirits are also able to enter human beings, and the result may be either good or bad depending on the circumstances. The spirit may use an individual as a medium for communicating with the family or community. These mediums or prophets may be possessed only once in a lifetime or on a regular basis.[36] On the other hand the possession may become so dangerous to the person and the community that exorcism is required.[37]

Just as a spirit may take possession of an animal or a man, even so it may enter a material object such as a stick, a hoe, a piece of cloth or a graven image. This is the basis for "fetishism."[38] It is of course a misnomer to suppose that the African does obeisance to material objects. He does not worship sticks and stones as such; his concern is rather centered on the spirit who is believed to reside in the object. He does not talk to the image but to the spirit who resides within the image.[39]

Smith is of the opinion that the same phenomenon is at work in so-called "nature worship," and once again he believes that this aspect of African Religion is closely related to the ancestor cult. He calls attention to the great African interest in the rivers, mountains, lakes, forests and the sea:

> That in one way or another, the Bantu are deeply impressed by these things nobody can doubt who knows them. But does their awe arise from, or induce, a belief that these things are in themselves animate and divine, or that they are the dwelling place of spirits? And if the latter, are the spirits the same as, or are they different from the ancestral spirits? Probably all three varieties of the belief exist among the Bantu.[10]

He records several examples which seem to indicate that such natural phenomena as the great rivers of Africa are not merely the abode of spirits but are themselves spirits. However, he goes on to quote Junod to the effect that a deeper probing into the matter usually results in the discovery that the lake and river divinities are none other than ancestor gods.[41]

Smith reminisces to similar effect about his own experiences among the Ba-ila. When he was building the mission station at Kasenga in the early part of this century, an old chief came to warn him not to cut down certain trees or to use specific anthills for building purposes. The explanation given was that the spirits who dwell in them would be resentful. Smith supposed that he had here a clear example of nature spirits, but in the final analysis the spirits in question proved to be the chief's own ancestors. He concludes: "The more one investigates the spirits believed in by the Ba-ila, the more they resolve themselves into spirits of human beings."[42]

In his book *African Ideas of God*, Smith seems to qualify his position with the suggestion that nature spirits are "for the most part personifications of natural phenomena."[43] However, he goes on to surmise that this conception may be more characteristic of the Northern Negroes than the Bantu-speaking peoples, the latter apparently following the pattern which Smith elucidated in his earlier studies:

> In their cosmology the Bantu appear to give a lesser place than the Sudanic Negroes to these nature spirits. The spirits of the Bantu are mostly those of human beings who continue to live in the unseen world. These may take abode in trees or mountains or waterfalls or rivers.[44]

Role of Divinities

According to Edwin Smith, there are four grades of ancestral spirits or divinities which, in their relationship to a living person, may be understood in terms of four concentric circles.[45] The nearest circle is occupied by the individual's own guardian spirit or namesake. The second circle is composed of the family spirits, the ghosts of his parents and grandparents and other close relatives. An examination has already been made of these two sets of relationships.

With the third and fourth circles the discussion moves into a new phase, for it reaches beyond the immediate family to the community and tribe. Smith defines the community divinities as the family spirits of the village heads, whereas the tribal divinities are the spirits of the great national chiefs.[46]

Not uncommonly the village and tribal divinities are recognized to be the ancestors of reigning village head men and tribal chiefs. They were themselves at one time head men and chiefs. When they governed in the flesh, they looked after the interests of the community and nation; and now they are considered to carry on the same function, although to a heightened degree, in the invisible world. Generally their fame and importance in the flesh has a bearing on their continued influence over succeeding generations. It is in this context that Smith refers to the spirits as "gods":

> If one asks what difference there is between a divinity and a god, it must be admitted that the difference is one of degree and not of kind; both classes are varieties of species, ancestral spirit. I use the word "god" to indicate that variety which is of greater importance, is revered over a wider area, and of which the human origin is quite forgotten, or almost forgotten.[47]

Another distinguishing feature of communal divinities, as contrasted with guardian and family spirits, is their permanence. The family ghosts of remote ancestors tend to be forgotten while communal divinities generally exist as long as the community itself. In many of his writings,[48] Smith alludes to *Shimunenga*, the principal communal divinity at Kasenga. Shimunenga was once a man, a chief of the Ba-ila.[49] All members of the village, from lowest slave to chief, put their trust in him. He is not approached for help in ordinary illness, which is the responsibility of the family ancestors, but he does play a major role in bringing wealth and protection to the village. When threatened by war, lions or pestilence, the villagers say: "Shimunenga, our *muzhimo*,[50] will save us."[51] Shimunenga's grave is surrounded by a sacred grove and is attended by a custodian. Some divinities have subsidiary groves, and in fact at Chitumbi and Busangu there are fig-trees dedicated to Shimunenga.[52]

Smith classifies the priesthood associated with Shimunenga as rudimentary in the sense that there is no hierarchical organization. Nevertheless, the office of custodian or priest is hereditary, and it is the priest's duty to make offerings for the people and to call them to periodical celebrations. He receives as wages a portion of the gifts brought to Shimunenga. Only the priest can enter the sacred grove and then only once yearly. The priest is not the only intermediary between the villagers and Shimunenga, however. At Kasenga there are (at least there were when Smith was there) two others who serve as mediums through which the divinity makes his will known. One of these is Nakahunga, a middle-aged man who has been "possessed" periodically by Shimunenga since childhood.[53] There are other communal divinities of importance in the life of the Ba-ila[54] although none so important for the people of Kasenga as Shimunenga.

Smith constantly calls attention to the parallels in thought between the experience of life on earth and that of the invisible world. The unseen is a copy of that which is seen. Therefore where kingship is highly developed, the king being far removed from his people and ruling through councilors and ministers, their view of "heaven" follows a similar pattern.[55]

The Ganda monarchy has been in existence for a thousand years and is much more unified from a tribal standpoint than the simple semi-autonomous village life of the Ba-ila. As the king—the *Kabaka*—has ministers through whom he rules the nation, even so *Katonda*, the Ganda name for the High God, also has ministers. Smith, quoting from Roscoe, alludes to forty such departmental gods, called *balubare*. These all appear to have been at one time human beings but are now deified and invested with superhuman power and influence. The chief minister of Katonda is *Mukasa*, who is a helpful healer of man's infirmities. His wife, *Nalwanga*, who is recognized as a goddess, is of special help to women. Mukasa's brother, *Kibuka*, is the god of war and his father, *Mususi*, the god of earthquakes. His grandfather, *Wanga*, is the oldest of the gods. The elaborate system includes also gods of birth, death, plague, hunting, agriculture, etc.[56]

Among the Ashanti of West Africa, the "lesser gods" are called *obosom*. According to Ashanti legend, *Onyame* the High God had a number of sons who were sent to earth to bless men and receive their gifts. Today the important rivers and lakes of Ashanti-land, such as Tano, Bosomtwe, Bea and Opo, bear the names of the sons of God and are considered to hold the power of the Creator.[57]

Beyond the sons of God, the Ashanti reserve an important place in their thought for *Asase Ya*, old Mother Earth.[58] Though lacking temple and altar, she is universally recognized and is especially remembered at planting time.[59] Smith quotes the prayer of an Ashanti farmer, as he sacrifices a fowl to the earth:

> "Grandfather so-and-so, you once came and hoed here, and then you left it to me. You also Earth, Asase Ya, on whose soil I am going to hoe, the yearly cycle has come around, and I am going to cultivate; when I work, let a fruitful year come upon me; do not let the knife cut me, do not let a tree break and fall upon me, do not let a snake bite me."[60]

The cult of the ancestors is generally carried on without recourse to priestly intermediaries. Each individual is responsible for relations with his own tutelary genius; relationships with the family divinities are maintained by the father of the family, whose duties are assumed by the eldest son upon his death. However, in the case of the community and tribal deities, not uncommonly (although not invariably) a temple or sacred grove is established to his honor. In such case a priest, or with more important deities a number of priests, are appointed to care for the shrine and lead the community in its necessary devotions.[61]

Important as these lesser gods are in the life of West Africa and among the Bantu-speaking people, it is still true to say that for the daily life of Africans they cannot rival in importance the ancestors, the individual and family divinities who are intimately concerned with the living members of the families of which they are themselves a part. This is the significance underlying the prayer of the Ashanti farmer, quoted above, where the entreaty to Asase Ya is combined with a plea to his deceased grandfather for help.[62]

Ancestors, Divinities and God

The ancestors are more important than the tribal deities in the daily life of Africans. They are nearer and more concerned with the fate of their own family members. The clan and tribal divinities are remote and are therefore uninterested in the mundane problems of man's daily existence. This statement also expresses accurately man's relationship with the Supreme God. Neither the tribal king nor God are to be bothered with the petty problems of men. One only comes before such high entities with matters of great import and when all other avenues of action have failed. Even when recourse is made to the intervention of the king, a lowly tribesman does not normally presume to go directly to him but makes his petition through his elders, the village head men and the clan chiefs, who act as his intermediaries at court. Even so the ancestors, communal divinities and tribal deities act as his intermediaries before the throne of God.[63]

The question of God's unity must be seen within the context of the diversity of the African spirit world: Is the African view of God to be characterized by the term monotheism or polytheism? Is God one or many?

Smith's answer is equivocal. God—that is, the Supreme God—is clearly one, but there are many divinities who encroach on Him, indeed who receive more attention and "worship" than God.[64] It depends upon whether one is thinking of the unique belief of the Africans in the Supreme God or whether one's thought is centered on the pantheon of ancestors and lesser deities which is no less significant.

Smith never specifically calls African Religion monotheistic. On various occasions he records without criticism the views of other commentators who do make such an identification.[65] However, it is clear that, for Edwin Smith, the decision as to whether African Traditional Religion is to be identified as monotheistic or polytheistic is contingent upon the definition given to those terms. Of Schmidt's concept of "primitive monotheism" he says: "Evidently Father Schmidt's definition of monotheism is not rigidly exclusive: it does not rule out other worshipful beings."[66]

Smith definitely considers the religion of West Africa polytheistic and approves Parrinder's identification of it as such.[67] Furthermore, he does not hesitate to label as polytheistic the highly developed system of departmental gods characteristic of the Ganda. In fact he sees Ganda religion as comparable to the religion of ancient Greece.[68] If it were only a matter of the "spirits," as contrasted with the "gods," he would be willing to call the religion "polydemonism" rather than polytheism;[69] but one runs into the other, making a clear line of demarcation impossible.[70] Nevertheless, Smith argues that a distinction should be made between the Ganda and that which characterizes the Bantu as a whole:

> I need not dwell upon the dynamism and animism [of the Ganda], but must say something about the polytheistic system which differs from what we find commonly among the Bantu.
>
> . . . .
>
> We feel in regard to this elaborate system, in which, as in the Greek mythology, gods and goddesses preside over various departments of life and death, that we are outside the main stream of Bantu thought, though the Bechuana also had their subsidiary gods, such as Cosa, the god of destiny; Nape, the god of divination.[71]

The difference may be only one of degree, not of kind; for Smith also says: "The Bantu creed is something much less than a pure monotheism."[72] At yet another point he comments: "It is only natural that they [the Ganda] should have developed ancestor-worship into a more elaborate polytheism than can be found among other Bantu tribes."[73]

CHRISTIAN CONTRIBUTION

Edwin Smith was no iconoclast. Christianity did not come to destroy African Religion but to fulfill it. This has not always been seen by missionaries; and where they have been inadequate in presenting the Christian conception, Smith does not hesitate to criticize them.

Although African Religion is not the final expression of God's will for men, it is nevertheless of great value and significance. The African perspective is fertile soil for the precious seed of the gospel. Together they can produce a luxuriant growth. There are some weeds in the garden of traditional belief, which must of necessity be pulled out; but it is by no means a garden merely of weeds. Some of the plants may be pruned to produce new flowers. Moreover, the pruning and planting takes time. It cannot all be done at once.[74]

Emphasis on Supreme God

Edwin Smith sees values in spiritism, values of eternal significance, values which not only should be retained but which serve to strengthen the Christian witness to the world:

Whatever view we take, we cannot deny, I think that "ancestor-worship" comprises values that should be conserved; and it becomes a question of how the Church can retain those values—that sense of continuity with the past, that reverence for established things, that intense awareness of the immediacy of the spiritual world, that sense of dependence upon unseen powers.[75]

The African is profoundly aware of the reality and significance of the spiritual world. He finds offensive the philosophy that man can live by bread alone or that life may be summed up in terms of the things that can be felt or touched. The assumption that death is the end of all things is to him inconceivable. The Christian missionary does not go to Africa to inform the people that there is a spiritual world or that the personality survives the grave. Africans know this from their own experience. This may be assumed *a priori*. Smith says: "If ever there was a people conscious that they are surrounded by a great cloud of witnesses it is the Bantu."[76]

In addition, the African is aware of his dependence upon unseen powers. He knows that in himself he is inadequate to live his life meaningfully. This sense of dependence obviously includes his recognition of the importance of the living members of his family and clan; what is of special significance in this context is that his sense of dependence goes beyond the seen to the unseen. Of modern-day interpreters of religious philosophy, Smith believes that Schliermacher came closest to the truth in defining the essence of the religious emotion as "the feeling of an absolute dependence."[77] He goes on to cite Radcliffe-Brown's observation that dependence on the ancestors includes the two elements of possibility and obligation. The ancestors not only *can* be depended upon, they *must* be depended upon:

"What I am calling the sense of dependence always has these two sides [the *can* and the *must*]. We can face life and its chances with confidence when we know that there are powers, forces and events on which we can rely, but we must submit to the control of our conduct by rules which are imposed. The entirely asocial individual—*and the entirely irreligious*—would be one who thought that he could be completely independent, relying only on himself, asking for no help and recognizing no duties."[78]

Important as these values are, however, African spiritism is not without its problems. Especially when viewed from the Christian perspective, it is found wanting; and its inadequacy is precisely its tendency to stifle or suffocate the belief in the High God.

Clearly for the Africans all power does not reside in God nor in any one of the unseen spirits but is distributed among them. They are all capable of making man happy or unhappy. Therefore it is only reasonable for the individual to seek the help of them all.[79] Smith reproduces the answer of an old Ashanti priest when asked why he did not trust Onyame for all things:

> "We in Ashanti have a fear of worshipping *Onyame* only, or the female Earth-god only, or any one spirit. We have to keep ourselves safe from, and make use of when we are able, the spirits of all things in the sky and upon earth."[80]

This world is a very complicated place in which to live. There are evil forces at work in it. Life is a mystery. One never knows when tragedy will strike. A wise man keeps up his relationships with the whole host of spiritual powers. He recognizes their presence, he speaks to them and brings them gifts.[81]

The essential problem involved in this view is not merely the fact that God is consigned to a relative position of being one among many. In the practical life of Africa, God tends to be crowded out entirely, or nearly so.

While acknowledging that virtually all Africans believe in the existence of a Supreme Being, Smith indicates that such a belief plays an "unproductive part" in their lives. It is not a "vital, effective" conception for them. This is especially true of the Bantu.[82] The divinities have temples or groves, God usually has none; they have a priesthood, He has none; they receive regular offerings, He receives them very rarely; they are constantly prayed to, He is addressed only in time of great necessity. Smith says:

> In all these respects there is, in the mind of the Bantu, a great and striking difference between the ancestral divinities and the Supreme Being. The latter is away on the fringe of their consciousness, the former occupy the center of attention.[83]

The belief in God's absenteeism from the ordinary affairs of man's existence is a cardinal belief in African Traditional Religion.[84] "Ancestor worship" draws attention away from God, thus contributing to His remoteness. The Ashanti priests affirm that "suman (fetishes) spoil the gods."[85] In addition, as cited earlier, there is an Ashanti myth to the effect that fetishes were not in the original order of things but came in as a result of the Fall.[86] In most literature dealing with African Traditional Religion, the term "fetish" is used, not for an amulet, but for a material object which is thought to be the temporary abode of a spirit. Hence the term "fetish," which admittedly is an ambiguous word precisely because of the confusion alluded to here, may refer to both dynamism and spiritism. However one regards the term, the references to "fetishes" among the Ashanti make clear that spiritism as practiced in Africa severely compromises the African conception of God:

> It is profoundly significant, I think, that as the old priests testified, Africans themselves, pagan Africans, recognise a lack in their beliefs—"fetishes spoil the gods."
> And not the fetishes only. The prevalence of ancestor-worship also tends to draw the minds of Africans away from the pure worship of the Almighty God of whom they are aware.[87]

In the final analysis, the great contribution of Christianity is the conception that God is near and concerned, the source of all power, the supreme help in time of need and deserving of the center of man's attention and worship. This is uniquely the message of the life and teachings of Jesus.[88]

Answer to Spiritism's Fears

Even as "fetishism" is related to both dynamism and spiritism, in the same way fear is a factor in these two aspects of African Traditional Religion. The fear connected with spiritism assumes various guises.

First of all, there is a fear connected with some funeral practices in Africa, namely the killing of slaves, wives and children in order to accompany a deceased chief into the other world, what Smith calls "the cruelest of all the cruel practices of the Bantu."[89] The following account shows the basis for anxiety:

> More than this, a man, especially a man of consequence, has need, the Bantu argue, of slaves and wives and children to serve and cherish him in the world to which he is going. There is only one way of providing him with them, they must be killed.[90]

Smith goes on to quote Bentley's experience among the Kuba of Congo. First the slaves are dealt with:

"The unfortunate slaves are brought. One of them is placed in the seat and fastened to it. A tall flexible pole is stuck into the ground at some distance behind the seat. From the top of the pole a cagelike arrangement is suspended by a cord. The pole is bent down and the cage is fitted to the unfortunate man's head. He is blind-folded, but he knows what is coming, for he has been present before, at like functions, when others were placed on the fatal seat with laughter and much merriment. The executioner commences to dance and make feints; at last, with a fearful yell, he decapitates his victim by one sweep of the huge knife. The pole thus released springs the head into the air. The crowd yells with delight and excitement. The body is unbound and a new victim placed on the seat."[91]

After the slaves have been dispatched to the other world comes the turn of the wives. The names of the four chosen to accompany the deceased are withheld until this moment:

"The marked women are seized, four of them; a few blows with a heavy stock suffices to break their arms and legs and they too are placed in the grave, living, but unable to scramble out. The body of their dead lord is then placed upon the groaning women and the earth is filled in."[92]

It is difficult for Westerners to be objective in analyzing this evidence. Undoubtedly the fear generated among Africans in the face of such practices is not the same as that which would inspire Christians in similar circumstances. Only this can account for the fact that women would sometimes jump into the grave voluntarily in order to be buried alive with their husbands.[93]

Nevertheless, it is impossible to imagine the above-mentioned violence without fear—if not in the wife, most certainly so in some of the others.[94] Therefore, it is not to be wondered at that, before the arrival of Christianity, Africans themselves questioned the propriety of these actions. Smith remarks that the custom apparently never existed among the Ba-ila proper; and by the time of his arrival it had disappeared throughout the area. Furthermore, he calls attention to the disapproval expressed by the Ganda when their chief sought to visit his predecessor more than once yearly. The tribe was quite frankly fearful of the consequences of the royal visits; and the violence attached thereto was ultimately eliminated.

In opposing such conduct, Christianity tends to strengthen the latent African disapproval of it. These are some of the "weeds," needing to be pulled out, mentioned earlier. In all of his writings, Edwin Smith sounds a clarion call, pleading with Europeans (missionaries included) to try to understand rather than condemn African thought and customs. Nevertheless, he is not a sentimentalist or a romanticist. He loves and appreciates the Africans, but he also knows that the "noble savage" is a myth. There is an unpleasant side to African life. It is possible for a missionary to be "so busy seeking to understand that he fails to resent the evil as sin and is led into an easy tolerance of wrong."[95] In the sense that Christianity contributes to the elimination of these customs, it may be seen as a factor in the eradication of fear as well.

A second area where fear is associated with spiritism is in "ancestor worship" itself. As mentioned earlier, Smith minimizes this fear. He does so precisely because so many other commentators on African Traditional Religion have given so much attention to it. However, this does not mean that it is of no significance. Fear is an element although not the major one. The fear may even be salutary in that it contributes to reverence and trust.[96]

Nevertheless, "ancestor worship" is not all salutary fear. Smith makes clear that the ancestors not uncommonly make their presence known by causing sickness. In such cases the family calls on a diviner to inform them as to which divinity is angry and why. Recognition is then made of the family's failure to fulfill its duties and offerings are given to appease the offended spirit.[97] The element of fear, or at least of uneasiness, is obviously heightened by the African conception of the ancestors as jealous and capricious, in short as beings bearing the same emotions as the living.

Although the fundamental conception of African Traditional Religion pictures the ancestors as good not evil, whose role it is to bless not curse, some fear is also involved. The following brief quotation seems to support such a generalization:

> To some extent it is quite true that fear enters into their worship of their ancestors, the fear of the consequences that will follow any failure in their pious duty. Their real feeling is a mingling of trust and fear; does it not merit the name of reverence, that highly compound emotion which is a blend of wonder, fear, trust, gratitude and subjection?[98]

Christianity's contribution lies in the transfer of dependence from the ancestors, who are good but capricious, to the Supreme

God, who revealed Himself in Jesus Christ not only as completely good but also as the Saviour and Healer of man's infirmities.[99]

Yet a third realm where fear enters into spiritism—and here Smith is unambiguous—is the African belief in the existence of evil spirits. These are universally believed in and feared. They were at one time humans living on earth, but for various reasons they left the realm of the living angry and disillusioned. Their main preoccupation now is to wreak revenge on the living. Smith indicates that this belief takes from the African experience of life much of its joy,[100] and he characterizes the effect on the people as one of "unmitigated dread":[101]

> It is difficult, and indeed impossible, for us to realise the intensity of this belief in the powers of evil spirits and the terror which it causes. Christianity appeals to the African largely because it comes as a redemption from his fears.[102]

Trans-tribal Community

The values attached to spiritism are not confined merely to teaching an awareness of the spiritual world and dependence on unseen powers. The ancestor cult is also a binding force in community life and serves an extremely important function in the creation and preservation of social solidarity:

> That this Spiritism has valuable social values we recognize. It is a consecration of the principle of continuity in human life; it tends to foster a conservatism that is salutary in many respects; it stabilizes custom; and it fosters respect for the aged.[103]

It is clear that there are two sides to the picture. Although the values are evident, there are also concomitant disadvantages. Continuity is good in human life, but change is also necessary. Custom must be stabilized if men are to live together, but custom may become fossilized. Respect for the aged is essential to social solidarity, but there must be a place for the young as well. Conservatism can be both salutary and unsalutary.

Edwin Smith is not guilty of perpetuating the error that African society is completely stagnant.[104] He recognizes that change occurs, but he questions the viability of some of the traditional mechanisms of change:

> Let us recognise that Spiritism exerts a powerful social influence. The ancestral spirits form the chief controlling force over the

living members of the community. To offend them by committing a breach of ancient customary law is sin which will bring punishment in its train. The fact that their bodies lie in the earth and the spirits hover about the villages, makes home and land sacred to the African, and out of that sentiment spring many virtues. We see at once the strength and the weakness of the African communal system—weakness because an intense conservatism is fostered by this devotion to the ancestors. Changes do come about, but slowly and only as they are sanctioned by the ancestors speaking through their mediums and representatives. But if there is weakness, there is also strength—strength born of loyalty.[105]

Smith's approach to the African view of community is characterized at every point by his feeling for its strengths and weaknesses. He admires the solidarity of African society, and he believes that there is a great deal here for Europeans to learn. Indeed much in the African conception is closer to Christianity than anything in the West. There are elements of eternal value to share with all peoples.[106]

However, Smith is also aware of the weaknesses of African society. All is not as it should and must be. He agonizes over the conflicting claims for individualism and communalism, and he finds himself unable to rest in either camp. He sees the break-up of African society due to the pressure of the European invaders.[107] At times he seems resigned to this process as inevitable: "All peoples have to pass that way. The British peoples have not been exempt from this law."[108] Nevertheless, he refuses to accept Western individualism as the final will of God for men. He longs for a system which will embody the strengths of both African communalism and European individualism, eschewing at the same time their weaknesses and errors:

> The pendulum swings to the tune of the Hegelian logic: thesis, collectivism: antithesis, individualism. The synthesis has not yet been found in a system which does equal justice to the social and self-regarding instincts of man. The Africans have hitherto lived in the collectivist stage: the community has been the unit; every individual interest has been subordinate to the general welfare. In many directions this excites our admiration—even envy. There is a solidarity that civilized communities find it hard to attain. The corporate sentiment that trades unions create among their members is but a faint reflection of the brotherhood found within the African's clan. The Africans have, it is true, to pay

heavily for their collectivism, in the injustice done to personal strivings and aspirations; just as we pay heavily for our individualism, in selfishness and greed.[109]

Hope for the future lies in Christianity. The synthesis of individualism and collectivism is found in only one place—the Kingdom of God. The Kingdom is more than a social ideal or a new world of equality and freedom. It is God's rule. It is the Family of men in which God is recognized as Father and King. The Christian life must be lived and realized in community. The individual is important to be sure; but the truly personal must also be social, for it expresses itself in love. The Kingdom is both present and future. Christians do not make or build it. They simply declare it, as Jesus did.[110]

Smith recognizes that missionaries coming from the West with their emphasis on individual conversion[111] have contributed to the disintegration of African society. Nevertheless, Christianity builds up as well. Much depends upon the missionary and the wisdom of the methods used.[112]

He believes that the opening up of Africa to the West would in any case, irrespective of Christianity, result in a serious challenge to the traditional society.[113] Looked at from this perspective, Christianity actually serves the useful purpose of providing a cushion for African society in its traumatic encounter with Western culture:

> Instances will presently be adduced to show that while some amount of temporary confusion has attended the introduction of Christianity—confusion that is due, perhaps, more to its presentation than to the Gospel itself—its intention, its tendency, and its achievement on the whole, have been on the side of the integration of African society.[114]

The close links of the Africans to their land are largely due to their belief that it is the dwelling place of the ancestors. The fertility of the soil and the health of their animals are assured as long as the ancestors are respected.[115] But the result of the European invasion is a radical alteration in the relation of the people to their land. Sometimes Europeans simply steal the African land;[116] sometimes they misconstrue agreements for land use to signify sale;[117] sometimes they press the Africans into forced labor gangs to work on European plantations;[118] sometimes the lure of the city lights and the attraction of industrial jobs is enough to induce them to leave their land.[119] The result of all these forces is a separation of the African from his land and his ancestors, resulting in an almost inevitable disintegration of his society:

> Anything that tends to separate the living from the dead is inimical to the social structure. In these days, thousands of Africans leave their homes for long periods to work for Europeans. They who go are absent not only from their tangible fellow-tribesmen; they depart also from the presence of the ancestors, for these remain attached to their homes. They do not travel. The man on a European mine or plantation is therefore cut off from the restraints which the presence of his ancestors exercises on his conduct, and almost invariably deterioration sets in. Almost everywhere this element of African religion is in process of decay. Unless something stronger is put in its place, the future is full of peril for the Africans.[120]

Smith recognizes the threat of secularism, but he continues to hope that Africa will accept the gospel of Jesus Christ as an alternative.[121] By transferring the allegiance of the African from the ancestor cult to the Supreme God, who is not bound to any one parcel of land, Christianity is able to introduce a new integrative principle into African life. Whatever the future may hold, the break-up of the ancestor cult is inevitable and irreversible.

This ought not to be construed to mean, however, that the continued disintegration of African communal life is a necessary concomitant. Christianity must see to it that it contributes nothing further to the destruction of African society. Smith calls upon his fellow missionaries to eschew their customary individualistic approach: "Since the African is accustomed to act as a member of a group, it would seem wise for the missionary to aim at, and expect, movements in the mass towards Christianity."[122]

Something also needs to be said regarding the exclusive nature of African society. The traditional African community is characterized by social solidarity, but that solidarity does not extend beyond the clan and tribe. There is no place in the traditional system for strangers or foreigners. They are, on the contrary, regarded as dangerous enemies. In a sense there is a logical inconsistency in African Traditional Religion in that it recognizes the reality of the Supreme God who is the Creator of all men, yet makes no provision for relations between the various tribes of men. The problem is precisely the one which has preoccupied Smith throughout his study, namely that the belief in the Creator

God plays by and large an unproductive part in their thought and life. Therefore, since the mainspring of attention is centered on their ancestors and tribal deities, concern on the human plane is also restricted to the members of their own family, clan and tribe.[123]

The question of the adequacy of the ancestral cult becomes crucial in the new Africa which is characterized by the creation of cities and the movement of people from one tribal area to another. There is no solution apart from a new allegiance to the Supreme God who is revealed in Jesus Christ.[124]

Edwin Smith believes that the Church is the answer to the communal-individual challenge which confronts Africa. The Church must embody the values of the traditional clan system while eliminating its weaknesses. The Church must itself become a clan, a new clan. While opening the door to membership for all, the Church must provide the same sense of community, of oneness in common endeavor and mutual support which was the strength of the old clan:

> And whether or no the clan system survives in the pagan society, it should be sublimated in the Christian Church. So I was accustomed to explain the Church on the analogy of the clan. Here, I would say, is a new clan, into which men can enter by adoption, a clan comprising men and women of all races, all united by the closest bonds of fellowship—the clan of the Bana-Kristo (the word "Christian" is so translated in our Ila New Testament), whose Head is the Lord Jesus Christ. The fault of a clan is, of course, its exclusiveness, its clannishness; sublimation comes in, when in the spirit of the Good Samaritan we can say, "Let us do good to *all* men and in particular to the household of the faith."[125]

As has been seen, Smith is critical of the individualistic approach of many missionaries.[126] Nevertheless, he insists that his description of the Church as a new clan is not only a pious ideal but a living reality in twentieth-century Africa. His concern is not merely the ideal Church but whether the African clan can really be transformed into a Church life which is manifestly better. He says:

> The true measure of the Church's success is the degree to which it has built up Christian communities—not of denationalized folk, but of Africans, organized on lines congenial to the native mind; not alienated from the mass of the people, but animated with a true spirit of brotherliness towards all; not disdainful of out-

siders but exercising a wide and elevating influence over the whole tribe or nation, and ever drawing into their circle those who have remained without, until the religious society becomes co-extensive with the civil community. . . .

Such branches of the Christian Church are in fact being formed in Africa, and prove by their measure of success that the social sense of the Africans can be utilised for high purpose. Take as an example, the Church in Uganda.[127]

The Church Missionary Society in Uganda wisely utilized the traditional civil system in organizing the Church and has from the beginning emphasized that Africa must be evangelized by Africans who are supported by their own people. The Ganda Church shows how effectively the clan feeling can be sublimated in the Church.[128]

Christianity was fortunate in Uganda in that the Ganda were highly organized under able leadership, and the work was well established before European colonists arrived in large numbers. Although this has not been the case everywhere, the Church has often been able to make a significant contribution to the reorganization and reintegration of society:

> In other parts of Africa the Missions have had to do with broken and scattered remnants of tribes and have played no small part in their reorganization. In Basutoland and Nyasaland, to name no other territories, and scarcely to a less degree than in Uganda, Christianity has exerted and still exerts, a tremendous social influence.[129]

4

Disposition:
Does God Love Man?

TRADITIONAL VIEW

One of Edwin Smith's favorite stories, coming from his experience among the Ba-ila people, is the legend of a very old woman who left home in search of God, in order to ask Him to explain the tragedy that so besets the lives of men on earth. In the story Leza is identified by His epithet, *Shikakunamo*, "the Besetting One," the One who cannot be shaken off. It is well to quote his account of it, for it provides an excellent introduction to Smith's understanding of the disposition of God in African Religion:

> In very ancient times . . . an old, old woman was the victim of his besetting. He slew her mother and father while she was yet a child; and in the course of the years all her relations perished at his hand. Surely, said she, I shall keep those who sit on my thighs; but no, even these, the children of her children, were taken from her, and she was left alone, alone. Then came into her heart the desperate resolution to seek out the Besetting One, and to demand the reason of it all. Somewhere up there in the sky must be his dwelling—if only she could reach it. She made several vain efforts to construct a tower of wood that would reach to the sky, and upon which she could mount up to God. But the tower always fell before it was high enough.[1]

Thwarted in her attempt to reach God by means of a tower, the old woman devised another scheme:

Far away upon the horizon she could see where earth and sky met, and she thought that if she could but reach that spot she would find a way to God. She set out, and as she passed from country to country, people asked her: "Old woman, where are you going all alone?" And she replied: "I am seeking Leza." "Seeking Leza! What for?" She told them, and they said to her: "You are bereft of friends and kindred. In what do you differ from others? Shikakunamo sits on the back of every one of us and we cannot shake him off!" The old woman never obtained her desire—never found God to ask that poignant, Why? And from that day to this, say the Africans, no man or woman has solved the riddle of this painful earth.[2]

There are several ideas in this legend which need to be considered in seeking to understand the African conception of God's disposition.

Tragic Sense of Life

The first thing of significance in this story is the tragic sense of life evident in African experience, and God's relationship to it. The old woman personally encountered one calamity after another. She begins life as an orphan and ends it alone and in despair: those who speak with her on her journey have had the same experience. Moreover, this tragedy is all in some strange manner related to God. In the *Ila-Speaking Peoples'* version, the men retort: "In what way do you differ from others? Shikakunamo sits on the back of every one of us, and we cannot shake Him off!" And she dies of a broken heart (*yamuyaya inzezela*).[3]

It must be said that there are variations between tribes and even within any given tribe. If life is happy, God tends to be identified as good; whereas for the one experiencing sorrow, He is cruel.[4] All Africans do not connect God directly with the ambiguity of life. The Pare people of Tanzania, for example, say that they know nothing more about *Kyumbi* than that He is the Creator of all things; beyond that He is not interested in them nor they in Him. Others picture God as so kind and good that He never causes distress, hence there is no reason to fear or propitiate Him.[5] However, these are exceptions. Most Africans, as with the old woman of the story, turn to God for the explanation of events which are otherwise incomprehensible.[6]

To understand this, it is necessary to recognize that for the

Africans natural causes do not serve as final explanations. Every event has a reason and a personal cause. Africans are often called illogical; but as Smith says, they are ruthless in their logic.[7] They are not satisfied with secondary explanations and have no appreciation for the concept of coincidence. The question "why" is fundamental for them.[8] When illness occurs, merely listing the cause as a disease, which would probably satisfy a Westerner, is of only relative interest. The African wants to know *why* that particular person contracted the disease in question.[9]

In the case of death, Africans seek to find out *why* it occurred and specifically *who* was responsible. The main recognized causes are witches or evil spirits; but when there is no other explanation, they say: *ndufu lwaka Leza,* "it is a death which comes from God."[10]

Smith notes that the Africans are not comforted, but rather filled with fear, by the thought that God's eyes may be upon them. The Ba-ila say for example: *Notangala Leza udikubwene,* "if you are happy, God sees you." Contrary to what we might suppose, the idea is not that happiness is related to being in the presence of God. The saying means that all has gone well and now a sudden disaster may be anticipated. The Ba-ila call the one who experiences this unexpected sadness *mulabile-Leza,* "one upon whom God's eyes are fixed."[11]

It is true that all of life is not tragedy. There are also joys and happiness. Hence while it is correct to say that tragedy comes from God, goodness also comes from Him. The Ashanti of Ghana apply to Onyame the praise-titles: *Amosu,* "Giver of rain"; *Amovwa,* "Giver of sunshine"; and *Tetereboensu,* "Wide-spreading Creator of water."[12] The Ba-ila are especially impressed with God's bounty in giving the rain. They call Him: "*Muninde,* 'the Guardian'; *Chaba,* 'the Giver'; *Luvhunabaumba,* 'Deliverer of those in trouble'; *Shintemwe,* 'the Compassionate'; *Shichenchemenwa,* 'the Good-natured one'."[13]

However, even in God's gifts, one sees the ambiguity of life. Leza is Chaba, "the Giver"; but He is also *Ipaokubozha,* "He who gives and causes to rot." Moreover, He is *Chaba-wakeaba-ocitadiwa,* "the Giver who gives also what cannot be eaten."[14] Smith says:

> He gives things, but His gifts are not permanent: fruits fall from the trees and decay; the rainy season passes into winter: the corn in the bins is spoilt by weevil, etc.[15]

Running through all of this is a fatalistic view of life. God is *Ushatwakwe*, "Master, Owner, of His things." All things belong to Him and He determines the fate of all. One old man described life to Smith as similar to the work card given by the European employer to his laborers: You cannot leave work until your time comes, but then you must go at once.[16]

There seems to be an effort on the part of the Africans to blame agents other than God for the tragedy of life, and most especially death. Sometimes man himself is blamed. Smith repeats one such story told to him by an old member of the Ba-ila tribe:

> Long ago, when Leza caused men to descend to earth, he gave them grain and told them to take good care of it. They sowed and reaped an abundant harvest. They gathered it into their garners, and began to eat. But the food was so abundant that they contracted extravagant habits; they were not content with a single meal eaten in the evening; no, they took to eating also in the daytime. But the grain was so abundant still that their gluttony made little impression upon their stores—the grain-bins were still full to over-flowing. Then the foolish people said: "We have eaten and eaten till we are full, and yet there is plenty. What is the use of all this food? Let us burn it."[17]

The result of their foolishness was that they were soon hungry and famine made its appearance. Nevertheless, Leza did not abandon the people but gave them wild fruits, admonishing them that henceforth they would have to be content with roots and berries.[18]

In this example God is pictured as concerned about men, providing for their needs, upset with their foolishness and attempting to alleviate the suffering they have brought upon themselves. At least in the beginning things went well between God and man; but man ruined it all by his perversity.

African myths concerning the origin of death are very widespread, and most reveal an attempt to exonerate God from the blame for this calamity.

A common way of telling the myth is that, after men were created, God sent to them Chameleon to inform them that they would not die and Hare[19] to tell them that they would. Unfortunately Chameleon was too slow and Hare arrived first. By the time Chameleon finally reached them, it was too late. Another version pictures Chameleon as sent to deliver a message of death, with Hare carrying later a message of life. Hare arrived first;

but when Chameleon came on the scene, he disputed Hare. In anger Hare returned to God in order to complain, but God allowed Chameleon's message to stand. In both stories, Chameleon is the villain, and this explains in no small measure the African hatred and fear of that animal.[20]

The Ashanti say that God sent Goat to men with the message that, although they would die, they would not utterly perish but would go to be with Him in heaven. On the way, Goat stopped to eat from a bush. When God saw that Goat lingered, He sent Sheep with the same message. However, Sheep perverted the words and told men that they would perish with no final place to go. When Goat finally arrived, the men would not believe.[21]

In the account of the Kaonde of Zambia, God gave to the bird, Honeyguide, three pots to take to the first man and woman, two of which contained seeds for planting and the third to be kept shut until God's arrival. On the way, Honeyguide opened the two with seeds and shut them up again. Then he made a hole in the third as well; and out poured cruel animals, disease and death, so much so that even God could not repair the damage.[22]

Sometimes man himself is made responsible. The Lunda of Zambia say that Nzambi ordered the first man and woman to remain awake while the moon was in the sky, with death the punishment for disobedience. After the man grew old and was in poor eyesight, one night the moon went behind the clouds where the old man could not see it; and he died in his sleep.[23]

These examples illustrate the African attempt to exonerate God from the full responsibility of bringing death and disaster on men. Obviously some do this more thoroughly than others. But in all there is ambiguity. Smith says:

> It would seem that the Africans wished very much that God was benevolent. But the facts have been too much for them. They have not succeeded in proving the goodness of God.[24]

God Absent and Remote

A second matter of significance in the story of the old Ba-ila woman, whose life had been marred by sorrow and tragedy, is the fact that God is absent.

Her grievance is real. She was orphaned early in life and has known nothing but misery since then. All her children have been taken from her until she despairs even of her own life. Why?

Why should this be? Then she hits upon the desperate resolution to seek out God and ask for His explanation. But where is He? He certainly is not here on earth. He must be somewhere up in the sky: Oh, if only she could find Him! God's absence from the world is a very important theme in African Traditional Religion.

It would be wrong to see God's absence as an absolute separation in a deistic sense. God does send the rain and is intimately connected with the crises of life. Moreover, some of the epithets of God picture Him as being everywhere. Among the Ba-ila, for example, He is called *Mutalabala* which is derived from the verb *kutalabala*, "to be age-lasting, to be everywhere and all times, equivalent to the phrase, *Uina ng'aela* ('He has nowhere, or nowhen, that he comes to an end')."[25]

However, this ought not to be construed to mean that God is present and active in the ordinary affairs of the life of men. Smith notes that Donald Fraser, in his book *The New Africa*, does indeed attribute this belief to the Africans: "God is in the world to-day, not an absentee God, but living and working."[26] Smith indicates that such a belief is rare in Africa:

> The old men agreed that God must be present and active; but that is precisely what many Africans would deny. God made things at the beginning; He may control the great cosmical forces, rain, lightning, thunder; He has ordained the destiny of all creatures; but they would not admit that He can come into immediate relationship with individual men in the affairs of everyday life.[27]

It may be that Fraser, or the African elders with whom he talked, had in mind God's action in the great celestial phenomena or His role in the ambiguities of life. Be that as it may, Smith challenges the statement that Africa does not believe in an "absentee God."

Many of the African myths concern themselves with God's departure from the world, and Smith notes the parallel between them and the myth of the Fall of Man in biblical literature. He examines the evidence for both African influence on the biblical ideas and contrariwise the influence of biblical sources on the African myths. He concludes that the African myths do not owe their origin to Judeo-Christian sources:

> While some of the myths may contain ideas, much diluted, derived from biblical or pre-biblical sources, I do not believe

that the myths which contain such material owe their origin to
the Bible. The myths may legitimately be used in the study of
the African doctrine of God.[28]

In the stories of God's departure there appears a similar
phenomenon to that noted in the myths of the origin of death,
namely, an attempt to exonerate God from the responsibility for
His absenteeism.

In the conception of the Ashanti, long ago Onyame lived with
men on earth. All went well and they were happy together.
However, one day God watched some women pounding grain.
For some unknown reason, they were annoyed at His presence
and told Him to leave. When He did not hurry fast enough,
they beat Him with their pestles. Therefore God left the world
to its fetishes; and until today men sigh at how happy they would
be if it were not for "that old woman."[29]

The Ewe tribe, also of Ghana, have two explanations for the
distance between man and God. In their view Mawu has always
had His dwelling in the sky; but in the early days the sky was
very near to earth. Some say that it was the smoke coming from
man's fires which got in God's eyes, making Him withdraw.
Others say that men cleaned their hands by rubbing them on the
sky and pushed their grain stompers into God's face; so Mawu
became exasperated and moved to a safer distance.[30]

According to the Barotse of Zambia, in the beginning *Nyambe*
and His wife *Nasilele* lived on earth together with God's
creatures, including *Kamonu*, the first man, and his wife. Everything God did, Kamonu copied. One day Kamonu watched God
smelting iron; immediately he made himself a spear and killed
a lechwe with it. He also hunted other animals for food. God
was angry since He wanted Kamonu to think of the animals as
his brothers; so Kamonu was sent away for a year. When Kamonu
returned, God forgave him and gave him land for farming; but
the buffaloes and eland destroyed his crops at night. Again
Kamonu put them to death. Nyambe crossed the water to be
away from man, but Kamonu built a boat and followed. God
climbed a mountain and man pursued Him. By this time the
whole earth was filled with Kamonu's children. So God pressed
Spider to spin a long thread up into the sky and Nyambe and
Nasilele ascended into heaven by it. They put out Spider's eyes
and cut the thread. Kamonu tried to build a tower to God, but it

came crashing down, killing all the workers. Then Kamonu gave up his attempt to find God.[31]

There are many other stories of God's departure. They are all different, yet strangely alike. Smith sums up the matter in these words:

> These stories make clear the belief of a great number of Africans, possibly of most of them, that at the start when God had made men, He and they were living together on earth, living in harmony as friends; and that they are separate today, man on earth and God in some far-off living-place, because of man's wrong-doing or foolish behaviour.[32]

As noted previously, the Africans' conception of God is strongly influenced by the social organization of the tribe in which they live. In societies where the idea of kingship is strong and the king is remote from the people, their conception of the Supreme God follows a similar pattern. Again the Ganda may serve as an example. The Kabaka traditionally rules the people through his ministers, to whom he delegates certain powers. The common people have little contact with him. When they have problems, they do not present them directly to the king but to his mediators.

God is conceived in a similar way. One cannot go to Katonda directly but only through the ancestors and the local gods, especially Mukasa, His first minister. There are other gods, each with his or her own function. Of Katonda little is said. He does not come to earth or become involved in the affairs of the world. All this is the responsibility of Mukasa. Katonda was busy at the creation of all things; now He is to be left alone.[33] A similar phenomenon is noted among the Ashanti.[34] Smith says:

> Similarly, we may expect that social organization will be reflected in religious belief and practice. Where the kingship is strong, and the king is hedged about with divinity and only to be approached through a graded hierarchy of underlings, it is natural that the Lord of the universe should be thought of as a remote chief with whom communication is possible only through intermediaries.[35]

Man's Search for God

Yet a third element enters into the story of the old Ba-ila woman, namely, her search for God. She was neither satisfied with her lot nor with God's absence; and so she set out on a journey to find Him. She sought both a new understanding of her situation and a new relationship with the Author of that situation.

The search for God is a common feature of African Religion. At one time God was near and lived close to man. Through man's wrongdoing or foolishness, God left him and made His dwelling high in the sky. He does not want to be bothered with man any more.

Nevertheless, man is not satisfied with that state of affairs. He wants to find God, not just to provide an explanation for the ambiguities of this present life but also to restore a relationship which through man's own stupidity has become an estrangement.

The story of Kamonu illustrates man's attempt to search for the missing God. Kamonu builds a boat to cross the water. He climbs a mountain. He builds a tower. But it is all to no avail.

Stories of attempts to build a tower to heaven appear in many cultures and many different African tribes. The Pare people of Tanzania tell the story of Kyumbi, the Supreme God, and *Kiriamagi,* the first man. Once again man's disobedience and God's departure are evident. A new element, although not un-related to the experience of the Ba-ila woman, is added when Kiriamagi urges his people to build a tower in order to make war against Kyumbi. As they build, God looks at them with disdain as if they were but ants. Then there is a great earthquake which puts an end to both the tower and the laborers. The result is that God moves to an even greater distance; He is now far, far away. Still men are not satisfied and desire to induce Him to come down, but Kyumbi will not listen.[36]

The old Ba-ila woman did not find God. Her whole life was one great tragedy, and she was frustrated in her final quest. The story ends in pathos: "She never obtained her desire: she died of a broken heart (*yamuyaya inzezela*). And from her time to this, nobody has ever solved her problem!"[37]

Donald Fraser's book, *The New Africa*, is of interest because it furnishes a glimpse into the evangelistic methods used by this able and sensitive missionary. In a certain district where Fraser worked, many Africans had become Christian, but the elders remained outside. Fraser questioned them as to their reason. "We are too old to understand the new doctrines and the new God," they said. When Fraser insisted that the Christian God was not a new God, the old men agreed to listen to him.

As Fraser moved step by step, he discovered that the elders had no question about God's existence or His activity in the world. However, the conceptions of God as "good" and "love" were new doctrines for them, and they found them hard to believe.[38]

In the final analysis the African God is distant and little concerned with men and their problems. The Africans long for a different view, but they do not seem to find it in their own situation. The last word on the question of God's benevolence in African Traditional Religion is at best ambiguous and uncertain. Edwin Smith concludes:

> The voice of Nature is equivocal, uncertain in meaning. Yes, God is Chaba, "the Great Allotter", who bestows blessing upon us, say the Ila; but He is also Ipaukubozha, "He who gives and rots". The riddle of this painful earth afflicts and perplexes Africans as it does ourselves. This gives them pause when they would think of God as only good. In their myths they try to exonerate God from the responsibility of causing death to come among men who were intended to be immortal; they ascribe much sickness, misery and death to the malice of evil spirits and of men; some, as do the Hottentots and Bushmen, assign all evil to the agency of a great Bad Spirit. But the doubt remains—the doubt that Dante puts in the mouth of Francesca of Rimini: *Se fosse amico il re dell'universo:* If the king of the universe were a friend . . .[39]

CHRISTIAN CONTRIBUTION

The legend of the old Ba-ila woman, who knew only tragedy in life, serves not only to show the African conception of God's disposition, but by contrast it reveals the Christian position as well. Although there are signs of God's love manifest in the traditional theological outlook of Africa, that picture is ambiguous and unclear. Christianity, on the other hand, insists unequivocally that God is deeply concerned about men and that "love" is the best word to describe His attitude toward them. Indeed God made known the depths of His love by coming among men in His Son.

God's Search for Man

In the African view the essential reality is man's search for God, while God remains indifferent and reluctant. Man takes the initiative in his quest, but he is unable to find or prevail upon God.

In the beginning all went well between God and man, but man broke that relationship of harmony by his foolish and wicked ways. Man's perversity caused God's departure, and now no amount of pleading can induce Him to return.

The myths of God's departure are African equivalents to the Fall of Man in biblical literature;[40] furthermore they do not owe their origin to the Bible but are indigenous to the African situation. A comparison of the African and Judeo-Christian view of God's reaction to the Fall is therefore important in a consideration of the question at hand. The Bible agrees with the notion that there was an original harmony which was broken by man. The result was man's expulsion from the garden. However, in the biblical account, this does not provoke God's departure but rather provides the impulse for a series of new ventures on God's part, in order to restore the original relationship. Smith does not mention God's activity in the pre-historical and Patriarchal periods, but he does refer to God's initiative at the Exodus and the revelation of His name to Moses. By leading the Israelites from Egypt, He shows Himself to them as Guide, Helper and Saviour. God takes the first step; so the Exodus must always be considered a proof of His love.[41] He leads them in the wilderness. He goes before them as a cloud by day and a pillar of fire by night.[42] He forms an agreement with them, and the ark is a sign of His presence. In the various crises of life, God sends them His prophets to show them their errors and to lead them in His way. All of this is by way of preparation for His great and final revelation in Jesus Christ.

Jesus' teaching displays an emphasis on God as a Seeker of men. This is made clear by Jesus' use of such parables as the Lost Sheep:

> God's acts are not only kind; He not only has no desire to take His good things from the men who give no thought to Him: He has a strong desire to get wrong doers to come back to Him, even as a keeper of sheep is moved to go looking for his wandering sheep. . . .
>
> These sayings of Jesus, and others, make quite clear what His thought was about God. Their sense is that God is the Father of all. His great design is that all the best things are to be for all men. It is for all men, in their turn, to be true sons of God, pleasing Him, living in harmony with Him.[43]

Not only did Jesus' teachings identify God as a Seeker of men, His life and death also manifested it in a supreme way. He was the Son of God, but He came among men and made Himself one with them. He identified himself with *all* men, even to the most hated and despised among them.[44]

Jesus' death on the cross was the supreme manifestation of God's search for man. The cross shows the lengths to which God will go in identifying Himself with men and effecting the restoration of the broken relationship between God and man. The cross also shows something else. It provides a new perspective from which to look at the evil of the world and the ambiguity of life; and it reveals God as the Healer of man's ills, not his enemy. Smith says:

> By becoming a man Jesus made Himself one with us. He took upon Himself the weight of evil which is upon us, all the pain and shame of it. The shame of men who put Him to death was the true cross which was upon His back and in His heart. . . . In Jesus we see God Himself taking upon Himself the pain and shame of man's sin. From the cross comes a ray of light upon the darkest of our questions. In the great fight against evil on earth and in our hearts God is not at a distance and out of touch. He is in it with us. And the cross lets us see how far God is ready to go, and does go, for the salvation of men. He goes as far as love will go—to the very limit.[45]

Smith notes that Africans would like to believe that God is on their side, but their thought is confused by the evil of life. They can accept the thought that God pities man, but they find it difficult to believe that God is a Saviour who desires their deliverance from evil. This concept of God came to Africa in the good news of Jesus Christ.[46]

It is this belief which has captured the thought of countless Africans. Smith records the reaction of one such person, an old African woman, to the preaching of the gospel: "There now! I was certain in my heart that there is a God like that!"[47] James Aggrey, that great African Christian of the Gold Coast, put it in these words:

> To the African's soul the name and personality of Jesus and Him crucified alone answers all questions. We always felt there ought to be somebody like that. Africa is a-hungering for the Christ, and Christ Jesus can take that continent in a generation if His disciples will give Him a chance.[48]

God Near and Concerned

In the African view, God is pictured as being far away and uninterested. In essence God is not concerned about men. He was interested. In the beginning it was different. God lived on earth and men lived in harmony with Him. But that is all changed now. God has His dwelling in heaven; man lives on earth; and the two have few dealings with each other.

Smith sees a parallel between African and Jewish views. The Jews also came to place God at a distance from man, thus creating a gap between *Yahwe* and Israel. Only the designated religious officials—the priests—had contact with Him, and they acted as the intermediaries between God and His people.[49]

Jesus came to bring a different view. God is near. He is in your midst and in your heart. Look at the birds and how God feeds them! Look at the flowers and their colors—more splendid than King Solomon! And if God cares for these things, will He not care for you as well?[50] God is not far away but near. Men do not need to take Him offerings or come to Him through a priestly intermediary. They can approach Him as a child does his father.

Smith generally tries to avoid placing the Christian view of God in opposition to the African conception, preferring to see Christianity as the fulfillment of African Religion.[51] Nevertheless, there is an unavoidable opposition involved:

> No doubt there were good men and women among the Jews, even as there are among Africans, who were conscious that God is near; but the general belief, it is true to say, was that God is at a great distance. Their idea was such that there was no pleasure in having Him near.
>
> No, Jesus said to men and women, your idea of God is all wrong. He is Father; at all times He is near; and if you will only see Him in your hearts as He is you will have joy in feeling Him near.[52]

In the African conception, God is seen as King and Chief; and the more highly developed the concept of kingship in the tribe, the more they conceive of God as remote and unconcerned. In many African tribes the chief has become so high and lifted up that the people are not permitted even to mention his name. Among the Banda of South Africa, for example, Chief Tangana, the progenitor of the tribe, may not be mentioned by name, nor may any other word with the same derivation pass the lips. As a result of this prohibition, the people use the word *igabade* for *tanga* when referring to the English word "pumpkin."[53]

This same prohibition occurs for the name of God in some tribes. Among the Tswana of South Africa, the word *Modimo* is taboo; and children are taught that if they utter the word, they expose themselves to the danger of death.[54] In this sense Africa exhibits a reluctance to speak the divine name similar to that which existed among the ancient Hebrews.[55]

The Jews were noted for their circumlocutions. In the public reading of the holy books, they regularly used *Adonay* for Yahwe. They spoke of "The Holy One," "the Highest" and "the Everlasting," and in oaths they used the words "Heaven" and "Jerusalem" in place of God.[56] Out of both fear and respect, they avoided the divine name, to the extent that later generations did not know how to pronounce it.

Smith suggests that such deep respect has much to commend it, but it runs the danger of removing God from the life of the common man. It was precisely this tendency which Jesus sought to reverse. And he accomplished his purpose by identifying God as *Abba*, Father. The word was used so often by Jesus that it appears in the Gospels in both its Aramaic and Greek forms.[57]

God's kingship and fatherhood are not contradictory qualities but two ways of looking at the same quality. They reveal the belief that the same One who is Creator and Lord of the universe is man's Friend. One is never complete without the other.[58]

Smith does not deny that the Africans and Jews conceive God as a Father. Indeed some Africans, in contrast to the Jews, picture God as both Father and Mother.[59] But he does insist that Jesus brought a new conception of fatherhood because of His own rich communion with God:

> So when Jesus in His teaching said that God is our Father it was not a completely new thought. But words which are old may be used with a sense which is much wider and deeper than before, so much so that they seem to be completely new. And the sense in which Jesus said "Father" was quite new. On His lips it was not one of a number of names for the Highest Being. It was the sign of a new experience of God.[60]

The significance of Jesus' emphasis on God as Abba, Father, is that it brings near the High God. For men who do not know Jesus, God is far away and unconcerned. Jesus makes Him a present reality:

To men who are without Jesus, God seems to be far away and uncertain. Jesus makes them conscious that He is there, near at hand, present at all times, and their Father. Through the Son men may come to have that sense of harmony with God, that feeling of being at one with God, which is the true and only possible knowledge of God. This is the revelation of God which comes to us through Jesus.[61]

God's Goodness and Love

The final contribution of Christianity to this aspect of African Religion, as seen by Edwin Smith, is the Christian conviction that God is both good and love. These concepts are already implied in what has been said about God as the Father who actively searches for His children. However, several further comments are needed.

The African view of God is ambiguous. God does good things for men, to be sure, but He also does things which cannot be characterized as good. He gives the rain, but He also withholds it. He gives food, but He also causes it to rot. He sends Chameleon with the message of life, but He also sends Hare with the message of death. He gives man the blessing of offspring, but He also takes them away. Man cannot count on God's goodness, let alone His love. At the moment of greatest joy, the threat of disaster is nearest.

The Africans question God's goodness. When Donald Fraser talked of it, the elders considered it a new doctrine. Nevertheless, Jesus insisted not only that God is good but that only He is good. Jesus would not even accept the appellation Himself. Smith notes the biblical accounts in both Mark and Matthew and then comments:

> Jesus had no desire to be given a name of honour, such as "good master", till a man was conscious of what he was saying. He said in effect: You say that I am good—you put a question about the good. Be clear in your thought what you are saying. *Who* is good? What is *good?* There is only one answer. God is the only good Being. All others may become good: only God is good— completely and eternally good. He is the fountain of everything which is good and true and beautiful.[62]

A corollary to this view is the idea that God is love. The elders who spoke with Donald Fraser could not accept that belief. Moreover, according to Smith, such an identification is not evident in either African Traditional Religion or in Judaism: "God is Power; God is Spirit—yes, most Jews and possibly most Africans would be in agreement with these sayings. But it did not ever come into their mind to say: God is love."[63]

This does not mean, of course, that Smith saw no allusions to God's love and goodness in Judaism or African Traditional Religion. Clearly he did. The Jews had a concept of the love of God, although they never formulated exactly the phrase "God is love." Smith himself alludes to God's love at the Exodus.[64] He sees the same in the Prophet Hosea.[65] Furthermore, the idea at least in germ is not unknown in African Religion. Some African people, according to Smith's testimony, say that God is "so good and kind that he never sends trouble or distress, and therefore men have no need to fear and propitiate Him."[66]

In this context once again Smith speaks of Christianity as the fulfillment of African conceptions, and he quotes Fraser to similar effect.[67] The essential problem of African Traditional Religion is that, although there are glimpses of the goodness and love of God, the picture is never clear. There is always an uncertainty and an ambiguity created by the calamities and sorrows inherent in life. It took a radical action of God—the intervention of His Son—to show men that Heaven really was on their side. God showed His love for men not only in the life but most especially in the death of His Son. Here is seen love in its fullest and best. Here the heart of God is laid bare.[68]

Throughout the story is heard the mournful cry of the old Ba-ila woman: "What have I done to Thee that Thou Afflictest me in this manner?"—a cry which might have sounded on the lips of the Son of God Himself. The legend ends in despair: "She never obtained her desire: she died of a broken heart (*yamuyaya inzezela*). And from her time to this, nobody has ever solved her problem!"[69] The Christians do not agree, for they believe that Jesus has already answered her cry.[70]

The African view of God's disposition was mixed and confused, but the Africans longed for a clarification. Only this fact can explain the acceptance of the gospel by so many Africans. Smith says:

> When the Christian missionary comes with the Good News of God revealed in Jesus Christ as a loving Father—whatever else in his teaching they find it hard to accept, this at least they readily take to their hearts.[71]

5

Revelation: Does God Reveal Himself?

TRADITIONAL VIEW

African experience is characterized by a constant coming and going between the worlds of the seen and unseen. This contact also has implications for the concept of revelation. The initiative comes from both sides: those living in the flesh seek light from the invisible world to illumine the problems of their daily life, while those who inhabit the other side attempt to influence the living members of the community.

Purpose of Divination

When Africans seek for an understanding of life's enigmas, they often go to a diviner for help. The Ila word for diviner is *musonzhi* from the verb *kusonda*, to divine. The divining instrument is called a *chisondo*.[1]

There is a difference between a doctor (*munganga*) and a diviner. The latter's task is to make known mysteries which are hidden to the common man:

> Although we speak of him in this chapter devoted to Leechcraft, his art takes a much wider sweep. He is essentially a revealer: things that are hidden from ordinary view he can discover and make known. Hence, he is called upon to find things that are lost, to detect thieves, to trace straying cattle, to deter-

mine the identity of the child that is born, and so on. His importance in the present connection is that he is the diagnoser of disease. He reveals not only what the disease is, but also its cause, and often tells what the medicine is and from what doctor (*munganga*) it may be procured. He tells also whether the death was due to witchcraft or to the divine will, i.e. of Leza.[2]

Smith describes ten different divining techniques found among the Ba-ila. Not all are common. In several cases he has not personally witnessed their use but merely records the descriptions of his informants.

The *Shimubi* divining rod is used by many diviners and is especially appropriate for finding lost articles. It is a bow-shaped piece of wood, one and one-half inches thick, with a snake's head carved on one end. The inquirer pays his fee, which is calculated according to his ability and the value of the object sought; and the diviner goes to work. He first places live coals into a bowl and covers them with dry leaves from several bushes. He chews some of the leaves and rubs some of the juice on the divining rod. He puts *Shimubi*'s head in the smoke and talks to it:[3]

> "You hear what is said. This thing that is lost, discover it. It is an axe. Perhaps it is on the ground, or on a tree, wherever it is find it. It is you who know where it is."[4]

Two men take hold of the *Shimubi*, while the diviner shakes a rattle and goes on with his exhortation: " 'Now, arise and go . . . Go on, man . . . Where is the road? . . . Arise, my friend . . . You know where this thing is . . . Come along, now do'."[5] The men begin to walk, insisting that the wood draws them toward their destination. The diviner accompanies them, shaking his rattle and pleading with the *Shimubi* until the lost object is found.

A smaller rod (*Shimubi mwaniche*) is used for diagnosing disease or locating game. The preliminary process is as listed above, but the diviner works alone. The rod rests in his hand; and as he talks to it, it begins to jump as if automatically. He may ask if they will find eland in tomorrow's hunt. If *Shimubi* taps the ground, the answer is "yes"; silence indicates "no." Other questions follow: Will the game be found soon? Will they succeed in killing the animals? The diviner often leaves himself a loophole in case the quest is thwarted. At the end he may say that success depends upon the shooting accuracy of the hunter.[6]

In case of illness, the diviner will seek to discover from the rod the name of the spirit offended and the necessary remedy. In death, especially where witchcraft is suspected, the diviner may address *Shimubi* in these words:

> "O Shimubi, you see these people in trouble; they are in tears; they are weeping. They want to know from you the cause of this death. Tell them. If it was *lufu lwa Leza* ('a death to be ascribed to Leza'), well, there is nothing for it but to go on weeping. But on the other hand, if it was caused by a fellow-man— tell us, O Shimubi."[7]

Shimubi's movement may indicate that witchcraft is indeed involved. Moreover, the warlock may be a close relative, identified by name. For verification the diviner suggests that they consult the *mwazhi* ordeal, described below.

Other divining methods follow the same general principles as described with the *Shimubi*, although not all are as rigidly controlled by the diviner. In the *Chipa*, the diviner uses a small pot placed on the sharp edge of an axe and balanced with an arrow on either side. If the pot remains rigid when questioned, the answer is "yes"; movement of the pot indicates "no." The *Kasambi* method is the same except that the pot is balanced on bark string.

It is possible to divine with an axe. In this case, the axe head is placed on a piece of iron bent double. The diviner hits the axe head down to push it on to the iron and forward to see whether it will move. Upon questioning, if the axe head goes forward the answer is "no"; lack of movement indicates "yes."

The *Impindo* technique involves the use of a walking stick and two pieces of root. As always, drugs are chewed by the diviner and the juice spat on the stick. Without the proper medicine, the endeavor would be fruitless. After placement on the stick, if the roots fall, the answer is "no"; if they remain the answer is "yes." Other methods are described by Smith, but it is unnecessary to list them here.[8]

It is important to comment further on the *mwazhi* ordeal, referred to above. The test may be administered in two ways, either in the form of hot water or poison. In the case of the former, the accused must put his hand in boiling water and not unusually is required to pick up a stone or other object at the bottom of the pot. If his hand or arm become blistered, he is guilty; otherwise he is innocent. Smith notes that he has never personally witnessed the ordeal, but he has seen the variable results on those who have taken the test.

In the case of the poison oracle, the poison (which is prepared from the *mwazhi* shrub) is usually administered to a dog or cock. Clansmen of both the accuser and accused are present when the poison is administered, the exhortation being made in such words as these:

> "You, O dog! We give you this *mwazhi* to drink. If it be that our relation died simply of disease, why should you die? Let it go west! *Kashia mumbo*, i.e., 'It is no concern of yours.' If he was bewitched, why, then, to-day you must not see the sunset!"[9]

If the dog fails to die, the accusers must pay a ransom to the accused; but if the dog dies, the accused is presumed guilty. The dog's tail is deposited with the chief. The *mwazhi* may then be administered to a cock for further clarification. As a last resort, where the accused insists that he is innocent, he may request to take the *mwazhi* himself.[10]

It is important to ask from what source the revelation comes in each of these cases. In the hot-water and poison ordeals, Smith suggests that dynamism may be at work and that oaths and ordeals are not different in principle. "Each is an appeal to the hidden forces to show the guilt or innocence of the person—the innocent escapes the penalty, while the guilty succumbs."[11]

According to the diviners themselves, the revelation of the *Shimubi, Chapa, Kasambi,* Axe and *Impindo* comes from the ancestral spirits. Smith accepts this although he seems to indicate that dynamism may be at work as well.

> In these five kinds of divining the the thing addressed is the *muzhimo,* the ancestral ghost—so the diviners tell us; it is the ghost with its supernormal knowledge that guides the *chisondo* and thus gives the answer. But if we had not been expressly told that, we should certainly have said that the power of divination was in the *chisondo* itself, and that the medicine was to enable it to perform its office, or, in other words, to release its energy. For it is the *chisondo* that we heard addressed; though there was much that we could not catch that might have been addressed to higher powers.[12]

Most Africans have a firm belief in the power of divination, although some laugh at it. Smith himself remains skeptical although characteristically he is gentle in his utterance of it. He and Dale once put a diviner to the test, offering a reward for finding hidden objects, but the diviner was unable to find them. He suggests that foreknowledge and shrewd guesses sometimes contribute to a diviner's success.[13]

Significance of Dreams

In the African view it is not merely a question of the living trying to communicate with the dead. The spirit world also seeks to enter into contact with those in the flesh. This communication from the invisible world may take various forms. Dreams play an especially important part.

For the African, the world of dreams is as significant as the world of consciousness.[14] The things which happen when an individual is asleep, and which he remembers the next day, are real events.

Smith notes the extraordinary impression that dreams make on the people and the complex nature of dream interpretation.

Often there are commonly recognized signs, some Ba-ila examples of which may be mentioned here: Dreams about love-making with relatives indicate meat and suggest that the dreamer should go hunting. Those which include tobacco have the same significance since the tobacco is symbolic of the livers of animals. Dreams involving weeping are cause for anxiety since they forebode the mourning of a dead person.[15] Fish is also a bad omen, telling of death, while one who dreams of flying through the air is certain to live long and well.[16]

Sometimes dreams are interpreted as contraries: If a dog bites a man's father in a dream, it means that someone other than his father is bitten by a lion. Dreaming of the death of his father signifies the death, not of his father but another. However, if a man dreams that his father is fat or well clothed or that he is being carried, his father is dead.[17]

Conversation with the dead is presumed to record a real communication of the sleeper's spirit with the ancestral ghost:

> According to the Ba-ila, the ghosts often make their appearance to the living in sleep. To them the dream world is as real as the waking world. When a man sees in his sleep the phantom of a person he knows or used to know, he has no doubt that the person's ghost has actually visited him.[18]

In making their appearance to an individual during sleep, the spirits not uncommonly give him information which is useful. In cases of illness, they reveal the names of leaves which should be made into medicine. When things are lost or needed, they tell where to look. To hunters they show the hiding places of game. For those facing court judges, they provide instructions regarding the proper conduct of the case.[19] When danger threatens, they make known the action of witches and the composition of charms.[20]

Through all of this is seen the benevolent action of the spirits in looking after the needs of the family, warning them in time of danger and revealing to them the hidden mysteries which make life more bearable.

All of the above examples refer to the relationship of an individual with his ancestors, his guardian spirit and family divinities. And it must be stated that the common daily occurrences of communication between the two worlds tend to follow this pattern. Nevertheless, there are also times when the village, clan and tribal divinities communicate with the living by means of dreams or spirit "possession." In such cases they reveal information or make known their will for the community as a whole. The persons who serve as the recipients of the revelation are then looked upon as mediums or prophets.

Role of Prophets

Spirits may enter the living either on an occasional or permanent basis.[21] This is not reincarnation, which pertains only to new births, but the "possession" of an individual after birth.[22]

Some cases of possession are accompanied by ecstasy. The spirit comes and goes, his presence signified by a trance or violent movement, during which the spirit communicates his message to the medium. At other times the spirit is believed to reside more or less permanently in the chest and speaks his message through the brain and mouth of the prophet.[23] In such cases the prophet may identify himself with the spirit and may be recognized as such by the people.[24] Smith lists a number of examples of spirit possession from his own personal experience among the Ba-ila.

In 1911 Chief Sachele, who had died earlier in the year, began to send messages to the people through a prophetess. According to the testimony received, he had been prevented from visiting his mother (who was herself a famous prophetess while alive) because of her resentment that he had been buried with dogs rather than slaves. Sachele's prophetess informed the people that all who paid their respects to the deceased chief would be blessed with rain; others would experience famine.[25]

Another prophet appeared at Kakoma's village, near the Nambala mission station, about the same time. He prophesied that there would soon be an abundance of rain and fish. The latter would be found on the banks of the river, some already cooked. He demanded a young boy as a slave, and his request was granted by the people. When his prediction that an eland would be found in a game-pit came true, his fame grew accordingly. The old women warned the children that they were to honor him as a prophet and do as he said. Smith adds this comment: "The missionary was not very pleased with him, as he told the people that praying to God was all nonsense and that they could get no rain at the Mission!"[26]

Not uncommonly, the prophet's message is of national significance. Smith records an incident which occurred after the great chief, Sebetwane, had led his Makololo tribesmen from Bechuanaland to the Zambesi River and was looking for a place to settle:

> But there now intervened one of those very interesting persons who so frequently figure in African history, for good or evil— the *senohi*, 'seer' or 'prophet'. This man, Tlapane by name, brought Sebetwane a message from the ancestral spirits. Pointing to the east, he said: "There I behold a fire; shun it; it is a fire that may scorch thee. The gods say, Go not thither!" Then he pointed to the west and told of a nation owning red cattle. Sebetwane's destiny was to rule them.[27]

These examples show that the Africans have a lively view of revelation. The visible and invisible worlds are not so far apart as to exclude contacts between them. Rather entreaties are constantly raised from the visible world, with replies from the "dead" no less abundant.

Prophets generally appear on the scene in times of trouble, when there is war or famine or drought, and this explains their wide acceptance by the people. Sometimes their message is directed to the preservation of the *status quo*, alleging that all the evils of the present are due to the tribe's failure to abide in the old ways. At other times the prophet becomes an innovator, stating that the problems of life can be resolved only by walking in new paths as he directs.[28] It would be impossible to overestimate the significance of these prophets as sources of both stability and change in African life.[29] However, their effect on the life of the people is not always beneficial. Smith comments:

> These prophets play a very important part in the life of the Ba-ila. As the mouthpieces of the divinities they are the legislators of the community and, generally speaking, they receive a great deal of credit. Sometimes the message they deliver is harmless enough, sometimes it is distinctly good, but sometimes it is noxious. The word of a prophet is sufficient to condemn to death for witchcraft a perfectly innocent man or woman. And such is the extraordinary credulity of the people that often they will destroy their grain or their cattle at the bidding of a prophet.[30]

One of the most notorious examples of the negative results of prophetic influence is that which occurred among the Xhosa in the last century. At the urging of Mhlakaza and his daughter Nongquase, the people killed thousands of their cattle in the vain hope that it would bring success and happiness.[31]

The African people are generally long suffering with one who purports to be a medium,[32] but there are limits to their tolerance. They sometimes lose patience and declare such a one a false prophet.[33]

Prophets from God

On occasion prophets claim to receive their messages directly from God. When the Matebele reached the Matopo hills in 1837, having been driven from the Transvaal by the Zulu and the Boer *Voortrekkers*, Mziligazi consulted *Ngwale nkolo*, the oracle of *Mwari*, the great God of the Karanga. Smith records the result in these words:

> The message came through the lips of the old priest. "Beyond the Zambesi," he declared, "there are villages so numerous that they cannot be counted. In every village there is a herd of fat cattle. Their king has a great store of ivory, for elephants are there as plentiful as hares." "So they have a king!," said Mzilikazi, "Yes, their king is Sebetwane who came from Kuruman many moons ago and he has eaten up all the Chiefs near the river."[34]

Sometimes the prophet identifies himself with God. In 1909 a man appeared among the Batwa, calling himself *Chilenge*, "the Creator." He insisted that he would rid the country of a grub which was attacking the local crops. Although the people followed him diligently, his prescriptions had little effect on the grub. Notwithstanding, he extended his predictions to include the destruction of the railroad and the bridge over the Kafue River, a six-day eclipse of the sun and the expulsion of Europeans from the region. The only requirement was that the people should kill all their cattle, which they proceeded to do. The prophet was arrested and imprisoned by the government authorities.[35]

Another prophet, Mupumani, appeared at Nanzela in 1913.[36] He was a leper of middle age and apparently had only one vision in his life. One night, as he was sleeping at home, he heard a movement above and saw a leg hanging over the roof. The full body of a person soon appeared and proceeded to carry him to a place where he had never been before. The face of the visitor remained hidden, but Mupumani surmised that he must have been a ghost. Soon the prophet found himself in the presence of *Namulenga*, "the Creator," and another figure who was not identified. Namulenga wanted to rid Mupumani of his leprous body, but the other figure warned that the people would die in amazement to see him cured. Then the Creator gave him a calabash of blood which he was to pour out in order to do away with the people, but again the mysterious second person intervened. Namulenga insisted that Mupumani inform the people that some of their tribal customs were contrary to His will and must cease. He was especially upset about the killing of cattle and mourning at funerals: Men both die and are reborn by the decree of the Creator; so it is not for men to mourn the dead but to accept God's will. Moreover, Mupumani was to deliver a message of denunciation against witchcraft. He was warned to persevere despite resistance to his message.

Mupumani ultimately found himself back in his own house, although he was unable to record how. His reputation grew with the preaching of his message, and people came from remote areas to hear him. At first he accepted no gifts except a small ring of beads which is placed on the little finger of every recognized prophet. However, the people insisted that he show them signs and wonders. They pleaded for medicine to hasten the growth of their corn and to give success in hunting; and he acceded to

their entreaties. He gave them what they wanted, and they paid
for his services. Nevertheless, he was not happy with the result.
He later testified:

> "They still kill cattle at the funerals. You know the Ba-ila never
> listen well to people who tell them to do things. At first I told
> the people about the calabash of blood and then I did not.
> Perhaps I made a mistake in not always speaking about it; they
> would have been afraid of that and listened to Leza's voice."[37]

There are several sequels to the story of Mupumani. While on
a visit to Lubwe, Mungaba, from the village of Mala, heard of
the prophet but refused to believe. On returning home, one of his
children died mysteriously. As he was wondering at the cause of
death, one of Shimunenga's prophets fell into a trance and uttered
these words:

> "I am Shimunenga. Mungaba's child has been slain by Leza be-
> cause he scoffed at Leza's messenger. It is your habit, it seems,
> to scoff at those who come from Leza. The missionary, too, you
> do not listen to him. Look out for yourselves."[38]

Nor was this the end of the affair. Shortly after the death of
Mungaba's child, some women, who had been gathering firewood,
ran to Mala in haste bearing word that a huge tree, known to have
been blown down in a storm, was now standing. The excitement
was overwhelming! Smith himself went with the villagers to
examine the tree. Most assuredly, it was standing upright, and
no one could doubt that it had previously lain on its side. Indeed
the marks of where it had rested were clearly visible in the soil;
the white ants had already begun to devour that side of the tree,
and the opposite side was charred by a fire which had swept
through the forest. Smith confesses his consternation, for it was
a very great tree:

> For a time I was puzzled, and then the explanation dawned upon
> me. When the tree was torn up by the gale a deep hole was made.
> The women came and lopped off many of the branches, and
> they dug away under the lower end of the tree to get at the
> roots. Thus they had lightened the tree at the top, and had
> enlarged the hole, until the tree, weighted at the lower end by
> the great mass of earth attached to the roots, had simply tipped
> up and stood erect. This, it seemed to me, is what had happened;
> but the explanation did not commend itself to the people. They
> were convinced that occult powers had been at work.[39]

Yet another event followed. While returning from hunting one evening, some men of the village saw a "tall figure clad from head to foot in white." They followed for a distance before the figure vanished in front of them. They later surmised that it was a ghost although they were at a loss to explain his white raiment.[40]

Smith affirms that he never in his life had such a receptive audience for the preaching of the gospel as the village of Mala at that time.[41]

Although several examples of communication from God have been described in some detail, it would be a mistake to assume that these are common occurrences. The conception of God's remoteness and absenteeism, noted throughout this study, is also a factor in the African view of revelation. An individual is addressed directly by his guardian spirit or family ancestors, and he seeks their advice and help in time of need. The village, clan and tribe in turn receive their messages from the communal and tribal divinities. Generally God interferes only in unusual circumstances, in times of national danger or disaster. Examples of a permanent oracle of the Supreme God, such as recorded among the Karanga, are extremely rare in Africa.

CHRISTIAN CONTRIBUTION

Edwin Smith questions some traditional explanations given to interpret the revelatory phenomena of African Traditional Religion. He doubts the validity of divination. He laments that the prophets do not focus more attention on the behavior of the people and that their message is often detrimental to African life.[42] As always he is concerned that the attention given to the ancestors and tribal deities tends to crowd out the belief in the Supreme God. In spite of these inadequacies, however, he is thoroughly convinced that African Religion contains elements of true revelation. Indeed the twilight of revelation in African Traditional Religion forms an important foundation for the full revelation of God in Jesus Christ.

African Religion and the Jews

In his writings[43] Edwin Smith shows an intense interest in the traditional literature of Africa. It may seem strange to refer to African "literature" in that Westerners normally confine their thought regarding that term to the written word. Although Africans had no written literature, they did have an oral lore of considerable significance.[44]

The religious value of African myths and legends has been recorded. Knowledge of the proverbs, riddles, conundrums and folk tales is essential to understanding the mental and moral constitution of the people.[45]

The evening is the proper time for telling stories, as the people gather about the fire. The purposes are many. The stories serve the useful functions of providing recreation, release for pent-up emotions, and education. They illumine facts about the nature of the environment and mould the ideals of youth. They tell about the world and explain the origins of the many curious phenomena which surround life.[46]

If people are to live together in harmony, there must be standards of conduct. This moral instruction is transmitted from generation to generation by means of precepts, maxims and proverbs, but the favorite and most effective mode in Africa is the story.[47] The Africans have no professional story-tellers, but some are geniuses at the art. The finest Smith ever heard was his friend Mungalo whose use of gestures, pauses, pitch and description excited the admiration of all. When he was in form, every animal spoke in his own voice; and his audience was held spellbound. No one ever tired of listening, although they may have heard the stories many times before. Smith affirms that it is impossible to transcribe adequately such narration to the written page.[48]

The moral of the story is not always self-evident. Sometimes it is necessary to search for it. Smith, who in all his writings displays a refreshing humor, makes this comment: "Africans are like the little girl you have all heard about, who said: 'I like the preacher's stories but I don't like his morals!' A wise story-teller does not force his lesson upon his listeners."[49] If the narrator were to attempt to do so, it would be resented by the people. He would thereby imply that they were not intelligent enough to grasp the point by themselves. Smith urges his missionary colleagues to see the implications of this approach for their own actions in Africa.

The significance of this discussion for understanding the relationship of African Religion to the Jews is seen within the con-

text of Smith's belief that folk tales offer an African equivalent
for the Old Testament:

> I think that of many of them [folk tales] it can be said they
> possess real religious value. Some are told openly on any occasion;
> others are the sacred and guarded possession of a few selected
> elders of a tribe and constitute what Rattray calls "the African's
> Old Testament."[50]

There are close parallels between the life of Africa and that of
the ancient Hebrews. In terms of general culture and approach
to the world, they stand on the same ground. There are similarities
in ideas and language. The result is that Africans appreciate more
and have deeper insight into many biblical texts than Europeans.[51]
This is especially true of the Old Testament:

> Africans and other peoples live much at the same stage of
> culture as peoples we read of in the Old Testament, and their
> vocabularies provide exact equivalents of various Hebrew words
> used in connection with religion and magic.[52]

According to Edwin Smith, the Africans have a religious heritage which is directly comparable to that of the Jews; and as God
prepared the Jewish nation for the coming of Christ, even so
has He been at work in African life and thought. His approval of
Rattray's identification of African folk tales as the African's Old
Testament has already been noted. In his commentary on the
LeZoute conference of 1926, he quotes Archdeacon Owen to
similar effect.[53] He goes on to state that since the African has a
similar heritage through which God has been working to prepare
him for the coming of His Son, it is possible to lead him directly
to Christ from his own experience in African Traditional Religion.
It is not necessary that the African make his approach by way of
Judaism:

> They have a heritage from God which we can only compare
> with the heritage that God gave the Jews in preparing them for
> Christ. We have not got to make the African a Jew before we
> make him a Christian. It is not necessary to teach him the story
> of Adam and Eve before we can bring him to Christ. You can
> approach the African at the point to which God has brought
> him and teach him Christ at once, and he will respond.[54]

All of this tends to suggest that, for Smith, the Old Testament
is unnecessary and irrelevant in Africa. However, this is clearly

not his purpose. In his book, *The Shrine of a People's Soul,* he eloquently argues for the possibility and necessity of translating the entire Bible into African vernaculars. Furthermore, he thought Bible translation so important that he spent the greater part of his active life as literary superintendent for the British and Foreign Bible Society. He states openly his conviction that the Bible is the greatest gift that Great Britain has to offer to the native peoples of the commonwealth.[55] But, in the light of all that has been said above, it is important to ask why the Old Testament is so necessary. Smith answers quite simply that the New Testament is incomprehensible apart from the Old:

> But permanently to deprive the Christians of the whole of the Old Testament, other than the Psalms, would be to inflict upon them a very great loss; for, after all, the New Testament cannot be understood apart from the Old.[56]

However, it is not merely a question of understanding. The Old Testament, when looked at closely, contains religious insights which go beyond anything which Smith has been able to detect in African Traditional Religion. This is especially true of the great Hebrew prophets. To be sure, Africa also had prophets who were of significance for the life of their tribes and nations. These correspond to the early Hebrew prophets.[57] With the later prophets a new stage is attained. It is not possible to attempt here an analysis of the messages of the various Hebrew prophets. Nevertheless, Smith clearly sees new insights emerging from them, which have no African equivalent, and which reached their culmination in the advent of Jesus Christ.[58]

One example will perhaps suffice, that of Jeremiah, whom Smith considered the greatest of the prophets:

> Jeremiah made a change in the very idea of religion. The Jews, like the Africans, had the idea that religion was the business of a group. Jeremiah said it is at all times a business between a person and his God. Society may be broken up, old ways of life may be quite changed, but so long as a person has a living faith in God, and a living desire to do what is right, it will be well with him. The Jews were to put this idea to the test while they were living in a strange land. Numbers of them came to see it was true. Africans may put it to the test today when the old conditions are giving place to new conditions. They will see it is true.[59]

African Religion and Jesus

In all of his thought Edwin Smith is dominated by the theory of evolution. The same is true of his concept of revelation. Revelation is progressive. Men are led step by step into an understanding of the mysteries of God. The Africans and Jews are parallel entities. They are both in the process of development. In some ways the Hebrew prophets have moved further in their religious quest, but this is a difference of degree, not kind.

Before schools were established in Africa, the elders had their own methods for training youth in their social responsibilities. It could not all be done at once. Learners had to pass through different stages of growth. In the educational process youth learn new things, but they are also taught to put away things which are no longer useful. It is not that the things are in themselves bad. Some may be but they are not all so. They were perfectly good for the stage through which one was passing, but their validity has terminated.[60]

Smith uses this analogy to lead his readers into an understanding of God's revelation. In the school of life God is the great Teacher and the students are not merely individuals but nations.[61] The history of the world is the story of the education of the nations in God's school.[62]

If man knows God at all, it is because He has revealed Himself. God has always wanted to reveal Himself completely; but given man as he is, it could not all be done at once: "You are not able to put all the water of a river into a water-pot. You are not able to make a little child have knowledge of all the laws of the tribe."[63] A wise teacher does not try to impart all his knowledge at once. He leads his students step by step.

Even so God reveals Himself little by little as men are able to understand. God reveals Himself to men through other men, who are themselves weak. No one man can grasp all that God has to say.[64] But when the time was prepared, God revealed Himself by means of a Son who was equal with God.[65] The old teaching was good but it was incomplete. The good is made better by being brought into that which completes it.[66] And where there are errors, they are also illuminated by the full light.[67] All of this means that Jesus reveals God in Himself.[68] Jesus unveils the hidden God for all men to see:[69]

All through the years men have put the question: What is God like? The full answer came with Jesus. God is for ever what Jesus was in the days when this earth was His living-place in the form of man. He is not all of God; the eternal One, Maker of earth and Heaven, was not able to put all of Himself into the little life of man. But there is all we have need of. Our deep desire is for knowledge of God's heart, and that we have in Jesus. In reading the Gospels we see how good He was, how He went about doing good; we have no doubt about His love for God and men. And all over that beautiful life we see the words: This is what God is like![70]

As the one who reveals God in Himself, Jesus becomes the measure of all value. He is the touchstone by which all things are judged. All beliefs and actions are evaluated in the light of His Person.[71]

The Bible is the greatest of books; but it is not in itself the full revelation of God, although it witnesses to that revelation: "We say truly that this greatest of books is a word of God to men. But the Lord Jesus is *the* Word of God."[72]

The Jews were students in God's school, and God led them step by step. They did not always understand God's will and ways. They made errors. Some of their thoughts about God were wrong. When the Christian reads the Jewish Scriptures, he recognizes that there are some things in them which are not in harmony with the revelation of God in Jesus Christ. Therefore he avoids such things, thankful for the further light which has been given to him. At the same time he recognizes that from the beginning the Jews were not devoid of true light, and once again he gives thanks to God who did not withhold His light from any nation.

An example of Smith's approach to the Old Testament is his comment on the action of the prophets, Elijah and Elisha, in putting to death the prophets of Baal:

> From our point of view as Christians, we say that these were cruel acts of blood. But they did their work. In later years nobody ever made an attempt to put another god higher than Yahwe in His land of Palestine. His power as owner of the land was no longer doubted.[73]

The Christian approach to Africa and African Traditional Religion must be the same. God does not restrict His light to only one nation and let the others sit in darkness. The Africans have true knowledge of God. He has revealed Himself to them. In all things He is their guide. To be sure, there are aspects of their life and thought which cannot be harmonized with the mind of Christ. Here the Christian will naturally choose to follow Jesus rather than the tribal elders. But even where the full revelation of God in Jesus Christ serves to correct African belief and practice, the Christian will never despise or lack respect for that which went before. He will know that those who preceded him were students in God's school and that they prepared the way for the full light which has now made its appearance:

> If we see that some things which they did and said were not in harmony with the mind of Jesus, then we will take the way of Jesus and not the way of our fathers. But not for a minute will we be without respect for them. They, like other men, were learners in God's school. We may put their beliefs and acts to the test, saying: What is the opinion of the Lord Jesus about this and that? And when we come upon things which are good and true we will give praise to God from whom all the good and the true and the beautiful comes.[74]

General and Special Revelation

All that has been said thus far is relevant for the controversy regarding general and special revelation made famous in theological circles by Karl Barth and Emil Brunner. Smith mentions briefly the debate in his book *African Ideas of God;* and as might be expected, he takes sides with Brunner against Barth. However, the total testimony of his writings seems to indicate that he approaches the question differently from both of them.

He is strongly critical of Barth. He believes that Barth has misunderstood Christian doctrine, and he quotes Brunner to the effect that "Karl Barth is inconsistent, now admitting and now denying universal revelation."[75] He negates the thesis that a belief in general revelation compromises the uniqueness of the revelation in Jesus Christ:

> That the full and complete revelation can only come through the personality of Jesus Christ—that "God has been unfolded by the divine One, the only Son, who lies upon the Father's breast"— this all Christians believe; but this is not to deny that God has set His splendour high in heaven and that, through nature, finite man can in some measure reach Nature's God.[76]

Smith insists that the African conception of the High God requires a belief in general revelation. This is manifest in the selection of terms for translating Christian teaching and doctrine. Although some missionaries have preferred to transliterate Latin and Greek terminology, most have used African names for God.[77]

Those who refuse to do so maintain that it is never possible to express Christian truth in pagan terms. Smith argues that the practice of the pioneer African missionaries has a clear precedent in the Old Testament itself.[78] *Elohim* for example was originally a class-name including many different supernatural beings; but through prophetic teaching, it came to represent the one God of Jewish monotheism. In the Septuagint Elohim was translated into *Theos* and Yahwe into *Kurios*. Whatever those terms signified to the ancient Greeks, the meaning was clearly not synonymous with that of St. Paul and the early Christians who used them. In the end Christianity succeeded in infusing them with a broader content. If they had represented wholly different concepts, without points of contact in their original context, it is difficult to see how they could have been so appropriated.[79] Smith observes:

> Christian missionaries in Africa differ from their predecessors in Europe for they have generally adopted not class-names like *theos* and *god* but personal names like Nyame, Leza, Nyambe. But the principle is the same—that of meeting pagans on their own ground, adopting for Christian use terms which fall short of Christian significance, but which by preaching and teaching may be given a new and fuller meaning.[80]

Smith has good reason for his insistence that the African names for God be adopted for Christian usage. The God of African Traditional Religion and Christianity is in fact the same. The God who revealed Himself fully in Jesus Christ is none other than the One who has continually made Himself known to African religious experience. When men attempt to understand the Power which they observe to be working in all creation, they give witness to a hunger which God has put into the hearts of all men.[81] When the African elders replied to Donald Fraser that they were too old to understand the new doctrines and the new God, he insisted that Christians do not worship a new God.[82] When the missionary hands the African a Bible, he brings him a message from the African's own God.[83] Whatever is true in African Traditional Religion is due to the work of the God of all men and all nations.[84]

Smith quotes from Frazer's Gifford Lectures, "The Worship of Nature," to the effect that man seems to have an instinctive, irresistible impulse to search beyond the phenomena of sense:

> Whence comes that "irresistible impulse"? Are there influences coming from without that set up that impulse and lead to the formation of religious ideas? Are men in touch with ultimate reality, or are the ideas mere projections of their wishful thinking? I personally believe that they are the responses of what in man is likest God to the initiative of the One who wills to make Himself known to all men.[85]

The point where Smith is perhaps most critical of Barth is in his understanding of Scripture. He quotes from Acts 14:15–17;[86] Romans 1:19–20 and Romans 2:14–15 and affirms that these texts pertain not merely to events of the distant past but to the present and continuous self-revelation of God.[87] He concludes:

> It seems passing strange that in face of this positive assertion (which by no means stands alone in Scripture) a school of Christian theologians should deny a general revelation and say that it is only in the Word not in Nature or History that God makes Himself known, or that if Scripture teaches otherwise it is only a "side-line".[88]

Of other passages of Scripture used for the same purpose, two deserve special mention. One is Matthew 5:17, Jesus' affirmation that he did not come to destroy the law or the prophets but to fulfill them. Smith states that the passage is as significant for the relationship of Christianity to African Traditional Region as it is for the relationship of the New Testament to the Old.[89] The words make clear Jesus' view that the old teaching was of value but was incomplete. Jesus' coming was to give full effect to that which had gone on before. Until Jesus' arrival, God had used the law and the prophets to illumine the way for men. Jesus did not come to put an end to the light revealed to those who had gone before. He did not come to say that theirs was a false light. He came, rather, "to make the glory of God's light complete."[90] An interesting feature is Smith's use of the text in practical missionary and church policy. He admonishes his Christian colleagues to recognize that, although Christianity signifies revolutionary change and a transmutation of values, its spirit is not iconoclastic. It is not the task of missionaries to barge in, smashing left and right. Rather they need to learn from Jesus who came to fulfill, not destroy.[91]

Another passage which Edwin Smith singles out for special mention in many of his writings is the Logos passage of the Gospel of John. Once again he emphasizes its relevance for the discussion of revelation in African Traditional Religion and Christianity. He believes that Justin Martyr has correctly interpreted the reference to the "light which lighteth every man," and he attempts to show how the rays of light in Bantu experience serve as precious elements for the foundation on which Jesus Christ builds.[92] The recognition of African Traditional Religion as a preparation for the gospel is indispensable to the proper self-understanding of the Church in Africa, and the influence of that recognition is felt in every phase of the Church's life:

> The attitude which we adopt towards the African's past will colour and shape everything we do—not in evangelism only, but in education and the building of the Church. If we really believe that the Divine *Logos*, who lighteth every man, has shone in the souls of Africans, we shall endeavor to trace that working and find therein the *preparatio evangelica*, and the conviction will regulate all our dealings with the people.[93]

It may be, as mentioned above, that Edwin Smith and Emil Brunner disagree on some matters relating to revelation. Specifically Brunner and Smith seem to define differently the limits of special revelation. For Brunner Israel and the Old Testament are obviously included in that category. Smith, on the other hand, approaches the question from a different perspective. To be sure, he recognizes the indispensability of the Old Testament for understanding the new dispensation in Jesus Christ and thereby appears to agree with Barth and Brunner about the special role of Israel in the history of salvation. Yet he also goes out of his way to show the parallels between African Traditional Religion and the ancient Hebrews, thus giving the impression that the distinction between them, as far as revelation is concerned, is one of degree not kind. It may be justified to conclude therefore that Smith identified both ancient Judaism and African Religion as general revelation, with the term special revelation confined to the gospel of Jesus Christ.

6

Ethics:
Does God Require Righteousness?

TRADITIONAL VIEW

Africa is distinguished by its close-knit society. Customs and laws for regulating conduct and inter-personal relations are complex.[1] The rules are not always obeyed nor expectations fulfilled, as is true of all human experience, but the continent is not characterized by anarchy either in theory or practice. Indeed African life is governed by an elaborate system of guides and sanctions.[2]

The Ila language contains a variety of words to express approval and disapproval: pleasant-unpleasant, heavy-light, good-bad, straight-crooked. All embody moral connotations.[3] Therefore, it is important to inquire concerning the African standard of judgment, what makes some things good and others bad. Smith replies that the norm of right and wrong is custom; that is, the good is that which receives the community's approval, the bad is that which is disapproved. The right builds up society; the wrong tears it down. One is social; the other anti-social. The African is taught to revere custom and resent change. This does not mean that African life is stagnant. Change does occur. Customs are altered through prophetic action, but this is usually a traumatic experience for the tribe, one more likely to occur in times of national disaster.

Edwin Smith lists three types of sanction for African customs and behavioral patterns—the traditional, the religious and the magical. The first is the simplest and may be defined briefly in this context; the other two require more extensive elaboration. In making reference to "traditional" sanctions, he means that, when questioned regarding a particular custom, Africans reply that they do it merely because their fathers did it and taught them in like manner. By the mere fact that they are passed on from generation to generation, customs tend to be hallowed by time. They may have at one time rested on religious sanctions, but these have been lost or forgotten; so that today the only answer given to the question is that this is the way it has always been.[4]

Concept of Taboo

Edwin Smith believes that the magical sanction is the oldest and strongest and therefore has the greatest influence on African behavior. In essence the sanction is built on the concept that some things are inherently harmful and are therefore taboo.

Offenses against tribal law may be divided for convenience into three categories, characterized by the Ila words: *chisapi, buditazhi* and *tonda*.[5]

Chisapi is defined as indecorum. A *shikisapi* is a rude person who commonly breaks tribal etiquette. He may be rebuked or chastised, and he is resented by his fellow tribesmen, but his crime does not merit the retribution of invisible powers, nor is he likely to be taken to court.

Buditazhi is a more serious offense. As with *chisapi* the offender is not liable to occult retribution, but he is in danger of being severely punished by his fellow tribesmen. Because of his misdeed, those wronged gain power over him. Redemption is possible only by the payment of a fine.[6]

The word *tonda*, the adjectival form of the verb *kutonda*, and the noun *mutondo*, taboo, is much the more significant word for an understanding of African ethics. It may apply to any person or thing and signifies invariably a total interdiction. If a word or an action is *tonda*, it is prohibited; uttering or doing it is full of peril. If a person is *tonda*, he is under a ban; to enter into contact with him is to court disaster.

When a man commits *buditazhi*, he puts himself in the power of another who exacts personal punishment for the misdeed. By breaking *tonda*, however, the offender places himself in the power of hidden forces which exact their vengeance upon him directly.

The essential characteristic of taboo therefore is automatic retribution. Smith says:

> Dynamism is also an ethic which can be summed up in one word: taboo. Anything is taboo, not when it is prohibited by the chief or by the chief's council, or by the law of God; but when its result automatically follows upon performance. You do or say something which, as it were, springs back and punishes you.[7]

As noted in Chapter 2, taboo is intimately related to the African understanding of *mana* or *ubwanga*.[8] In itself *ubwanga* is neutral, but like electricity it is highly dangerous. Certain actions or things unleash this energy and are therefore taboo. An ordinary person does not interfere with them or he will cause damage both to himself and the community.[9] *Ubwanga* may be used for good or evil, but to break taboo is to assure oneself of releasing its evil consequences:

> I can only register my conviction that without presupposing a belief in *mana*, it is impossible rightly to appreciate many things in the African's life. Their religion consists largely in getting (as Dr. Codrington said of the Melanesians) this *mana* for one's self, or getting it used for one's benefit. Here is the fount of taboo which so largely regulates the African's life. He must not do this or that, say this thing or the other, eat this or that, because otherwise some evil consequence will follow.[10]

It is difficult to generalize regarding taboos since they are so all-pervasive in African life. Smith does attempt a rough classification, grouping the taboos under the qualifying adjectives: physiological, occupational, special, dietary and personal. Physiological taboos are those relating to the vital bodily processes, especially the relationship of the sexes and rules governing menstruation, pregnancy, nursing and the life of widows. Occupational taboos relate to the work of traders, hunters, warriors and iron-smiths, the contravention of which means not only failure but quite possibly death as well. By special taboos, Smith means those which may be of concern for only limited periods of time and for special purposes as for example during the treatment of disease. Dietary taboos include both general and specific prohibitions, some for a lifetime, some for shorter intervals. Personal taboos are highly individualized and may be assumed on the person's own initiative, somewhat as a Westerner might conclude that certain foods do not agree with him and are therefore to be avoided. As can be readily seen, the categories are not mutually exclusive but run into each other. This is particularly true of dietary taboos; for although there are general dietary prohibitions for the clan, food interdictions may be involved in any of the categories mentioned above.[11]

It is not possible to furnish here an exhaustive account of African taboos. Smith does present such for the Ba-ila people in his book *The Ila-Speaking Peoples of Northern Rhodesia*. References to taboo and descriptions of how it functions appear throughout that work. The most that can be done in this context is to provide a few examples in order to show something of the complicated nature of African taboo.

Iron smelting is a difficult venture and therefore is surrounded by carefully defined restrictions. All the smelters are in a state of the strictest taboo. There must be no sexual intercourse in the village. The women are not allowed to wash, nor use ointment and ornaments; they must act like widows. While the kilns are being moulded, the men are permitted to drink only *namenze*, not water. If while asleep a man should dream of sexual intercourse and have an emission, he must confess it at once and be purified of his uncleanness by the doctor. The doctor is also taboo. Not only is he forbidden contact with women; he must also avoid cutting his hair or shaving. Menstruating women are not admitted near the camp, and anyone wearing a dark garment is also excluded because black is an unlucky color. Although adultery is strictly forbidden, swearing and stealing are encouraged. Indeed the work is accompanied by the singing of obscene songs. Any transgression of the rules will thwart the efforts of the smelters and cause failure of the operation. In such a case the doctor seeks to discover the offender who is identified as a witch.[12]

Restrictions on sexual intercourse are extremely complicated and are by no means confined to smelting operations. The same prohibition obtains when women are making beer, as well as during the agricultural tasks of sowing, threshing and storing grain. Men must avoid intercourse before beginning a journey, trading or business activity, fishing and hunting, although some Africans consider the sexual act a lucky charm in the hunt. During war sexual intercourse is strictly taboo, an infraction causing death to the individual and provoking the loss of the battle as well.[13]

A knowledge of the magical aspects of African ethics make possible an understanding of one of the most curious phenomena of African life, namely immorality.

The use of the term "immorality" in this context is not meant to suggest a judgment of African morality from the Western or Christian perspective but from the African's own perspective. Nor is it a reference to the failure of an individual to live up to the standards which society imposes on him.

What is meant rather is that there are times when society itself recognizes not only the right but even the duty of individuals to contravene the rules which normally govern it.

An allusion has already been made to obscenity during smelting operations. Another such occasion is a funeral. After the corpse is buried, the mourning increases in intensity. The women throw themselves violently on the grave and begin singing. Smith expresses his astonishment at the songs. He expected them to reflect upon the paradox of life and death or at least to extol the virtues of the deceased. But in reality the songs are lewd, mostly phallic, in nature. He translates some of them:

> "Come, select your paramour: go take her out. Dear oh dear, select her, go take her out" . . . "You who were at the rains get up and lie with me, get up and lie with me" . . . "I have not yet been concerned in *lubambo*. Have a try at *lubambo!*"[14] . . . "Dear! Dear! Dear! His great penis is a size! It is a thing without an end. It must have had a long unwinding!" . . . "Most energetic in copulation (remember that) the old house is only made of grass." . . . "As for us the penis is erect; as for you the clitoris is small."[15] . . . "In my fellow wife the clitoris is very black. In myself there are small and pretty labiae."[16]

In the ordinary course of life both men and women are prohibited from voicing such sentiments in the presence of the opposite sex. However, a funeral is not an ordinary event, and the rules which generally govern life are altered. It is a time of license when men and women are free to act as they please.[17] Not only is there relaxation of the sexual mores; thatch is torn from houses, fields are robbed and other violence occurs—all without complaint. Smith states that by the time he began his research among the Ba-ila, the practice of levying fines for some of the abuses attending upon funeral celebrations had been introduced.[18]

It is not an easy task to interpret the significance of this transmutation of values. Edwin Smith confesses that he does not have a completely satisfactory explanation for it.[19] Nevertheless, he suggests that the immorality in such cases acts as a charm to normalize the normal:

That the neutral force may be turned to good or bad use explains many curious things in the practices of the Ba-ila. Incest is one of the things that bring men into violent connection with it, and is therefore taboo. The incestuous person is expressly called a *mulozhi* ("a warlock"), a trafficker with forbidden powers. But incest under certain conditions, i.e. when a man is wishful of special good fortune, is not only permitted but enjoined.[20] So with words. Phallic songs that on ordinary occasions are *tonda*, must be used on the occasion of a funeral, during smelting operations, and on other occasions when the forces are intimately in evidence. In normal times the abnormal is taboo, but in abnormal times the abnormal things are done to restore the normal condition of affairs.[21]

Ancestral Sanctions

If one asks the African why some things are *tonda* and others are not, a question which deals ultimately with the origin of his tribal mores, he may not go back beyond the traditional answer: "We do it because our fathers did it."[22] More often he is likely to say that the customs of the tribe rest on the will and desire of the *mizhimo*, the ancestors.[23] The real dynamic at work may be largely magical in nature, based on the automatic retribution involved in the abuse of *ubwanga*, but the explanation given may be either traditional or religious, the latter understood as resting on the authority of a god or God. In reality it is not possible to maintain clear distinctions between the magical and religious sanctions. They are often found at work together.

As an example, it may be useful to cite another case of "immorality" among the Ba-ila—the yearly fertility festival of Shimunenga. This occurs at the beginning of the new year. Shimunenga's representative cuts a path into the center of the sacred grove and talks with the god. Then he goes to the surrounding villages urging the people to begin brewing beer. All being prepared, the feast begins. On the first day the women gather at the grove to sing and dance. The next day belongs to the men. They bring their cattle to the grove, and parade them to the river and back, all the while singing, dancing and drinking beer. Both the men and women invoke the name of the divinity: " 'Shimunenga, Lobwe, Udimbabachembe!' ('Shimunenga, Gatherer of men, Giver of virility to males!')."[24] As at funerals, the songs sung by the women are mostly phallic in nature and there is general license.

A recognized part of the feast is the *Lubambo,* which literally means "an arranged thing." In ceremonial fashion a man and woman publicly announce that they are lovers and gifts are exchanged to signify the relationship. The woman's husband cannot complain because he does the same thing. It is not merely a temporary arrangement during the feast but may go on afterward. The system is accepted by the men because they also benefit from it, but they are sometimes resentful of a wife who shows too much affection for her lover.[25]

The significance of the festival is apparently to please the god so that he will bless their agricultural endeavors in the new year. Concerning the interplay of dynamism and spiritism, or magic and religion, Edwin Smith makes this comment:

> Just as a living chief is pleased and complimented by an exhibition of his people's happiness and wealth, so Shimunenga is thought to be gratified by this display—so gratified that at this critical season of the year he will in return do his utmost to increase their prosperity. So far, we may say that the festival is religious. The accompanying immoralities and singing of ribald songs by women and men are, I think, in the nature of a charm, intended to work directly, that is to say, by "magic" force, upon field and herd.
> . . . If I am right in my interpretation of the sexual irregularities, magic and religion combine in this festival in a manner similar to that in which they are combined in the rain-making ceremony.[26]

To speak of religious sanctions in African ethics is to recognize that the ancestors are the trustees of tribal morality. Although there are differences in the attitude and approach of the diverse African peoples to the ancestors, everywhere they are regarded as being intimately concerned for the living members of the community. Some are recognized as personal guardians. Others look after the welfare of the village and tribe. But all have the best interests of their people at heart. The ancestors seek for the health and well-being of the tribe. They know the mysteries of life. They know what is good and bad, what builds up and tears down, what is beneficial and harmful. Therefore they can be depended upon to guide the visible community in the ways of happiness and prosperity.

Anyone who fails to abide by the tribal mores is an offender not only against the living members of the society but the entire com-

munity, composed of both the living and the dead. Indeed they
thereby commit a special crime against the ancestors whose task is
to look after the welfare of all. Smith says:

> In a great continent like Africa there is necessarily great diversity
> in the way in which these ancestors are regarded, but every-
> where they are recognised as having close connexion with the
> life and well being of their descendents. They are the guardians
> of the tribal customs, and any breach of inherited morality is
> an offence against them.[27]

The ancestors have established the norms for the good life and
serve as the protectors of tribal morality. Where changes are
necessary, they make their will known through their representatives—the prophets.[28] It is not the task of an ordinary individual
to alter the established practices of the community. Anyone who
should attempt it would be classed as a witch, that is, one who is
anti-social, and would suffer the consequences:

> Indeed it is dangerous to attempt to do anything contrary to the
> general practice, as the community is always on guard to protect
> itself against any innovation. Should a blacksmith conceive the idea
> of making better hoes—it is never done! Should a man wish to
> introduce new methods of tilling—it is never done! If either of
> them persist, they will probably be accused of, and condemned
> for, the most horrible crime known to Africans—witchcraft. This
> is not to say that no change ever takes place in African society.
> It only means that there are recognised instruments of change,
> and it is not for an unauthorised individual to strike out on his
> own. If he sets out to be more clever than his fellows, and should
> succeed in becoming more successful than they, his action would
> be regarded as evidence of traffic with forbidden powers.[29]

Contravention of the ancestral norms, either those long established or those recently revealed to the prophets, may result not
only in the accusation of witchcraft but automatic retribution as
well. It is often the visible retribution which confirms the truth of
the prophetic utterance. It is not to be presumed that the teaching
of a medium is always accepted. In reality it may not be accepted
at all. Changes are not easily effected. Factors influencing the
matter are the prophet's reputation and confirmatory signs.

Smith tells of one prophet who proclaimed a message from Leza
that the *kamwaya* bush was no longer to be used in scattering
storm clouds. Shortly afterward two men were caught in a

thunderstorm, and one began waving *kamwaya* branches to chase the clouds away. The other warned him of the prophet's words, but his warning fell on deaf ears. Suddenly there was a crack of lightning and the offender fell dead. Word spread rapidly. Villagers took it as a sign of the truth of prophetic teaching.[30]

Role of Supreme Being

The reference to Leza in the *kamwaya* bush example leads logically to a consideration of another aspect of religious sanctions, namely, the relationship of the Supreme God to tribal customs.

Smith makes it clear that many of the tribal customs of the Ba-ila are regarded as owing their origin to Leza. Of some taboos they say: *chifundo chaka Leza.* The word *chifundo* refers to a line on the ground which cannot be passed, thus giving to the phrase the meaning of something prohibited by God. The first time that Smith ever heard the phrase was after he and Dale had doctored to health a young man seriously injured in an encounter with a leopard. Smith asked the man's father for the leopard skin as a remembrance of the event. The father reluctantly refused, explaining his decision with reference to *chifundo chaka Leza.*[31]

In the Ba-ila conception God is referred to as lawgiver.[32] Many of the tribal norms and customs owe their origin to Him and thus obtain their validity through His authority.[33] Yet the Ba-ila do not seem to be conscious of a clear ethical relationship between themselves and God. Smith says:

> Leza is regarded as having founded many of the customs, and . . . certain laws or regulations are said to be *shifundo shaka Leza* ("God's prohibitions"). But too much must not be made of that. The relation between Leza and men is not to be described as ethical. He has no title of Judge. It is true that at times when they see a circle around the moon the Ba-ila will say: "Today there is a *lubeta* above" (*Kudi lubeta kwizeulu*), using the word describing the meeting of the chiefs and people to try a case. But this is no more than a picturesque description today, whatever it may once have meant. That Leza should take cognisance of all the doings of men, and regard them with approval or disapproval, is an idea quite foreign to their minds. In all their invocations of Leza there is no confession of sin.[34]

Only in the atonement for homicide is there an idea of sin against Leza; yet even here the offering of oxen is not made directly to God but to the communal divinity, Shimunenga. The idea is that Shimunenga is responsible to Leza for the lives of all the members of the community. Hence in the case of murder, Shimunenga is in debt to Leza. Shimunenga receives the gift and in turn offers the ox's spirit to God as propitiation.[35]

Smith has difficulty in making generalizations about the African conception of God's ethical concern. His early books tend to minimize God's role. In speaking of Bantu Religion he says:

> That God should take note of all doings of individual men and should reward and punish them according to their deeds is an idea quite remote from the Bantu mind. Yet in some faint way they have a notion that He makes for righteousness.[36]

His strongest expression of God's disinterestedness is found in *The Secret of the African:*

> As a general rule Africans do not associate morality with their belief in God; men are not more honest, truthful, and virtuous because of their awareness of His existence. The Creator rules in the cosmical sphere and is the Supreme Arbiter of human destiny, but he does not bring men into judgment now or here-after. He does not mind whether a man is good or bad.[37]

In his book, *African Beliefs and Christian Faith*, Smith qualifies that statement by reference to the practices and beliefs of other Africans. For some tribes at least God is both law-giver and judge.[38] The Bacongo not only speak of *nkondo mi Nzambi* (laws of God); any contravention of them is called *sumu ku Nzambi* (act against God) and is punished by *lufwa Nzambi* (a bad death).[39] They insist that the automatic retributive death for breaking the incest taboo comes directly from God.[40] Although by no means a common belief in Africa, the Bacongo declare that a man's life after death is influenced by his actions in the present.[41]

The Chagga people of Tanzania affirm that *Ruwa* punishes a disobedient child, a thief and a traitor to his tribe, while rewarding with cattle, goats and children those who are upright in their relations to others.[42]

The Konde of Nyasaland assert that *Kyala*, disguised as a lion or snake, visits men when there is great evil and punishment is re-quired. Smith observes that such a belief does not appear to be a comforting thought for the people:

For that reason the desire of the people is that God will go away again. "Go far from here. O God, go to the Sango, because your house is great"—this is a prayer not uncommonly on the lips of the people when it seems to them that God is near.[43]

In spite of these examples, however, one ought not to conclude that Africans have an unclouded picture of the relation of the Supreme Being to the moral life of men. Addressing himself to the question: "How far are Africans conscious that in doing wrong they are acting against God?" Smith replies: "It seems that some light, though not a full light, has come to Africans on this point. To some it has come more fully than to others."[44]

Another factor, already mentioned in some detail,[45] adds to the ambiguity of present conceptions, namely, the myths of God's departure.

In the beginning all went well between God and man; but because of man's foolishness or wickedness, which is often expressed as his willful disobedience, God left him to his own devices. The parallels between the story of the Fall in Genesis and the myth as told by the Chagga of Tanzania, for example, are astonishingly close.

The Chagga say that Ruwa committed to the care of the first man a banana garden. At the center of the garden he placed a plant called *ula* or *ukaho* and ordained that the man should not eat of it. There appeared one day at the house of the village chief a stranger asking for food. He was informed that he could go into the garden but was not to partake of the *ula* for that was prohibited by God. To this the stranger replied that Ruwa Himself had sent him to cook the *ula* so that all might be happy together. A cooking pot was provided and a meal eaten of the forbidden fruit. When Ruwa heard of it, He was angry and cursed the chief and his people, stating that their bones would be broken, their eyes cut to pieces and death would overcome them. That was the last of Ruwa's messages to man. Man's problems began when he disobeyed the divine will.[46]

CHRISTIAN CONTRIBUTION

In the field of morality, once again Edwin Smith calls for the sublimation of African conceptions in the Christian Faith. He is convinced that the position of African Traditional Religion encompasses both strengths and weaknesses. Some of the latter are inherent in the African ethical system. Others are aggravated by the particular situation in which Africa finds itself today due to its encounter with the West. A distinction between ethical and non-ethical aspects of behavior and a new motivation based on a deeper understanding of God are both essential. As always Smith calls upon his missionary and African Christian colleagues to correct the weaknesses without overlooking the strengths of traditional belief and practice.

Strengths and Weaknesses

Unquestionably there are values in taboo morality. For one thing, taboo instills within the African an innate sense that there is a distinction between good and evil, right and wrong, clean and unclean. All actions are not the same. A person is not free to do just as he pleases. There are consequences to man's deeds. To the one who fails in his duties, taboo teaches not only the necessity but also the desire for purification.[47] Among the various taboos, some are undoubtedly of importance from a health standpoint and therefore add to the happiness of the people. All serve the useful purpose of providing for discipline in life and contribute to the African's recognition that he is not self-sufficient but dependent upon that which lies beyond himself. Smith remarks:

> They [taboos] are valuable from our point of view in the testimony that they bear to a recognition on the part of the people that their well-being depends upon obedience to something external to themselves; and this discipline has, on the whole, been salutary. Some taboos are the first form of hygienic and medical interdictions.[48]

Many African taboos are of high ethical value. In discussing the role of traditional literature in Africa, it was noted that folk tales form the equivalent of the Old Testament. Furthermore, Smith explicitly states that "the pagan Bantu conscience . . . approves the greater part of the Decalogue."[49]

Smith is under no illusions that African and Western views are the same, but he does not insist that where different the Africans are wrong and Westerners are right. He is fully aware of the fact that, although African practices sometimes seem shocking and silly to Europeans, European practices have the same effect on Africans.[50]

Both Africans and Westerners oppose incest, for example, though they define it differently. Smith does not assume that one definition is necessarily of higher value than the other.[51]

The African Church should be indigenous, and the African Christian should remain African. Nothing disturbed Edwin Smith so much as the suggestion that, to become Christian, an African had to become European.[52] The African should not assimilate unthinkingly the mores of the West, nor should he substitute the tribal customs of Europe for those of Africa.[53] Missionaries must learn to work *with* not *for* the African Church.[54] They are still needed, and theirs is a noble work,[55] but they are not a permanent factor in the situation.[56] The Church must be placed as soon as possible under African leadership where Africans can develop their own genius and make their unique contribution to the universal Church and the world.[57]

It is true that some African customs cannot be completely harmonized with the Christian view of life, nor are all judged alike from the Christian perspective. Smith divides them into several different categories.

Some are clearly incompatible with Christianity. In this group is listed such conduct as the killing of people at funerals and infanticide, especially the killing of twins. This latter practice is grounded in the belief that abnormal births are bad omens and will therefore bring evil on the community. Smith sees no way to harmonize these actions with Christian teaching. He believes that Western influence will before long result in their elimination.[58]

Some customs need to be baptized. They are not in themselves necessarily evil, but they contain elements which require alteration. Many African practices fall into this category, and it is not possible to explain in detail the often complex approach which Smith takes to them. Examples include a number of sexual practices,[59] payment of bride wealth,[60] and initiation rites.[61] Polygamy is a special case in that Smith seems to see monogamy as of the *bene esse* of life, both from the standpoint of Christianity and traditional African conceptions, without judging polygamy as necessarily wrong.[62]

With yet other customs, Smith judges the action right but the motive false. He notes that people commonly abstain from stealing when protective charms are placed in a field, since they are fearful of unleashing the power of evil resident therein. Certain kinds of adultery are taboo because, if they are indulged in, evil consequences will automatically follow. In each case Smith approves the result but questions the reasons which lie behind it.[63]

Although largely neutral from the Christian perspective, another group of customs are taboos which lack a justifiable rational basis. Many of the dietary prohibitions fall into this category. Certain things cannot be eaten. Other things cannot be done or disaster will come upon the individual. The idea that eggs cause sterility or impotence;[64] the view that a child must be protected from the evil eye of the blue jay[65] are examples. Smith observes that education tends to break down the fear attached to these practices.[66]

Separation of Ceremonial and Moral Law

One of the disturbing features of African Traditional Religion, according to Edwin Smith, is its lack of differentiation between the ceremonial and moral aspects of the law.

Taboo is a unitary concept composed of moral and extra-moral elements based on the assumption that any infraction will bring its own retribution. Obeying strictly the dietary regulations of the community is just as important as keeping its ethical rules. Indeed the former are not uncommonly considered the more significant.

The real difficulty of the African conception is that it makes no allowance for distinctions in ethical quality between different types of taboo:

> It is not easy for one trained in Christian morality to appreciate the position occupied by the taboo in the life of the Ba-ila. The things summed up in the word *tonda* include not only prohibitions due to a vague instinctive repulsion from deeds which the highest ethical consciousness recognises as wrong, but also others which to advanced thought have no moral significance. To our minds there is a world of difference between theft and, say, eating a quail; but it is a sign of the weakness of their ethical discrimination that a breach of what we should call the "ceremonial law" is rated a greater offense than a breach of the "moral law".[67]

Smith goes on to illustrate his judgment by citing the complaint of a highly intelligent Ba-ila man against a woman who had stolen goods from his house. The woman in question had recently aborted and was still "unclean." The woman was guilty of two crimes, but for the man it was manifest that her uncleanness was much more serious, for it placed in jeopardy both himself and his family. He was willing to forgive the theft, but the other crime could only be covered by a fine. Smith concludes with this comment: "We were amazed, and yet—why? From his point of view he was unquestionably right. And in all these matters we have to think ourselves back into their position."[68]

The battle for a differentiation between the ceremonial and moral aspects of the law is not a new one for Christianity, nor is the lack of distinction between the two strange to Christian experience. It was precisely the situation in the early history of the Jewish nation. The Penteteuch juxtaposes these two aspects of the law without distinction. The Hebrew prophets attempted to impress on the minds of the people the essential difference between them, but they did not achieve complete success. Jesus himself had to re-emphasize the point:

> At that time, as in Africa to-day, there were great numbers of taboos; this thing and that thing might not be taken as food, for example. The Law said that the taking of them made people unclean. Jesus said: "Nothing outside a man is able to make him unclean by going into him; it is what comes from him which makes him unclean. From inside, from the heart of man, the designs of evil come: sex evils, taking of other people's property, putting to death, bad desires, cruel and unkind things, deceit, envy, pride—all these evils come from inside and they make a man unclean" (Mark vii. 14–23).[69]

Inner Compulsion for Morality

Smith is concerned that a new motivational foundation be built to underpin those ethical practices which he believes are essential not only to Africa but all human behavior. The urgent need for this is the fact that the concept of taboo is seriously challenged by the introduction of science and Western education in present day Africa. Because of its unitary nature, a challenge to taboo's non-ethical aspects places in jeopardy its ethical elements as well.

A man goes away to work. Perhaps he seeks employment on a European plantation or in a mine near one of Africa's cities or towns. When he says good-by to his family, he also leaves behind his ancestral gods, for they are attached to the tribal home. He finds himself in a new place, together with men of other tribes and races who regularly eat food which he considers taboo. They laugh at him for his foolish ideas and by both precept and example encourage him to do the very things which he has been taught since birth to regard as wrong. Smith calls attention to the all too common result:

> The danger to him is that he may also disregard obligations with more ethical content than food-prohibitions. Men return home, in fact, with morals loosened. They may have found that they can live very comfortably without their gods, for no evil befell them through the neglect of tribal religious rites, and as a result they have not the respect for the gods which they once had. They have less respect too for the chief; they have learnt something of their own individual value, and look with scorn upon the restraints exercised by stay-at-home folk who have never travelled. In the old days, a charm placed upon a neighbour's pumpkin-patch kept robbers away; these men have learnt from sophisticated work-companions to pooh-pooh such silly things, and thieve with an easy conscience.[70]

Edwin Smith sees the distintegration which has resulted from the encounter of African culture with the West. He laments the loss thereby of much that was good. He is critical of the abuses of Europeans on the continent, but he is convinced that the encounter itself was inevitable.[71] Moreover, even if the European had been scrupulously fair in dealing with the African, a certain amount of dislocation could not have been avoided because of the very nature of the relationship of African belief and practice. Missionaries have also contributed to the destruction of traditional ways in Africa, although theirs is not merely a negative role:

> What is the effect of missionary teaching upon the Africans? Neither missionaries, traders, government officials, nor miners can be absolved from causing disintegration of African society. It is well for us frankly to admit this fact. It is often charged against us that we have no right to tamper with native beliefs. The answer is twofold: first, that all Europeans, whether missionaries or others, whether intentionally or not, are breaking down these beliefs; secondly, that only the missionaries are engaged in building up again.[72]

Unquestionably taboo has a salutary effect in protecting property and social life.[73] In addition, taboo accomplishes its task with a minimum of outward restraint. But when the concept of taboo is weakened or destroyed, as it is increasingly in Africa today due to the impact of Western culture, the question arises as to what will take its place. Smith sees little hope in more external control, such as the "gallows" for example. To say nothing more, it is a much weaker restraint than taboo. Taboo was inescapable, whereas one may by stealth outwit police and judge.[74]

The value of the European system of law, when applied to the African situation, may be seriously questioned, if for no other reason than that it attempts to substitute external fear and control for what has to date been internal restraint, albeit inadequate inner restraint for the present day.

The only real hope is that an inner compulsion for morality be created to take the place of the old taboo system. What is needed then is a new understanding of the restraint of conscience.

One of the greatest disasters that could happen to the African would be for him to receive only a secular, scientific education.[75] That he become educated is necessary. That he learn science is important. But he needs also a new motive for morality or disintegration will necessarily follow:

> As I showed in a previous chapter, the weakness of this dynamistic morality is shown when Africans are brought into contact with Europeans. The education which they are receiving inevitably saps this form of belief and practice: it cannot withstand elementary scientific knowledge. Its rational basis is too slender. The sophisticated young African realizes that many of the taboos that restricted the actions of his fathers are devoid of real foundation. Unless the restraint of an enlightened conscience replaces the old dynamistic controls, the youth falls into the danger of becoming morally an anarchist.[76]

The experience of education and contact with the world will of necessity challenge, but it must not be allowed to destroy, African life. To prevent this from taking place, Christianity has an important role to play. It must be the bridge between the old morality and that which is required for this new day. The essential Christian purpose therefore is not one of destruction but one of sublimation. African morality must be placed on new foundations, with a new motive force. Sublimation will accomplish its task "by transforming prohibitions into rational medical and hygienic regulation, by replacing imagination beliefs by stalwart religious faith, by transmuting the taboo into the sinful."[77]

Ethics and God

Edwin Smith believes that there must be rules for conduct if people are to live together in harmony, but he is also convinced that a society cannot rest entirely on the sanction of external law. There must be inner controls if life is to be bearable.[78] The most viable society occurs where its members are governed not by fear of the consequences of wrong actions but a love of the right and good. It is not enough to merely state that Africa is in need of a new inner compulsion for morality. The real question is how this can be obtained. Characteristically Smith sees the answer in a new emphasis on the role of the Supreme Being.

The problem of African ethics, both past and present, is precisely the problem of African Religion. Africans have a belief in God, but that belief plays only a peripheral role in shaping their behavioral patterns. To be sure, there is a relationship between the Supreme God and the ethical conduct of His people. He is recognized as the source of many of their customs, and among some African people He is also identified as judge. Yet even at its strongest, the belief in God plays a very limited part in governing their actions. Smith says:

> Among numbers of Africans there is, as we have seen—in great things if not in small things—a fear of God and what God will do if certain laws are broken. As a control of behaviour this fear is generally feeble.[79]

A new emphasis on the role of the Creator God not only deepens the motive for African morality, but it also broadens its base beyond the tribe. As noted in Chapter 3, there is an ambiguity in the African world view that retains the concept of the High God, the Creator of all men and all tribes, and yet makes no place in its system for those other men. Smith observes that the normal rules for ethical action do not apply to strangers and those of other tribes:

> Ancestor worship has some ethical implication. To be sure that influence is limited: a man will not desist from homicide, as homicide, out of reverence for, or fear of, his communal divinities. They are quite indifferent as regards the lives of people who do not belong to their particular community. As far as they are concerned, the killing of a stranger is no murder and no sin.[80]

The significance of this for the new Africa which is characterized by the migration of people and the creation of towns and cities can hardly be overemphasized.

The African clan system provides for an extraordinary sense of oneness and community. Men act and work together. They help

and protect each other when need arises. They live in brotherhood with their neighbors. The problem is that the clan is limited
in its boundaries. The feeling of oneness and brotherhood does not
extend beyond the ties of kinship. Those who are outside are
looked upon as foreigners and often enemies. Jesus brought a new
vision. He recognized no boundaries. In his thought all men are
of one clan—God's clan. This is the meaning of his parable of the
Good Samaritan.[81]

In the view of Edwin Smith, the key to real moral behavior is
one's conception of God. This is true not only for Africans but all
peoples.

Jeremiah's greatness as teacher and prophet was his understanding of this truth. He looked forward to the time of a new coven-
ant, when the Jews would know God and His will for them, when
God's desires and their own would be identical, when they would
do the right thing not because of some external law but because it
was the law of their own hearts.[82]

When Jesus came, the lives of most men were still governed by
the restraints of external law. Jesus did not oppose the rule of law,
but he insisted that the secret of life lies in love—love for God and
man. Smith expresses it in these words:

> In effect this was His teaching: Get right with God. Get the
> right idea of God as your Father and King. Go about things in
> God's way. . . . Let your behaviour be such that you will not
> be shamed by your thought of God. Be full of joy when you go
> about doing God's desire here on earth which is God's house,
> conscious all the time that He is near and loving. Not fear but
> love is to be your guide.
>
> Jesus did not come to give men a new body of laws in place of
> old laws. He did not make a new system of rules for the govern-
> ment of everyday behaviour. What He gives is a new outlook on
> life, a new measure of value, a new line of thought, a new sense
> of God. It is all based upon His view of God as Father and King.[83]

Something else needs to be said. The significance of the gospel
consists not merely in what it reveals of Jesus' thought and belief
about God. The Christian Faith centers itself in the Person of
Jesus as the one who unveils the hidden God and who by the
sheer attraction of his life calls men to be his disciples. It is because of his love that men love. It is because of the kind of God
that he revealed that men are challenged to follow in his foot-
steps.[84]

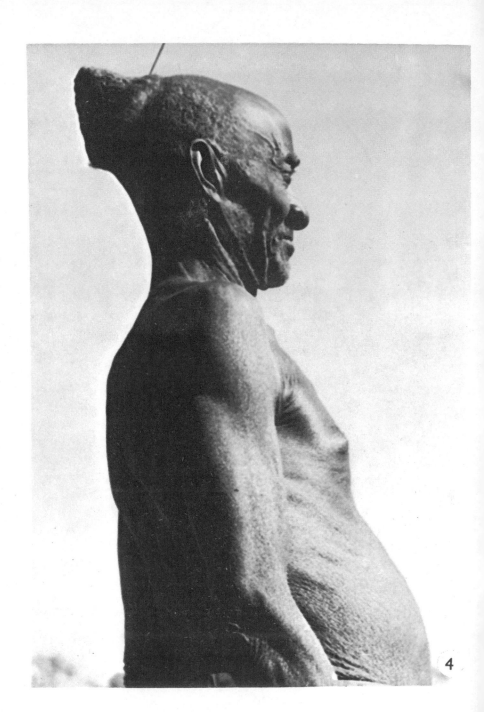

4

5

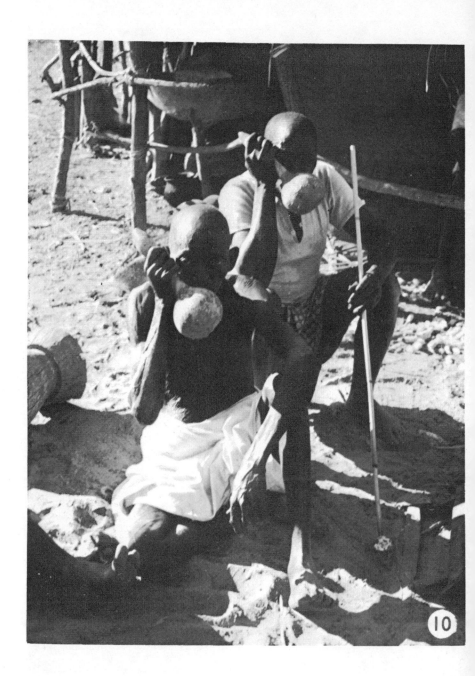

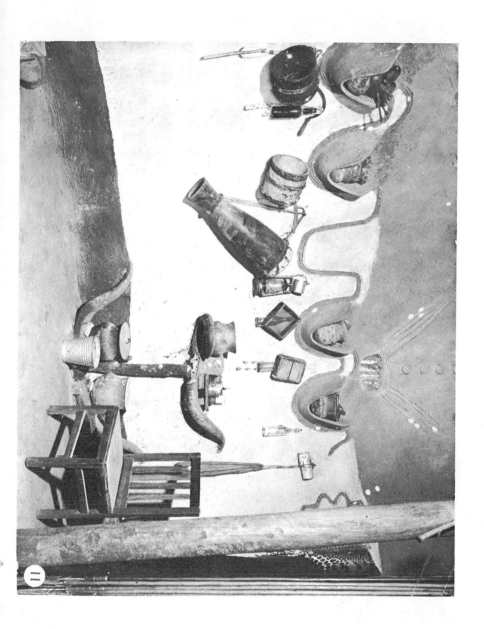

12

14

15

21

23

25

PHOTOGRAPHS

1. Edwin W. Smith and family. *Photo by Sayers, Great Yarmouth.*

2. Edwin W. Smith and family on their way to Zambia (1902).

3. Mrs. Edwin W. Smith outside her home on Nanzala Mission Station, Zambia.

4. A. Ba-ila elder displaying a traditional haircut (1948). *Photo by Zambia Information Services.*

5. A Ba-ila funeral (1948). *Photo by Zambia Information Services.*

6. Mourners at a traditional Ba-ila funeral (1948). *Photo by Zambia Information Services.*

7. A Ba-ila chief (1948). *Photo by Zambia Information Services.*

8. A Ba-ila blacksmith at work (1948). *Photo by Zambia Information Services.*

9. A Ba-ila woman with traditional pipe (1948). *Photo by Zambia Information Services.*

10. Ba-ila elders drinking from traditional gourd cups (1948). *Photo by Zambia Information Services.*

11. Interior of Ba-ila Chief Mukobela's house in Namwala District, Zambia (1948). *Photo by Zambia Information Services.*

12. A Maasai initiation ceremony in Kenya. *Photo by Nation Newspapers Limited.*

13. A modern-day Kenya medicine man (1964). *Photo by Nation Newspapers Limited.*

14. An assistant of Peter Njagi, a prominent Kenya medicine man (1964). *Photo by Nation Newspapers Limited.*

15. Market dispensary of Vice-chairman Thuita of the Kenya Medicine Man's Association, called in Swahili *Waganga wa miti-shamba* (1964). *Photo by Nation Newspapers Limited.*

16. A revival service in East Africa.

17. An African pastor with his parishioners. *Photo by The New York Times.*

18. Barundi women returning from worship.

19. A Christian school in Burundi.

20. The Feast of Timkat (Epiphany) celebrated by the Ethiopian Orthodox Church. *Photo by the United Nations.*

21. A parish church in Ugogo, Tanzania, built in the style of traditional Wagogo houses.

22. Bishop Ajuoga of the Church of Christ in Africa, an independent church in Kenya, exhorting the faithful to complete the building of their new cathedral. *Photo by The New York Times.*

23. Religious dance in Isaiah Shembe's Nazarite Baptist Church, an independent church in South Africa. *Photo by the World Council of Churches.*

24. Worship in the Cherubim and Seraphim, an independent church in West Africa. *Photo by The New York Times.*

25. Building the principal Kimbanguist Church in Kinshasa, Zaïre (1967).

26. Healing and exorcism in the Cherubim and Seraphim of West Africa. *Photo by The New York Times.*

7

Worship:
Is God Worshipped?

The African lives in a spiritual world. He is conscious of being surrounded by a great cloud of witnesses and by powers which are not fully intelligible. Both the world of the seen and the unseen are realities, and the living seek contact with that which is invisible. The sense of dependence in the face of the mysteries of life inspires the African with awe and reverence and impels him to enter into communion with the unknown. The African is deeply religious, and his religious sentiments express themselves in worship.

"Ancestor Worship"

African attention is centered on the ancestors who are looked up to as the guardians of individuals, families and the community as a whole. Those in the flesh constantly seek communion with the departed. It is therefore important to inquire regarding Smith's understanding of the relationship between the living and the dead as it is reflected in the worship experience.

A study of Smith's writings makes clear that throughout his life he was preoccupied with the problem as to whether the attention which the living give to the departed should be characterized as "ancestor worship." He was never absolutely certain on the subject, although the total testimony seems to indicate his qualified acceptance of the validity of the term. Several quotations will serve to illustrate this.

In his early study of the Ba-ila people, published in 1920, while discussing the Ila words for offerings to the divinities, he says:

> These words are not restricted entirely to the service of the divinities but are occasionally (and *kutula* more frequently than *kupaila*) used of presents given by one person to another, and especially of gifts to a superior. The word *kukomba* corresponds very well to our "worship" in the broad sense.[1]

His books of the 1920's show evidence of his conviction that "these acts of worship have a real religious value."[2] However, qualifications also appear, as for example the statement: "The ancestral spirit becomes the object of something like worship."[3]

In 1946 he notes with *some* approval the positions of Driberg and Young that so-called "ancestor worship" is not worship at all and that the relations between the living and the departed are secular, not religious.[4] This is repeated four years later, with a concluding remark that nevertheless this is something more than a "secular" concept:

> We may accept the caveat by T. Cullen Young and J. H. Driberg; but only on a narrow definition of religion can the ancestral cult be dismissed as "purely secular". If the essence of religion is the sense of dependence upon supersensible powers who are able and willing to help, then we are in the presence of religion when Africans commune with their kinsmen in the unseen world, who have enhanced powers associated with their new status and particularly as mediators between man and God.[5]

At a later point in the same book, he says: "Ancestors are not 'worshipped' (if worship it is) without discrimination."[6]

Smith's position represents a hesitant affirmation of the validity of the term "ancestor worship." It is essential to investigate further what is meant by those words, specifically the significance of worship in African life.

African Conception of Worship

African worship is a varied and complex affair. As to form, two main elements are involved: prayer and offerings.

Although most prayers are expressed in words, some Africans use gestures to communicate with the unseen. The Tswana for example use an elaborate system of signs in their worship. One method is for a man to put his hands on his chest. Another worshipper strikes his thigh, followed by the tossing of dust or pieces of wood into the air. In yet a third case a man wets the index finger of his right hand with saliva and points it skyward through the index finger and thumb of his left hand.[7] These are the equivalent of voiced prayers.

Prayers may be both regular and occasional, individual and communal. Some Africans make daily prayers, and many pray as a group at the sowing and harvesting seasons.[8] Prayer becomes especially important during the trials of life and, depending upon the particular crisis, may express the sentiment of an individual, a family or the community as a whole.

Offerings are also many and varied. Usually the gifts consist of the ordinary articles of daily use, not items of great value.[9] Almost anything may be given to the divinities. They need things as much as those who live in the flesh, although they only partake of their spiritual counterparts. Tobacco, beer, grain, cloth and hoes are all useful and are regularly presented. Water is a common offering and is usually given by filling the mouth and spitting it on the ground.[10]

Saliva is also tendered, not because it is needed by the spirits but because it represents a giving of oneself to renew the bond of relationship between the worshipper and worshipped:

> The simplest offering of all, and one which is the usual accompaniment of prayers in some tribes, is the saliva. We cannot easily bring ourselves to understand the condition of mind that sees religious value in such an offering; the idea of spitting as an act of worship is repellent to us. But if we think of the spittle as what it is,—a part of oneself—then perhaps we may begin to realize how it can come to have sacramental value as an offering. It is not that there is any intrinsic worth in the spittle, or that it can conceivably be of any use to the divinity; but simply because its value is nil, it acquires a real religious value. It is something like a lover offering a flower to his beloved. It creates a bond, or renews the bond, between the worshipper and his divinity.[11]

If one expectorates with force (transcribed as Thu!), it is interpreted as a curse. An offering is an easy expectoration, Tsu![12]

It is difficult to maintain a clear distinction between prayers and offerings. The "Tsu!" in question is an offering, but in practice it is usually little more than an interjection within a prayer.

Blood sacrifices are also offered to the divinities and usually signify a more important happening in the life of the community. Occasionally human sacrifices are involved, although this practice has not been common in Africa.[13]

Reference has already been made to the atonement for homicide.[14] The murderer pays a *lwembe* ("weregild") of up to twenty head of cattle, donated by his clansmen. Two are killed as a blood offering to Shimunenga. After the meat has been eaten by the people, the heads of the beasts are placed inside Shimunenga's grove. The priest receives one or two oxen as payment for his services and the rest are divided among the local chiefs.[15]

Solemn sacrifices are offered to the ancestors before new or dangerous ventures, such as the building of a village,[16] or going to war.[17] Strangers who receive permission from a chief to fish and hunt on land not their own must see to it that sacrifices are offered to the local ancestors to insure the success of their activities.[18]

Prayers and offerings are usually joined together in the worship experience of Africans. Prayers accompany offerings or sacrifices, and offerings are rarely presented without some verbal exclamation. This can be well illustrated by numerous examples of the relationship of a person with his namesake.[19] When a man sneezes, he expectorates an offering of saliva, saying: " 'Tsu! My namesake, stand by me always!' " Before hunting he makes an offering of meal at the public altar, praying:

> "Tsu! My namesake, let us go out together and hunt; bring the animals near to me, let the sharp stick sleep, let the fierce snake be far away. I want only meat. Give it me, O hunter."

After killing an animal, he offers portions of the liver, rump, heart and leg to the East, North, West and South, uttering in each case the phrase: " 'Thou in the East [North, West, South], here is meat!' " He lies on his back, claps his hands and says: " 'To-morrow and to-morrow give me meat!' " This is followed by a further offering (of liver and heart) and prayer to his namesake:

> "Here is meat, O my namesake, Pambala, pambala, a spirit does not refuse his own anything. To-morrow and to-morrow may I kill even more than this animal! Be thou around me, O hunter!"

When he returns home, he makes another offering.

The villages of the Ba-ila have both public and private altars.

The former, called *lwanga*, usually consist of a long pole placed in the center of the village. Charms are hung from it and offerings, such as meat from the hunt, are put at its base. If a man buys a new slave, he leads him before the pole and spits water on the slave and the altar. The ceremony is meant to cement the new relationship between the slave and master; the slave receives a new name to certify his changed allegiance. The village gateway is also regarded as a holy spot where offerings are left.[20]

Private altars are ordinarily devoid of distinguishing marks but are recognized as sacred places by the family, the most common being the central pole and the two sides of the doorway to the hut. The man's altar is to the right, the wife's to the left.[21] Since both belong to different families and the ancestors help only their own people, husbands do not pray or make offerings for their wives nor vice versa.[22]

The graves of the ancestors are sacred to the living. Sticks are planted around them and soon form a grove of trees identifying the spot. A small hut is often erected over or near the grave. If the village is moved, sometimes the ancestral houses are moved as well. Prayers and offerings are made at these sepulchral temples.[23]

Allusions have been made to funeral services and to the offerings and prayers at the burial service. These are meant to honor the deceased and to assure that he will be well disposed toward the living. Among the Ba-ila there are five set beer-drinking ceremonies of remembrance during the first year, and these are meant to fortify the ancestor's good favor. They are: (1) the *funku owetwe* ("beer of the ash"), which occurs several days after the funeral, when ashes of the mourners' fires are swept up by the relatives and thrown away; (2) the *funku owa nsako* ("beer of the shafts"), when the spears of the deceased are broken; (3) the *funku owa kuzhola munganda* ("beer to bring back the deceased into the house"), when the spirit is welcomed home; (4) the *funku owa mapai* ("beer of the offerings"), which includes the killing of an ox for the feast to honor the ghost; and (5) the *funku owa madidila* ("beer of the final weeping"), about a year following the obsequies. Usually this ends the formal ceremonies for family divinities, and they are attended to only when they cause trouble or when the living relatives need their help.[24]

A time of special need is when illness occurs to a member of the family. If the diviner affirms that the cause is a neglected divinity, the family head makes an offering and may pray in this manner:

"Oh, my father, if it be thou (who art troubling him) leave the child alone that he may go about alone. Tsu! Oh, my father, what is the matter? You divinities who are without, he doesn't see you (i.e. doesn't recognise you). Tsu! Oh, old man, leave him alone. If thou art crying for something to eat, he shall brew thee the beer thou criest for and make thee an offering. If it be thou, leave him alone that he may walk this very day. Tsu! Oh, my father, we worship thee!"[25]

If the head man is himself ill, he may offer this prayer:

"Tsu! If it be thou, O leave me alone, that I may be well. What is it thou requirest? See, here is tobacco, here is water, here is beer. Leave me alone that I may enjoy myself."[26]

Although prayers and offerings are usually petitionary in nature, Smith denies that they are meant as bribes.[27] The fact that most offerings are of little intrinsic value is proof in itself, but there are other factors. Some prayers are made up entirely of praise-names without any requests.[28] Others express the sentiment of thanksgiving. After a Thonga has made tobacco or snuff, he puts some on the family altar as a gift to the ancestors.[29] Many Africans put particles of food on the ground in the morning before they eat, or they blow their first puff-full of tobacco into the air as a gift to their guardian spirits.[30] Among the Ba-ila it is customary for a person, before eating in the home of a relative, to drop some food as a gift to the family divinities.[31]

Smith also denies that prayers are believed to have a magical efficacity. While not denying that this may be true in some cases, he affirms that most Africans look upon the divinities not as abstractions but as real men and women who lived at one time on earth and are concerned with the petitions which the living raise to them. He says: "The offerings create and renew the bond which unites them all, and in the contact the human soul feels itself lifted up and strengthened."[32]

The Ba-ila make no images of the ancestral spirits, but the Baluba, and those who have close contact with them, do. Smith tells of a visit he made to the temple of Chibaluma, chief of a mixed community of Baluba and Ba-ila background. It was a simple hut, surrounded by trees and located in the center of the village. Inside were found the chief's hunting trophies, valuable merchandise such as guns and drums, a bed on which the chief sometimes slept and two carved wooden figures. The heads of the figures contained holes in which medicine was deposited from time to time. The relationship between Chibaluma, his ancestral spirit and the images is close, although not fully clear:

> The hut is sacred to Chinenga, an ancestor of Chibaluma, removed three generations back, who was chief of the district and had his village farther west. He is reincarnate in Chibaluma and is his genius. It is believed by some of his people, and some of his sons, that Chibaluma's life is hid in these images; he himself told us that they preserve him from witchcraft. In some way his genius is bound up with the images, and the "medicine" is poured in at times to renew their power. On occasions, such as departure for a trading or hunting expedition, or before going to war, and when he is sick, he makes an offering before these images and implores the help of his divinity.[33]

Worship of Supreme Being

Africans conceive of God as far away and remote, and this conception has its influence on their worship life. In general they do not go to God directly or make regular prayers to Him. However, there are notable exceptions, illustrated in the beliefs and practices of the Ashanti and the Nandi.[34]

Every Ashanti compound contains an altar dedicated to the Sky God. It is a particular tree, called *Nyame dua,* "God's tree," planted in front of the house. From one of its forked branches is hung a basin in which are placed God's offerings. Smith quotes Rattray to the effect that hardly a day goes by without offerings being placed in the pot or thrown on the roof of the hut.[35] Although the gifts are clearly for Nyame, they are not always accompanied by prayers. Smith indicates that they may possibly be considered prayers without words.[36] This points up again the difficulty of maintaining a clear distinction between prayers and offerings.

The Nandi people of East Africa make daily prayers to *Assista,* the Supreme God, often in the morning and the evening. Smith quotes an early morning prayer uttered by the old men of the tribe:

> "*Assista,* in this way have I made my prayer to you. Keep watch over my children and my cattle. I have come near to you morning and evening. *Assista,* I have made my prayer to you. Do not now say, I am tired. O our spirits, keep watch over us who are

living on the earth, and do not say: We are put to death by men."[37]

There are other times when the Nandi pray directly to God: at birth, four months after birth, at planting and harvesting time, when building a new house, when making things and when the men are away fighting.[38]

The Ashanti pray to God when a girl comes into puberty, when a woman is in her sixth or seventh month of pregnancy and when drums are made.[39] Furthermore, the Ashanti dedicate temples to Onyame, which are "beautifully designed buildings" located within the older palaces.[40] The temples are attended by priests who are distinguished by their peculiar haircut, their ornaments and the figures drawn on their bodies in white clay.[41] The Ashanti have no images of God; and this is true of Africans generally, the only exception known to Smith being an image of Mawu found among the Ewe people of Togo.[42]

Saturday is the sacred day dedicated to Onyame by the Ashanti, and one Saturday each year is set apart as a day for special offerings. The priests cook yams which are mashed and placed on the altar, accompanied by these words: " 'My God, Nyankopon, I pray you for life and I pray you for strength'." A sheep is sacrificed, the blood falling to the ground; and after pieces of the meat are placed on the altar, the priest prays: " 'Here is a sheep I kill for you, take and eat, and give me health and strength'." Following the ceremony, the chief sleeps in the temple during the next eight nights. Afterward two white chickens are sacrificed, their meat being placed in the altar receptacle and their blood and feathers smeared over the sacred pole which holds the receptacle.[43]

As to the purpose of these offerings, Smith says:

> Most Africans would say that the Highest Being has no need for food but some of them do make Him offerings of such things as they themselves take as food, goats and beer and milk. These at least, in their opinion, are pleasing to Him because they are a sign of the worshipper's good feeling.[44]

Most Africans do not erect temples to God. Some state that the Supreme Being is the Owner of all space and therefore cannot be restricted to any location on earth. Others look upon certain natural phenomena as the localization of Deity. The Kamba and Kikuyu consider Mount Kenya the abode of Deity. The Konde call a holy grove of trees on Mount Rungwe the dwelling place of

Kyala. In addition they refer to the Rock of Kyala near Lake Nyasa, in the hollow of which is the House of God. The Chagga call Mount Kilimanjaro God's House, while the Karanga also believe that God lives in the hollow of a mountain.[45]

Smith calls attention to the difference between the worship of West Africa and that of the Bantu-speaking peoples. The Bantu do not have temples or priests dedicated to God, nor do they make regular offerings to Him.[46]

Different explanations are given by Africans to account for their sporadic worship of God. Some say that God is so good that it is not necessary to ask Him for anything. Others say that, since He owns everything and therefore needs nothing, it is unnecessary to bring Him gifts. Still others affirm that He is so far away that it is not possible to get in touch with Him anyway.[47] All are agreed that the best procedure is to offer prayers and gifts to the ancestors, who are near and concerned; and if that source of help fails, recourse can be made to the Supreme Being.

In times of great need Africans make their prayers directly to God. The Tswana tell the story of an old woman who, in a time of drought and famine, went out with the other villagers to seek food and drink. When she could go on no further, she was left by the others who went on in their search for water. As she prepared some roots for food, she prayed: " 'O God, my mother, make it so that this food may be with water in addition'."[48] When her people returned, they were amazed to find her still alive. She replied that after her prayer, she no longer needed anything to drink.

The following quotation reproduces the cry for help of a member of the Rolong Tribe of South Africa:

> God of our fathers;
> I am stretched out with no food,
> I am stretched out with a crying stomach.
> Others have taken food,
> They are stretched out full;
> Even if it is but a polecat,
> Or a little rock-rabbit,
> I would be pleased with it.
> I say the name of God.
> Father of my fathers.[49]

In the case of illness, the common procedure is to seek the guidance of a sign-reader to find out which of the ancestors is angry. Gifts and prayers are then offered to restore the broken relationship. When this brings no relief, God's intervention may be sought. In such a case the Ba-ila make this prayer, followed by the expectoration of a mouthful of water as an offering:

> "Leza, I pray Thee. If it be Thou who hast made our brother sick, leave him alone, that Thy slave may go about by himself. Was it not Thou who createdst him on the earth and said he should walk and trust Thee? Leave Thy child, that he may trust Thee, Eternal One! We pray to Thee—Thou art the great Chief!"[50]

When prayers to the ancestors have failed to cure sickness, the Chagga sacrifice a goat at midday. While spitting water on the goat's head, they say: " 'Here is the goat, Ruwa, my chief. You only have knowledge how you will do with this man as if you would let him come to birth again'."[51] Then they kill the goat and eat his meat.

Other occasions when the Ba-ila offer prayers directly to God are when no children have been born within a family, during travel and when the hunt has been unsuccessful.[52]

A crisis situation of unusual gravity is drought. Smith says:

> Even those Africans who do not regularly make prayers to God do so when rain does not come down at the right time. It is natural for them to do this seeing that they have a belief that God has control over the forces of the sky.[53]

The diviner is consulted to see if an ancestor is impeding the rainfall. If the verdict is negative, a prophet is called upon for help. Accompanying the dynamistic practices of the rain-maker, which were described in Chapter 2, the people sing and invoke the praise-names of Leza, saying: " 'Come to us with a continued rain, O Leza, fall!' " After the first rains, the villagers refrain from work for two or three days out of reverence for Leza. They warn one another: " 'Do not wound (him) with a hoe, do not wound his water, his urine'."[54]

Although elements of praise and thanksgiving are not excluded from the worship of God, the above examples make clear that the principal sentiment in the minds of most Africans, in making offerings and prayers to God, is one of petition. Smith remarks:

> We see what the purpose is of these prayers: it is chiefly, almost completely, to make requests for things which God is able to give and men are in need of: that is to say, food and drink,

strong bodies, help in time of trouble, increase of children and cattle.[55]

Role of Intermediaries

Having considered the worship that Africans offer the ancestors and the Supreme Deity, it is well to examine the relationship between these two types of worship. Before doing so, however, it will be useful to inquire into Smith's view of dynamism as a form of worship.

That there is a relationship between dynamism and theism is well illustrated by the rain-making ceremony. Smith insists that dynamism is "religion." He specifically repudiates the assertion of Marett that magic is only the raw material of religion, and not religion itself.[56] In addition, his affirmation of the validity of the term "ancestor worship" is due to the fact that "the essence of religion is a sense of dependence upon supersensible powers who are able and willing to help,"[57] which might be applied to dynamism as well as to spiritism. Indeed in commenting on the practices of the Ganda, Smith explicitly identifies dynamism as worship:

> They have always been a religious people, says Canon Roscoe, whose book, *The Baganda*, is a classic. The objects of their veneration and worship are fourfold: gods (*balubare*), fetishes (*mayembe*), amulets (*nsiriba*), and ghosts (*mizimu*). That is to say, their religion presents the features of dynamism, animism and theism which we have seen to characterize other Africans.[58]

Although magical practices accompany the prayer to Leza for rain, Smith acknowledges the difficulty of defining the relationship between the two, that is, whether they act together in a supplemental or a causal fashion:

> How does the rain-doctor's medicine act precisely? Is it conceived as acting directly on the wind and on the rain-clouds, or does it in some mysterious way wing the words of the people's prayer to the ears of the Power that can cause rain to fall, or does it act upon that Power in a compelling manner so that, willy-nilly he or it must respond? As I have said, it is extremely difficult to answer this question with entire satisfaction to our analytical minds.[59]

In fact Smith never attempts an answer; so it is impossible to ascertain whether the religious practices of dynamism may be considered as fulfilling an "intermediary" function with the Supreme Being.

Such is not the case when attention is turned to spiritism. As with dynamism, there is an intimate relation between the spiritism and theism of African Traditional Religion. Much has been said throughout this study on the relationship between the social structure of a given African society and its effect on the theological formulation of the people. In particular it has been noted that where authority is centralized, such as among the Ashanti and the Ganda, God tends to be conceived as remote from the people. In such cases God does not rule directly but delegates His power and authority to the lesser gods, who serve as his "lieutenants."[60]

Nevertheless, this does not rule out contacts between man and God, nor man's worship of the Supreme Deity. Indeed it is a fixed belief of the Ashanti, as well as other Africans, that they pray to God and the ancestors at the same time.[61]

When an Ashanti woman is in the sixth month of pregnancy, she gives a chicken and eggs to her husband, asking him to make an offering to his *ntoro*, his "familiar spirit," to make possible a successful birth. The chicken's head is severed, the blood falling to the ground, while the man prays to his guardian. The fowl is taken by another member of the family to God's altar outside the house, where it is plucked. The chicken is singed over a fire and returned to the husband for dismemberment. Some of the chicken is roasted. The man places between his lips the leaf of a certain shrub with salt; and after blowing them out, he utters this prayer: " 'O Supreme God, Onyame, upon whom men lean and do not fall, O my *ntoro*, O my breath, O my *obosom* (my lesser god), allow this infant to come forth peacefully'." The prayer is repeated three times, in each case with a new leaf and salt, after which husband, wife and children commune together from the sacrificed fowl. Smith calls attention to the significance of the prayer:

> The man offers it, you will observe, without the assistance of a priest: he enjoys direct access to the Supreme Being. But he does not pray to the Supreme Being alone; he addresses in one prayer the Supreme Being, his familiar spirit, his breath or soul, and his *obosom*, or lesser god.[62]

Another example, illustrating the same phenomenon, is the prayer and offering of an Ashanti woman when her daughter comes into puberty (*bara*). She pours wine on the ground and pronounces this prayer:

> "Supreme Sky God, Nyankopon, who is alone great, upon whom men lean and do not fall, receive this wine and drink. Earth Goddess, whose day of worship is a Thursday, receive this wine and drink. Spirit of our ancestors, receive this wine and drink. This child whom God has given to me, to-day *bara* state has come upon her. O mother who dwells in the land of ghosts, do not come and take her away, and do not have permitted her to come to womanhood only to die."[63]

It might be suggested that these prayers do not necessarily imply a causal relationship between the anticipated action of the Supreme Being and the lesser gods in blessing the one who seeks help. That seems to be the implication of the action of the Ashanti priest, who seeks the help of all spirits, no one of which has complete jurisdiction over the power necessary to assure success in life.[64]

However, it is also clear that in many cases there is a causal relationship between African prayers to God and those to the ancestors. Africans do in fact regard the ancestors as intermediaries between man and God, and this is true not only of the highly developed systems of the Ashanti and Ganda but also of the Ba-ila.

Attention has already been called to the intermediary function of Shimunenga in the case of the atonement for homicide. Shimunenga receives the sacrifice of oxen and in turn transmits it to God. Shimunenga's intermediary function is not confined to the sacrifice for murder. It is rather of a much more general nature.

> Shimunenga and the other ancestral members of the invisible part of the community, are regarded with awe but not with terror. They have power which living men do not possess; they are in contact with the Supreme Being and act as intermediaries between him and the living.[65]

The belief in the ancestors as mediators between God and man represents in reality a common conception in Africa:

> A very general belief is that these *mizimu* are go-betweens: they are in the middle with men on one side and God on the other. They are representatives of men to God, of God to men. God is so great and so far away that, in the same way as you do not put your cause straight away to a great Chief himself but only through his headmen, so in coming to God you come by way of the *mizimu*. These were men like ourselves; they still are men at

heart though out of the body. They have knowledge of our needs from the inside and have power to give us help. A Zulu put the general thought of Africans into words when he said: "We give worship to those who are of us and have knowledge of our way of living."[66]

CHRISTIAN CONTRIBUTION

The African people are intensely religious. If they err, it is in being, like the Athenians, not too little religious but too much. Aggrey of Achimota fame saw this very well. While calling attention to the African's "need of a clearer vision,"[67] Aggrey accomplished much good in showing the African search for God and counteracting the misconceptions of the Western view, for which missionaries bear no little responsibility:

> Aggrey often dwelt upon the African's capacity for religion and the higher elements in their indigenous faith. In this he was doing his people a real service for it has become a fixed notion, largely fostered, one must say, by some missionaries in the past, that the African's religion, if such it may be called, is a repulsive hotchpotch of cruel, stupid, superstitions, "fetishism", devil-worship, etc. etc.[68]

Smith's attitude toward missionaries is worthy of note. Throughout his life and writings, he considers himself one with them, and he is eminently fair. Nevertheless, he can be devastating in his criticism, even when he expresses it in gentle terms.

He has great esteem for Robert Moffat, for example, but he does not hesitate to point out Moffat's belief that the Tswana had no religion before the arrival of Christianity.[69] He concedes that the Tswana of the early nineteenth century did not represent the highest in African belief and practice; nevertheless, he censures Moffat and asks in that case why he should see fit to use the Tswana word for God—Modimo—in his translations.[70] He concludes that it all depends upon one's definition of religion: "As Mr. Thwackum says: 'When I mention religion, I mean the Christian religion; and not only the Christian religion, but the Protestant religion: and not only the Protestant religion, but the Church of England'."[71] Smith adds his own definition ("a felt practical relationship with what is believed in as a superhuman power") and concludes that the Africans are indeed profoundly religious.[72]

Not all missionaries are the same. Livingstone was openly critical of his father-in-law.[73] Part of the difficulty of the Moffats was that they wrote so many letters about the Tswana before they had properly learned the language.[74] At any rate, "there are missionaries *and* missionaries: as a friend of mine puts it, 'they don't all come out of the same bag'."[75]

Africans are religious and their lives are characterized by worship, but this does not mean that Smith finds no fault with their religious practices or their understanding of worship. Rather he agrees with Aggrey that they are in "need of a clearer vision," the kind of vision that Christianity can bring to them.

Worship Centered in Supreme God

Throughout this study one theme has predominated: God is far away and remote. He may have been near and concerned at one time, but that does not characterize His attitude and position at the present time. The manifestations of His absenteeism vary with different tribes, but in all there are deep implications for the worship experience of His people. Because the Supreme Being is so high and distant, the focus of religious attention is concentrated on those powers which lie close at hand.

The dynamistic and ancestral worship practices of African Traditional Religion interfere with the worship of the Creator God. This is well illustrated by the Ashanti, in spite of the fact that they have preserved a more intimate worship of God than most other African peoples.

Rattray tells of his experience in entering the temple of Tano, a son of the Supreme Deity and the greatest of the lesser gods. He was amazed to find no *suman* (charms) inside, nor were any charms found on Tano's priest. When questioned about it, the priest replied that, since Tano comes from Onyame, ordinary charms can add nothing to his power. At the end of the conversation, the old priest commented: " 'Suman spoil the gods, but I cannot stop most priests using them'."[76]

The same is true of spiritism. Although the Ashanti worship God directly, even to the point of dedicating altars, temples and priests to Him, the main influence in shaping their life is the ancestors. Even the sons of God and Asase Ya, the Earth-Goddess, are too remote to satisfy the daily needs of the people:

> "These great unseen powers [the Sky and Earth deities] are generally too remote or perhaps too mighty to be concerned very

intimately with the individual clan, much less with the individual member of that clan, and the predominant influences in
the Ashanti religion are neither 'Saturday Sky-God' nor 'Thurs-
day Earth-Goddess,' nor even the hundreds of gods (*obosom*)
with which it is true the land is filled, but are the *samanfo*, the
spirits of the departed forbears of the clan. They are the real
landowners, who, though long departed, still continue to take
a lively interest in the land from which they had their origin, or
which they once owned." This we have seen to be true also of
the Bantu.[77]

It is this preoccupation with the ancestors and lesser deities, to
the exclusion of the High God, which Christianity seeks to
reverse. In the traditional system, at best God is regarded as one
among many, at worst He tends to be crowded out entirely. The
Christian emphasis sets in motion a different tendency. The
Creator is brought back into the center of consciousness and is
invested with the sole claim to the worship of His creatures.
Smith muses:

> It seems strange to us Christian people that men should trust
> and worship a host of lesser spirits, human and non-human, and
> not give all their service to the one Supreme God whose existence
> they acknowledge.[78]

Christianity came to Africa with the message that the Supreme
God, the Creator of all men and all things, is not far away but near
and concerned. He is like a Father with His children. He cares for
them and seeks their fellowship. He is therefore the One who is
supremely worthy of worship.

True as this statement is, it does not exhaust the Christian contribution. Something else needs to be added. The real power of
Christianity is not its teaching that men should center their worship on God. The unique contribution of the gospel is that it
reveals in Jesus Christ the kind of God that men will want to
worship:

> When we see God unveiled in a person of such attraction as
> Jesus, we are overcome. Worship of a God like that is natural,
> we are not able to keep from it. It is a worship which is the out-
> come of love, not of fear; a true worship.[79]

Because of Jesus, Christians can appropriate to themselves the
sentiment of the Zulu tribesman quoted above: we give worship
to Him who is of us and has knowledge of our way of living.[80]

Sublimation of Form

Edwin Smith calls for the retention of as many indigenous elements as possible in the African expression of Christian worship.

Some of these are inherent to the traditional practices of the people. Written prayers and liturgical formulae will undoubtedly be helpful, but nothing should be done to interrupt the spontaneity characteristic of African prayers.[81] The African Christian should be encouraged to use customary posture in prayer: standing, bowing or kneeling as the case may be.[82] Although African villages have public and private altars, the people have traditionally not been bound to places in their worship. Christianity also should promote this sense of worship at any time and in any place. Public chapels and private altars are useful, but they must not become the exclusive premises for religious observance.[83] Especially in industrial centers churches should always be open for worship, and people should be inspired to pray at all times: "We are too apt to lead our converts to associate religion only with Sunday. The pagan Africans have the advantage of a better conception of the place religion should occupy in life."[84]

African music should be adopted to Christian worship. Missionaries have introduced Western hymns, often with good results, and the Africans seem to enjoy foreign melodies. Nevertheless, the result is often negative because the musical beat clashes with the tonal stress of the African words.[85] The African has an extraordinary gift of music, and it is a tragedy for him to assimilate the European system to the exclusion of his own. The solution is in the adoption of African tunes for Christian purposes. African musical instruments, such as reed flutes, xylophones and drums, should be used as accompaniment for vernacular hymns.[86]

Not only should the African musical genius receive a new emphasis, the same is necessary for the dance. In many of his writings Smith laments the suppression of dancing among Christian converts. He is aware that a censurious attitude is not without basis since traditional dancing often appealed to baser emotions; but he repudiates the suggestion that all dances are evil or that dancing is wrong in itself. Dancing is rather one of the African's most appreciated diversions and is as essential an element in his education as music. Both derive from a real need of the people which cannot be fulfilled if they are prohibited.[87] The dance is valuable not only for educational and recreational purposes; it can also become a valuable ingredient in the worship experience:

> Too often has dancing been banned. Many native dances are lascivious, but not all, and it is better to select and to purify what is after all a healthful exercise. David danced before the Lord with all his might and the Psalmist urged the people to praise God's name in the dance. We cannot imagine an Anglo-Saxon dancing as a religious exercise, but I can readily conceive of an African doing so. And why not? The African's natural histrionic gifts could well be utilized in his general and religious education. Miracle plays would appeal to them very strongly. In all these matters missionaries are too apt to take a repressive attitude.[88]

In terms of architecture, once again the Church must not ignore the African ethos. Although Africa may not offer the distinctive architectural styles of Asia, it is possible that such features as the *bwalo*, the open circular meeting place, may be adapted for Christian usage. In any case African ornamentation in colored native designs, pictures and wood carvings should be freely appropriated.[89]

To be true to African experience, it is necessary that Christianity address itself to the total experience of life. There should be room for variety, including not only the great celebrations of Easter and Christmas but also the agricultural and seasonal festivities of the year such as sowing, harvest, first day of fishing and other functions.[90]

The traditional naming ceremony can be incorporated into Christian baptism,[91] and features of African marriage can be taken over in the Christian service.[92]

In this way the African, whether as an individual or as a member of a family and community, will be able to sublimate his experience of worship in the Church. Most importantly, that experience will have for its center the High God who is the Creator of all things:

> At each event, God will be glorified as the source of life and of all we possess, and each ceremony will renew the sense of stewardship, that we hold the soil and life itself as trustees and are responsible to God for making the most of His gifts.[93]

Although he does present some suggestions regarding liturgies for First Fruits, the Harvest Festival and All Saints Day, Smith does not presume to provide a blueprint of all that might be included in Christian worship in Africa. Ultimately the task should be carried out by African Christians, who must be free to exercise their own genius. He hopes that Christian worship in Africa will not be characterized by a too rigid uniformity and that it will be both African and Catholic:

> What ultimately will be the characteristic marks of the African branch of the Catholic Church we cannot pretend to say. We hope that it will exhibit the spirit and external features of a true Catholicism, loyal to all that is true in Christian tradition and yet reflecting the African ethos. . . . We have no desire to see a strict uniformity of worship or organization throughout Africa. We think the African Christian should be free to borrow from any source the materials which may enrich their worship and not be forever tethered by the usages of the parent denominations; and we follow Madras in hoping that they will find within their own ethos much that will enrich and fortify their devotion.[94]

Sublimation of Content

The sublimation of the African understanding of worship in the Christian faith is necessary not only in its outward form but also in its inner content, and once again God is central to its expression.

Smith admits that Christians (missionaries included) have not always lived up to the magnificent promise that their faith has afforded and that traditional African practices retain understandings of the nature of reality which are of permanent value. He is especially critical of the missionary tendency to over-intellectualize the experiences of worship:

> Missionaries have been criticized for secularizing religion. An arid intellectualistic atmosphere with its appeal only to the intellect is foreign to worship and particularly fails to touch the depths of the emotional, mystical-minded African. Every possible resource should be employed to stir his sense of wonder and feed his imagination. Emotion may need control but it should not be repressed. The public service should be so planned as to afford an outlet for deep feelings.[95]

Edwin Smith wants the African to come to a new understanding of God, the recognition that the God of Christian experience is as near to the Church member as the guardian spirit of his pagan brother. He acknowledges the fact that thanksgiving, confession, adoration, intercession and supplication all have a part in African worship. In the Church these must receive new emphases.

Smith is concerned about the excessive emphasis placed on petition in African prayers. This is true of the African's total understanding of worship but especially so of his prayers to God. The narration of the plight of the worshipper and the supplication for help are essential to religious life, but in Africa they receive too much stress. The prayers to God are even more exclusively petitionary than those addressed to the ancestors. Although the petitionary element is strongly emphasized in "ancestor worship," Smith denies that that is its only sentiment.[96] Prayers to God, on the other hand, are "chiefly, almost completely, to make requests for things which God is able to give and men are in need of."[97] The essential problem is once again God's remoteness and the lack of a personal relationship between Him and the believer. Because the enquirer tends to reserve his prayers to God for crisis situations, the element of supplication is of necessity the dominant motif in his thought.

Confession is another area of concern and has a close bearing on the question of African ethics, discussed in the previous chapter. It will be remembered that the African testimony regarding the acknowledgement of sin against God is ambiguous. Smith does list some examples of such a recognition but at no point does he include any allusion to a confession of sin to God. Of the Ba-ila he specifically says: "In all their invocations of Leza there is no confession of sin."[98] This does not mean that the Ba-ila or other African peoples are ignorant of what is involved in confession. In discussing iron smelting, mention was made of the need to confess any transgression against the taboos associated with the process.[99] Many other examples could be listed. The problem essentially is one of bringing God into the center of man's failure and inadequacy; so that the words of forgiveness and the possibility of a new beginning may be heard.

Once again the concept of intercession is subject to an alteration of values in the Christian context. Africans do believe in intercession, and numerous examples of it, both in prayers to the divinities and to the Supreme God, have been cited in this study. Yet another may be added here. When a family member is ill, the advice of a diviner is sought, who may identify the cause as a neglected divinity. The head of the family may then make an offering and a prayer such as this: " 'Tsu! If it be thou [the family divinity] who art causing our child's sickness, see, here is the beer which thou wantest, and also some tobacco. And if it be Thou, O Leza! who art destroying me, I pray Thee let him recover.' "[100] The problem of African intercession is a lack of breadth rather than depth. It does not extend beyond the family and clan to embrace a wider circle. The African prays for his family, but his sense of brotherhood does not include those of other tribes. The failure of Christians to live up to their own high calling in regard to racial brotherhood is an ever-recurring theme in all of Smith's writings.[101]

In spite of its failures and weaknesses in practical living, however, Edwin Smith is convinced that Christianity brings to each of these areas a new understanding.

The sense of thanksgiving and adoration because of a new understanding of God, His nearness and concern, infuses the petitionary aspect of prayer, which in the traditional African expression is too pronounced, with a new humility:

> The intimacy with which he [the African] addressed his guardian spirit is retained when he learns that he can talk with God, no longer remote but near and attentive, but the intimacy is infused with a new humility. He no longer thinks of prayer only or chiefly as supplication for help.[102]

The element of confession, which was often required by the divinities before health and well-being could be restored, is transferred for the Christian into a sense of obligation to God and a recognition of the reality of forgiveness. Intercession, which in the past was confined to kinship relations, is broadened to include all men:

> Confession is not altogether a strange thing to Africans: there are occasions when the pagan knows that to obtain the help he or she needs from the divinities a frank and full revealing of past misconduct is necessary before his or her fellows. But now the Christian knows that to obtain forgiveness he must not cloak his sin but confess it to God. Adoration is not a strange thing to the African: it commonly takes the form of calling over the praise-titles which express eloquently the attributes of the divinity; and now the Christian can adore out of a fuller realization of what God is in Himself and in His relations to men. Nor was inter-

cession a strange notion: it was common for Africans to pray for
a relative's restoration to health. Now he learns to pray for
others.[103]

Communion of the Saints

As has been seen throughout this study, Smith sees Christianity
as the fulfillment, not the destruction of African Traditional Religion. Although some elements of traditional belief and practice
must be suppressed, this is not the case with the great majority of
them. Sublimation serves as the means whereby the African experience is appropriated and turned to a new purpose.

Since the ancestor cult is central to African worship and religious life, it is important to ask whether this element cannot also
be sublimated in the Christian faith.

Smith addresses himself to the question and shows that this is
indeed his purpose. The ancestor cult of African Traditional Religion must be transformed into the communion of the saints of
the Christian Church, a belief with broader implications than anything involved in the African conception today. In fact both the
African and the Universal Church are enriched in the process.

Although a radical distinction must be made between the worship of God and the fellowship which the living have with the
invisible members of the community, this should not signify the
diminution of the reality of the relationships involved. The communion of saints must in fact maintain a local as well as a universal
significance.[104]

In discussing the worship which should characterize Christian
families in Africa, Smith emphasizes the need of bringing religion
into the daily experiences of life, just as the African does in his
traditional activities: the offering of thanksgiving for daily food
and for healing; the use of appropriate ceremonies to celebrate the
birth of a child and during the stages of his growth; the dedication
of new tools and seeds for planting; the seeking of God's blessing
before beginning a journey; the celebration of the harvest gathering and the consecration of new houses. Although God is the
center of religious attention, the ancestors are not to be neglected.
Smith emphatically states in this context: "Nor would the invisible
members of the community be forgotten in the Christian family
worship."[105] As members of the family, they also have their place

in the family's worship. They are not themselves objects of worship, but they participate in the family's worship of God.

The communion of the saints cannot be confined merely to the family but in the Christian context must be broadened to include the wider fellowship of God's children—the fellowship which knows no distinction of race or tribe. The allegiance of the African to family and clan is broadened into the universal clan of Jesus Christ, the Church:

> Individual and family worship culminates in the public church service: the act of corporate homage rendered to God by the united Christian community. In this supreme act the local body represents the great fellowship of the Universal Church engaged in praise and prayer. It may be few in numbers but it is part of the Ecumenical Church, gathered from *every tribe and tongue and people and nation*, some in heaven, some on earth. The idea of the visible and invisible members joining thus in praise to the God and Father of all should come home readily to Africans with their awareness of being surrounded by a great cloud of witnesses.[106]

As to belief, Edwin Smith is thoroughly convinced that the greatest need of African Religion is a new and vital emphasis on the Supreme God who the Africans already recognize. He believes that Christian evangelization is the means by which that task can be accomplished. Concerning method, however, he is an immensely practical and patient man. He states that the Christian gospel will effect its own revolution in African belief:

> Can an intense reverence for the dead be regarded as incompatible with Christian faith? The danger is that lesser loyalty may usurp the supreme loyalty to Christ. We may expect that as the consciousness of God deepens and clarifies in the Christian African, all trust in the beneficence of ancestors will be transferred to God as revealed in Christ. No longer will it be thought necessary to approach a remote Creator through the mediatorship of our ancestors. The requests for help addressed to guardian, family and communal spirits will become prayer to the heavenly Father in the name of Christ. But while this true faith is growing, we would not too severely condemn a lingering belief in the aid of revered ancestors. Many good African Christians are, we know, helped by believing that their departed fathers and mothers are near and interested in them.[107]

8

Critical Analysis: Traditional View

MISUNDERSTANDING OF CENTRAL PARADOX

The central motif in Edwin Smith's approach to the African conception of God is apparent: God is remote. In the beginning it was different. God was near. He and man lived together in harmony. But because of man's foolishness or wickedness, God withdrew. He is now far away.

Most European students of African Religion, contemporary with Smith, have emphasized God's absenteeism. Indeed books are still being written which have little more to say of God than that He is remote. An example is Turner's recent study of the Ndembu of Zambia, which, although excellent in its interpretation of traditional ritual, characterizes the belief in *Nzambi*, "who is said to have created the world and then left it to its own devices," as "simple" and "naive" because the High God is after all "otiose."[1]

Transcendence and Immanence

African scholars are especially critical of the idea that the African conceives of God merely as remote. Danquah expresses this sentiment strongly[2] and even goes so far as to suggest that the Akan have no concept of the Fall.[3] Idowu does not deny God's absenteeism, but he insists that Westerners make a mistake in placing all their emphasis on this element.[4] Busia observes that the various tribes emphasize different aspects of God but that two thoughts are generally prevalent in all parts of the continent: God's nearness understood as omnipresence and His absence seen as inscrutability.[5] He draws the conclusion from the Ashanti myth of God's departure that God has removed Himself too far away from man for direct approach; yet this is accompanied by the Ashanti belief that everyone has access to Him.[6]

\ Mbiti expresses the same sentiment in these words:

> The transcendence of God is a difficult attribute to grasp, and one which must be balanced with God's immanence. The two attributes are paradoxically complementary: God is "far" (transcendent), and men cannot reach him; but God is also "near" (immanent), and he comes close to men. This could be taken as the general distinction. Many foreign writers constantly harp on the note that for African peoples God is "too remote" and virtually excluded from human affairs. This assertion is false, and the many facts contained in this book show clearly that people consider God to be both "far" and "near."[7]

This understanding of the African conception has not gone unnoticed by European scholars. Middleton calls attention to the two aspects of the Lugbara view: God in the sky and God in the streams.[8] God is the final source of power and order and is both far and near. As the transcendent One, He is called *Adroa* or *Adronga*, while *Adro* identifies Him in His immanence. Linguistically Adroa and Adronga are diminutives of Adro, and their relationship to each other has theological implications: "The diminutive is used because God in the sky is more remote, both spatially and in intensity of contact, than God on earth." Middleton insists that only in His immanence does God receive offerings.[9]

Lienhardt translates the Dinka word *Nhialic*, usually rendered "God," as "Divinity." In their sacrifices and prayers, both to Divinity and the lesser free and clan divinities, the Dinka sometimes plead with the spirits to come near and help, while on other occasions they entreat them to stay away and avoid troubling them. Lienhardt quotes from a Dinka hymn collected by Nebel which "explicitly refers to a paradox of nearness and farness, the conjunction and division of the above and below":

> Great Deng is near, and some say "far"
> O Divinity
> The creator is near, and some say "he has not reached us"

Do you not hear, O Divinity?
The black bull of the rain has been released from
        the moon's byre
Do you not hear, O Divinity?[10]

The Nuer take God's existence for granted.[11] The Supreme
Being has always had His abode in the sky, but He is not to be
identified with the sky.[12] In the beginning earth and heaven were
united by means of a rope. As men grew older, they were able
to ascend to heaven in order to be rejuvenated. One day the
hyena and weaver bird climbed the rope. They were captured
but later escaped, the hyena cutting the rope during his descent.
This explains the gulf between God and man.[13] But God is also
near. The Nuer insist that He is in fact everywhere. He is like
the wind and the air.[14] Evans-Pritchard concludes: "Nuer religious
thought cannot be understood unless God's closeness to man is
taken together with his separation from man, for its meaning lies
precisely in this paradox."[15]

Good and Evil

It is not an easy task to understand the juxtaposition of transcendence and immanence in the African conception of God. It
is much more than a spatial concept showing the fullness of the
African view, for it has moral implications as well.

The African God is not only present and absent, near and
far; He is also good and bad. Indeed it is the combination of these
two qualities in African thought which creates the real problem
of the African idea of God.

Lienhardt quotes a Shilluk proverb to the effect that " 'God
threads good and evil men on a single thread'." He goes on to
note that the Shilluk regard Him as hostile or friendly depending
on the particular situation since He is the "source of good and
evil."[16] Lienhardt insists that *Juok* (God) Himself is neither
good nor evil, although He is the explanation for what is good
and evil in man's life.[17]

Among the Dinka, the term Nhialic (Divinity) is used to
describe that which is unpredictable and accounts for both good
and bad fortune. If one asks why things happen as they do, the
Dinka evoke the name of Nhialic as the final explanation. The
thought is well expressed in this Dinka hymn:

Spring rain in a dry spell, strikes the ants on the
head with a club
And the ants say: My father has seen
And they do not know whether he helps people
And they do not know whether he injures people.[18]

Attention has already been called to the Lugbara conception of God in the sky and God in the streams as proof of His transcendence and immanence. It is God in His transcendence, remote in the sky and absent from men who is good (*onyiru*). The near God, manifest in the streams and close to men is bad (*onzi*).[19]

The Bacongo say: "God possesses us; He eats us," which means that He does with men as He wishes. If a Mucongo escapes danger, he exclaims: "God spoke to me; otherwise I would be dead." If he suffers misfortune, he says: "God did not give me a chance today."[20]

Van de Merwe calls attention to two Shona names for God: *Chirozva-mauya* "the one who has power to destroy the good and the bad" and *Chirazamauya* "the one who provides for good and bad." He concludes: "The VaShona seem to believe that God could also be the Author of Evil."[21]

Some African people emphasize God's goodness while acknowledging also His relationship to evil. The Banyarwanda see *Imana* as essentially good. They say: " 'Your enemy is digging a pitfall for you, *Imana* prepares your exit'." God is so good that no offerings are required by Him; the people insist: " '*Imana* gives, he does not sell'."[22] Imana is believed to shape men as a potter does his clay. When man is miserable or unsuccessful in life, the Banyarwanda state that he was created by *Ruremakwaci* which has led some commentators to suggest that there are two creators and a dualistic concept of good and evil. Maquet negates such a thesis: "As a matter of fact, *Ruremakwaci* is the name given to *Imana* when he does not create very successfully, when 'he is tired,' or, for some inscrutable reason, decides that a certain destiny will be unhappy."[23]

Other African peoples emphasize God's negative aspects while recognizing that there are also positive sides to His relationship to men. The Nyakyusa for example recognize Kyala as the giver of rain; nevertheless "it is the terribleness not the goodness or purity of God of which the Nyakyusa are aware." They say that a madman, who is characterized as having a loose heart (meaning that he is quarrelsome), has been " 'caught hold of by Kyala'."[24]

Fate or Destiny

Running through the African conception of God is a clear sense of fate or destiny.

The Ashanti affirm that God gives a bit of Himself to each man, and with that is bound up a man's destiny, what he is to do and be in his life.[25]

Idowu identifies Olódùmarè as the "Determiner of Destiny"[26] and devotes an entire chapter of his book to the relationship of God to man's destiny. He says: "To the Yoruba, the end for which a person is made is inextricably bound up with his destiny. They believe that man's doings have been predestined by Olódùmarè."[27]

The Nupe hold that there is one God who has existed from the beginning. He is related to the sky and is conceived as being far away. Yet he is always present and is found everywhere. He is the Creator of all things—good and evil. The Nupe sing this song: " 'Should you do anything that is beautiful, God has caused it to be beautiful; should you do anything evil, God has caused it to be evil'."[28]

M. Wilson indicates that Kyala is responsible for all the problems of life. If the log splits or the lorry skids, Kyala did it. If the potatoes are small, Kyala made them that way.[29] This translates itself also into a strong linguistic stress on God's will: " 'The medicine will be effective if Kyala wills'; 'rain will fall when the rainmaker soaks his stones if Kyala wills'; 'when the doctor treats the tails they "vomit" (froth over), then if Kyala has helped us the cattle give much milk'."[30]

The Lele of Kasai believe that Nzambi is the Creator of all men and all things. In their relations with God, men are like slaves before their owner. It is Nzambi who orders their lives, giving instructions, providing protection, making right their affairs and avenging their wrongs.[31]

The essential goodness of the Banyarwanda view of Imana has already been mentioned. Like the potter, Imana fashions a child in a young mother's womb, using clay and water left at the bedside each night. After birth Imana decides what the destiny of the child will be, whether he will be happy or unhappy. As Maquet perceives, the belief that Imana only does good is not fully consistent with the concept of an evil destiny. He replies that predestination is not taken too seriously by the Banyarwanda and that even the person who suspects an evil predestiny does everything he can to improve his situation.[32]

The Nuer also believe strongly in God's goodness,[33] yet insist that He is responsible for all things. If one asks the Nuer the origin or cause of something, whether it be an event of the past or a present phenomenon, they reply that God created it that way or willed that it should be as it is. Everything experienced by man in life takes place according to God's will. The Nuer are convinced of the reality of natural causes and the activity of lesser spirits, but God is always the final explanation. All secondary explanations are contingent upon the primary cause, for they are merely God's agents and instruments.[34]

Smith's Position

It is essential to understand that, although God's remoteness is the dominant motif in Smith's perception of the African God, it is not the sole motif or the only aspect to which he addresses himself. He is much too able an observer for that. As has been seen,[35] he does call attention to the manifestations of God's nearness as well.

Smith lists a number of epithets which the Ba-ila apply to Leza, all of which relate to God's omnipresence and cast doubt on His goodness: Shikakunamo, the one who besets another, clinging, adhering and persecuting by constant attention: *Sungwasungwa*, the one who stirs up another to do good and bad things; Shichenchemenwa, the one who, although good natured himself, takes advantage of a person's good nature by asking for unwarranted favors; and *Natamaukilwa*, the one who constantly changes his mind.[36]

Some of Leza's praise-names also show that He is not restricted to the sky. Three titles allude to His role as the maker of things: *Chilenga*, the Creator; *Lubumba*, the Moulder; and *Shakapanga*, the Constructor. If one asks what things Leza makes, the answer is unequivocal: "all things."[37] There are other names which allude to the all-encompassing presence of God: Mutalabala, the one who is age-lasting and everywhere at the same time; *Namakungwe*, the one from whom all things come; Ushatwakwe, the one who is Master and Owner of his things.[38]

Smith believes that there is a "deep underlying fatalism" in

Ba-ila belief[39] and that Leza therefore is blamed for much of the sorrow and evil which characterize life.[40] Attention has already been called to the expressions: *Notangala Leza udikubwene*, "when you are filled with joy, God sees you," meaning that disaster will soon strike; and *mulabile-Leza*, "one upon whom God has looked," used to describe those bereft of children. The common expression for death is: *Leza wakombola mungo wakwe*, "God has snapped off his pumpkin."[41] Indeed whatever cannot be explained by any other means is ascribed to God.[42] The same is true of other African peoples.[43]

Yet throughout God is also good. He is the "Guardian" and the "Giver." When asked about Leza, Kambunga, one of Smith's informants, replies that He is compassionate, merciful, good-natured and doing good at all times in spite of the people's complaints that He either makes it rain too much or not enough, and that he is responsible for it being either too hot or too cold.[44] Another informant, Shikanzwa, insists that life was happier and God was better disposed toward men at an earlier period; nevertheless Leza cannot be accused or questioned or charged with offense.[45]

The essential difficulty of Smith's approach is two-fold: first, he fails to draw out the implications of the paradox involved in the African conception of God. It is perhaps too much to say that he does not see the paradox, but it is true that he does not comment on it. He never uses the word "paradox," nor any equivalent, while discussing the conception of God and never attempts an explanation of it. He presents the evidence for the paradox: the transcendence and immanence, the far and near, the good and bad; but he does not discuss them as a unit. He sets them side by side and gives the impression that the ambiguity created by them is the result of "unclarity" in the African conception rather than seeing it as the manifestation of a deeper grappling after reality in the African search for God.

Secondly, Smith fails to see that it is only when these two—God's immanence and transcendence, His nearness and farness, His goodness and badness—are seen together, in their relationship to each other, that African Religion can be understood. This does not mean that the paradox is self-evident, but its depths cannot be probed until its dimensions have been defined.

Smith is correct in identifying God's remoteness as the most obvious characteristic of the African conception of God. But he does not explore the possibility that the most pervasive characteristic of African thought might be God's nearness or that God's all-encompassing nearness (as seen in His control of destiny) might be the root cause for His being pushed to the periphery of human consciousness.

The idea presents itself, therefore, that only superficially and secondarily is God too remote in the African view. Rather the underlying, fundamental and determinative element of that view is that God is too near. What is being suggested is that a God who is so near as to control man's destiny absolutely is a difficult God to live with, a God from whom one may wish to flee. This is especially true when life is seen for what it is—a mixture of good and bad, fortune and misfortune, joy and sorrow.

There is no problem when things go well, when there is success, health, life. But when things do not go well, when there is tragedy and failure, the tables are turned. If God is the author of this also, he may be seen as oppressive or even intolerable. In such a case, other sentiments come to the fore, a desire to push Him off at a distance in order to escape His all-embracing tentacles.[46]

The desire to be rid of the near God is not uncommon to African experience. This expresses well the sentiment of the Nyakyusa.[47] M. Wilson notes that it is precisely the Christian concept of "union with God which the pagans so greatly fear."[48]

Although in general Africans maintain a sincere respect for God, even in great adversity, sometimes their pain and spite express themselves in deep resentment, as for example in this verse sung by the Bacongo:

> Eh! Nzambi, sot que tu es,
> Eh! Nzambi, mange donc avec mesure,
> Eh! Nzambi, sot que tu es![49]

The Nuer insist that God is everywhere like the wind and the air, but He is also the God who has withdrawn Himself to the sky. They have a vivid myth of His departure. God determines everything and the Nuer insist that His fiat is always good. Yet He appears to be too good to be true, for His nearness is in fact oppressive:

> It is true that Nuer, like everyone else, fear death, bereavement, sickness and other troubles, and that it is precisely in such situations that they so often pray and sacrifice. It can be admitted

also that, in that these troubles are manifestations of Spirit, they fear Spirit and wish to be rid of it.[50]

Although he does not draw the same conclusion, Edwin Smith also provides testimony to the effect that it is the near God (in this case the One who is too "good" rather than too "bad") who must be driven away from the African consciousness:

> The Konde of Northern Nyasaland say that *Kyala* sometimes comes among men in the body of a lion or snake and sees their doings. He is a God of righteousness and comes only when evil is very great and punishment is needed. For that reason the desire of the people is that God will go away again. "Go far from here, O God, go to the Sango, because your house is great"—this is a prayer not uncommonly on the lips of the people when it seems to them that God is near.[51]

J. V. Taylor's interpretation of the African paradox is worthy of quotation:

> His immanence therefore is dangerous and consequently "bad." He is both welcome and unwanted. So it is not surprising that this paradox sometimes finds expression in a two-fold conception of God as transcendent in the sky and close at hand in the bush. But this, which has misled many European investigators into an over-simplified dualism, is only a symbolic or mythical way of expressing the unbounded fullness and variety of God. . . . I have long suspected . . . that the unceasing sense of this all-pervasive God was too much for African man and he sought an escape by elevating one of the ancestral heroes of the tribe and identifying him with the far-off aspects of God. By naming God in this way and fixing him in the heavens man was able to keep him at a safe distance.[52]

It may be seriously questioned whether Taylor, in this quotation, takes seriously enough the full significance of the African identification of God as responsible for the "good" and "bad" in life. Is not more involved in that than merely "a symbolic or mythical way of expressing the unbounded fullness and variety of God"? The position taken in this study is that such an "all-pervasive God" would be too much for any people. Be that as it may, Taylor has understood well that the African resolution of the paradox, namely by fixing Him at a safe distance in the heavens, results in a God who is "too remote to meet man's needs."[53]

Misplacement of Speculative Talent

The fundamental problem of Edwin Smith's presentation is that he fails to consider meaningfully the central paradox of African Religion, namely, how to understand the God who is transcendent and immanent, far and near, good and bad.

Although he is aware of the paradox, he does not discuss it to any significant degree. He mentions the fact that the Ba-ila conceive of God as present everywhere but has little more to say about it. He tends to see the paradox of God's responsibility for the "good" and "bad" as an example of unclarity in the African view. He is much more interested in God's absenteeism than His omnipresence, and his failure to consider them as a unit leads to distortion.

His approach is not determined by an unwillingness to engage in speculation regarding African Traditional Religion. As a matter of fact, he does speculate a great deal, the results of which are often questionable.

Origin of Religion

Throughout his life Edwin Smith is intensely interested in the question of the origin of religion. As a young missionary he avidly reads Frazer's books as they appear. He is also influenced by Marett and to a lesser extent by Tylor. He commends Parrinder's book, *West African Religion*, for "its minimum of speculation as to origins,"[54] but he never gives up his own quest. In his presidential address to the Royal Anthropological Institute in 1934, he notes the challenges to the evolutionary conception of anthropology but insists that it is an impregnable fortress.[55] He repudiates the view of Schmidt that there was a primitive monotheism which degenerated into the present confusion.[56] He also denies the view of Spencer and Tylor that one can explain the High God as the elevation of a deceased hero.[57] Rather taking his inspiration from Marett and Frazer, he sees dynamism—the personification of *mana* and especially the Cosmic Mana manifest in the celestial forces of the rain, thunder and lightning—as the way in which men were led to the belief in God.[58]

One area where Smith departs from many of his predecessors is in his recognition of a "Reality" behind all this evolutionary development.

Evans-Pritchard makes the point that many of the early anthropologists were themselves atheists or agnostics who felt that,
explaining "primitive" religion as a natural phenomenon, they
could discredit the so-called "higher" religions, especially Christianity, as well.[59] Smith clearly negates any such attempt:

> For us Christian people no theory of the origin of the Bantu
> conception of God can be complete that does not include the
> guiding Spirit of God who wills to be known of his children. He
> who believes in that Spirit will look upon dynamism as the path-
> way along which men have been led towards God.[60]

Smith sets a hopeless task for himself. Anthropologists are now
largely agreed that there is no way to investigate the question of
the origin of religion or the belief in God.[61] The various theses
are interesting but remain the pure speculation of the scholars.
There simply are no materials on which to base a final conclusion.
It is true that some anthropologists of the Durkheim school continue to insist that religion can be understood entirely in terms
of sociological analysis. However, Evans-Pritchard has argued
persuasively that, in making such an identification, they leave
the realm of ethnographical study and become themselves theologians, albeit negative theologians.[62] Herskovits also warns of
the "futility of the search for the absolute origin of any non-
material element in culture." He accepts the usefulness of such
categories as animatism, animism, polytheism and monotheism
as descriptions of religious experience but denies all attempts to
place them in developmental stages or evolutionary sequence.[63]
    Although E. Colson expresses enthusiastic appreciation for the
extraordinary contribution that *The Ila-Speaking Peoples of
Northern Rhodesia* has made to ethnographical study, she rightly
calls attention to Smith's excessive preoccupation with the question of origins: "The chapters on religion contain too many
echoes of Tylor and the search for the origin of religious ideas."[64]
While accepting the validity of that criticism, it is important to
mention again that Marett and Frazer influenced Smith more than
Tylor.

Influence of Social Structure

Smith's speculations regarding the relationship of the social
structure to the African conception of God are also less than

fully satisfactory. This is not meant to deny that such a rei
ship does in fact exist. After Durkheim it would be impossib.
make such an assertion; but it may be seriously question
whether Smith has properly grasped the dimensions of it.

Several references have been made to Smith's view that when
the structure of the society is complex and highly centralized,
with a paramount king who rules his subjects through a hierarchy
of ministers and lesser entities, the conception of God also follows
a similar pattern. Even as the earthly king is inaccessible to the
people, except in extraordinary cases, so the Heavenly King is
also inaccessible. He rules through intermediaries and is approached by means of mediators. Smith uses two examples to
prove his case: the Ganda and the Ashanti.

It is true that the analogy holds good for the structure of the
earthly and heavenly societies. Both God and the chief rule
through ministers and lesser entities. The structural parallels are
striking and are of considerable significance. However, the analogy
breaks down over the question of mutual accessibility. Among the
Ashanti, in spite of the fact that the Supreme God is high and
lifted up, and supposedly inaccessible, the Ashanti in fact offer
Him[65] more direct and constant worship than almost any other
African people—much more than the Ba-ila who have a less complex social structure. This does not in any way deny that "ancestor
worship" is more significant for the Ashanti than their worship
of God, nor that the ancestors act as intermediaries; but it is
clear that Smith's theory offers no explanation for the daily
offerings to God which are also a part of the Ashanti religious
experience.

Significance of African Myths

Once again Smith's interpretation of the meaning of African
mythology creates as many problems as it resolves. He suggests
that the myths are attempts to exonerate God from the full responsibility for His absenteeism and for bringing death and misfortune upon men. It may be seriously questioned whether they
are in fact meant to do this. If they are, they clearly do not
succeed. Even Smith notes this in stating that some are more
efficacious than others but in all the result is ambiguity.

If they are meant to exonerate God, they fail because they
raise even more questions about Him: If God gives Hare the

message of life, why does He also give Chameleon the message of death? Even worse, why does He allow Chameleon's message to stand when Hare complains?[66] Why does He trust the curious bird, Honeyguide, with such a crucial expedition? Why does He make death the penalty for sleeping when the moon is in the sky and still allow the man's eyesight to fade through old age?

Perhaps even more important are the questions raised by God's departure: Was God justified in leaving men because of such trivialities? Was it not an excessive reaction on His part to withdraw because of man's fires or the woman's grain stompers? How could man and woman avoid their use anyway?

Mbiti observes that God went away only partly due to man's disobedience. There was also an accidental aspect to the disaster.[67] The question follows as to why man must suffer the full consequences of an event for which he was only partially responsible, in some cases for which he was not responsible at all.

These questions are not merely the result of scholarly reflection on the matter. Village Africans are also aware of their validity. Lienhardt perceptibly observes that, contrary to Smith's contention, the myths actually show God's capriciousness and unfairness, which is another way of emphasizing the enigmatic mystery of life:

> The attitude of the Dinka towards the stories of Divinity's withdrawal from Man is of some interest here. Those who have commented upon these stories have sometimes made it clear that their sympathies lie with Man in his plight, and draw attention to the smallness of the fault for which Divinity withdrew the benefits of his closeness. The image of striking Divinity with a hoe or pestle often evokes a certain amusement, almost as though the story were indulgently being treated as too childish to explain the consequences attributed to the event. . . . Divinity's withdrawal from Man as the result of a comparatively trifling offense, by human standards, presents the contrast between equitable human judgements and the action of the Powers which are held ultimately to control what happens in Dinka life.[68]

Something else is accomplished by the myths. They not only point to the ambiguity of life; they also succeed in pushing away the Author of that ambiguity. It is precisely the near God who is intolerable and who must be thrust to the periphery if life is to be bearable. In telling of God's departure, the myths actually hasten His flight. Most important of all, they fix His absence into the consciousness of African thought from which He is not easily dislodged. The cultural and psychological mechanisms are extremely complicated, but they cannot be fully understood apart from their theological implications.

Concept of Personality

Edwin Smith spends a considerable amount of time on the question of personality. He wants to know whether the Africans conceive God as a person or a thing.[69] He admits that the evidence is ambiguous but concludes that it seems to point in the direction of personality. Since one is dealing with an evolutionary growth in ideas, it is not surprising that there is "unclarity" in the African view.

He assumes that, like Western man, the African also divides life into two categories: animate and inanimate or persons and things. Within that framework he asks to which category God belongs.

In this context Smith's approach to Tempels' *Philosophie Bantoue* becomes significant. For Tempels Bantu philosophy is centered in one concept: vital force. All behavior is concentrated in an attempt to achieve or improve this life force. The Bantu have no idea of "being" apart from "force." Being is that which has force, and force is the nature of being. That means that force is being, and being is force.[70] Tempels defines Bantu philosophy as embodying a dynamic view of being as contrasted with the static Western concept. He denies that the Africans are dynamists in the sense of believing in a universal force.[71] He insists rather that they distinguish between being as forces and emphasize the individuality of forces. However, this does not mean that a force is anything in itself, as is true of the individualized "person" in the Western view. The forces interact with each other and may be strengthened or weakened as the case may be. Moreover, the universe is organized into a hierarchy of forces having its apex in God the Creator. Life then is a web of interacting forces. Even as a man interacts with the other members of his family and clan, and has his significance within the hierarchy of those family relationships, even so his vital force interacts with the other forces of life such as animals, trees and stones, each of which exist in their own hierarchical orbits. Within this framework, some vital forces are endowed with intelligence and will while others are without reason. Nevertheless, they all interact in hierarchical fashion and receive their significance in their relationship to one another in the hierarchy.[72]

Tempels spells out the implications of his theory for an understanding of Bantu psychology and ethics, but it is unnecessary to comment on all the intricacies of his thesis.

Edwin Smith is very much attracted by Tempels' study, as evidenced by his long book review in *Africa* and his later comments in *African Ideas of God*. He conceded that Tempels' thesis offers a better explanation for metempsychosis than more traditional arguments.[73] As to Tempels' contention that there is no universal force but a network of individual forces, he suggests that Temples may have gotten the idea from Smith's book, *The Ila-Speaking Peoples of Northern Rhodesia*.[74] Nevertheless, he opposes the idea.[75]

Unfortunately, he does not address himself specifically to the crucial point at issue here—the personality of God—except to note that God is at the apex of the hierarchy of forces.[76]

As mentioned above, Tempels distinguishes between forces with reason and those without. Smith appropriates this suggestion and identifies the forces with intelligence and will as "persons," the others as "things."[77] However, there is a different dynamic involved, the implications of which he has not fully seen.

For the African, life in its totality is much more a unity than for Western man. To be sure, the African distinguishes between God, men, animals, plants and minerals, some having reason and some not, but all form part in a web of interaction. The African in traditional society does not distinguish as such between the categories of animate and inanimate, persons and things, "he" and "it." It is true that Mbiti sometimes uses the word "inanimate," but he also talks about the "life" of non-living things which raises a question regarding the meaning of the word "inanimate." His conclusion that "strictly speaking 'nothing is essentially dead or devoid of life(being)' in the sight of African peoples"[78] also finds echoes in Busia[79] and Sawyerr.[80]

Since in fact the web of interaction which encompasses reality is composed of "living forces," Temples might better have used the term "being" than "vital force" to translate the idea into Western thought.[81] In either case a re-definition of terms is required. However, it is necessary to see the essential oneness of reality.[82] The oneness of nature, man and God in the African view is a oneness based on relationship, not identity.[83] This is not oriental pantheism, nor is it Western theism; it is somewhere in between the two.[84]

Smith's difficulty is that he asks a Western question (Is God a Person?) and forces a Western-type answer. When the answer is not readily forthcoming, he falls back on "unclarity" as an explanation for the difficulty. What does not seem to occur to him is to ask whether his question is in itself legitimate or meaningful in the African context.[85]

Smith's preoccupation with evolutionary stages leads him to presuppose an inanimate stage when Africans did not distinguish between the sun or sky or rain and God. The idea that God is a personal Being separate from these natural phenomena and indeed their Creator, Smith believes, is a later development. But, as has been seen, there is no way to prove or disprove such a theory, nor is such an idea necessary since Africans today have no difficulty in using the same names for God and these natural phenomena without seeing them as identical.[86]

DISREGARD OF MULTIFORM REACTIONS

Because Edwin Smith does not see in its full proportions the significance of the central paradox of African Traditional Religion, he misses also an understanding of the dynamics of the African attempts to resolve it. He has glimpses of it. Indeed he has many of its elements within his grasp. His excellent research and his own extraordinary ability at field observation make these available; but at the crucial point of interpretation his speculative interests fail because they are largely concentrated in other directions.

That Africans are aware of the problem is manifest. It is also obvious that there has been a search for solutions. It is therefore of value to examine some of these attempts. As will be seen, each position is unique. It represents a special combination of the various elements which go to make up the total African world view.

Unity and Plurality

Smith's endeavor to deal with the totality of African Traditional Religion leads him into difficulty. He is most convincing when he concerns himself with the beliefs of the Ba-ila. Here he records and interprets what he actually observes. When he moves beyond the circle, he is on increasingly weak ground. In his book, *The Religion of Lower Races*, he expands his interests to Bantu thought in general; and *The Secret of the African* includes sections on the conception of God in South, Central and West Africa. In each case he interprets the evidence in terms of the beliefs of the Ba-ila.

He is aware of the problems involved in trying to deal with the fullness of the African religious experience. In his second presidential address to the Royal Anthropological Institute in 1935, he observes that, since knowledge of the subject is so fragmentary, "the time is not yet ripe for a comprehensive and synthetic work on African religion,"[87] ignoring the fact that he has already written two such tracts. His "Foreword" to Parrinder's *West African Religion*, written in 1947, supports the endeavor to bring together the beliefs and practices of diverse regions in a search for the principles which underlie them; yet he also commends Parrinder for not attempting the "impossible task" of examining the thought of all the people of West Africa.[88]

Nevertheless, in between these two comments, Smith himself is responsible for *African Beliefs and Christian Faith* (1936) and *Knowing the African* (1946). In *Knowing the African* he specifically discusses the question of the unity of African Religion. He perceives that there is a great variety but also insists that there is an underlying unity permitting one to talk about African Religion.[89]

There is no unanimity among scholars on the question.[90] Busia, while not discounting the variety in African belief, affirms that "it is possible to discern common religious ideas, and assumptions about the universe held throughout Africa, and which provide a world-view that may be described as African."[91]

A criticism of Smith's position in this regard should perhaps center itself not so much on his attempt to address himself to the "impossible task" as on his results. African ethnographical study and research would most certainly be less rich today if Smith had not ventured as he did; but it is also true to say that his framework is often inadequate to handle the different views which his research make available to him. To deal with the bewildering variety of evidence, he must often resort to a "some say this . . . others say that" approach to the issues.[92] Even more serious, he tends to conclude too readily that the African view is "unclear" because of a divergent witness coming from different quarters. This is not to deny the existence of ambiguity or even unclarity in the African view but merely to recognize the fact that Smith sometimes calls "unclear" diverse or conflicting ideas which he juxtaposes in his theoretical framework, whereas they are not necessarily so unclear in their original context.

Evans-Pritchard understands this better. He insists that, although there are common features among all African peoples (that is beliefs regarding theism, "ancestor worship," witchcraft, taboo and magic), the philosophy of each tribe is unique in the way it combines the various elements into a unified whole.[93] The focal point of each philosophy varies. Bantu thought is centered on the ancestor cult while the Azande emphasize witchcraft. For the Nuer, "Spirit," understood principally as the belief in God, is central. Other tribes are oriented to other notions.[94] In a perceptive remark of considerable significance for this study, Evans-Pritchard states: "The test of what is the dominant motif is usually, perhaps always, to what a people attribute dangers and sickness and other misfortunes and what steps they take to avoid or eliminate them."[95]

Misfortune as Good Fortune

The Nuer, who have been so ably studied by Evans-Pritchard, are a case in point. They share with other African peoples a sense of destiny and fatalism. They know God's nearness and farness. They have a departure myth.[96] Unlike many Africans, although they are by no means alone in this, they believe in divine retribution. The rules of society must be obeyed. Good follows right conduct while evil is the result of wrong actions. God will often overlook error so prayers are useful, but basically suffering entails guilt.[97]

However, the Nuer add alongside this another thought which is unique: a denial of evil's reality. Evans-Pritchard calls attention to the striking difference between the Nuer attitude toward God and men. In their relations with men, they are proud to the point of arrogance; but before God they are the humblest of the humble. They constantly confess their ignorance and weakness. They do not complain when misfortune strikes. It is God's will. He is good. He is in the right.[98] The deceased is God's man; so God only took what was His own. If one grieves overmuch, God will be angry. It is best to be content, for God is always in the right. He could have taken the person himself, whereas He only took his ox.[99] It is better not to be so rich anyway.[100] If one rejoices excessively over good fortune, it is sure to be taken away. The proper way is to be humble throughout and to recognize that misfortune is really good fortune![101]

The Nuer are among the most theistic of African people. "Ancestor worship" is definitely subordinate. Animism is practically non-existent, and both witchcraft and magic are insignificant; nor do they have any concept of *mana*. Evans-Pritchard suggests that these elements "are incompatible with a theocentric philosophy, for when both fortune and misfortune come from God they cannot also come from human powers, whether innate or learned."[102] This is a debatable statement, for in reality most African people blame both God and human powers for the ambiguity of life; but it does not invalidate his general interpretation of Nuer theology.

It would seem that both Nuer solutions to the central paradox of life are unsatisfactory in answering the African question. Neither the denial of the reality of evil nor the concept of retribution (which themselves cannot be fully harmonized when placed in one system), appear to speak to the deepest need of the African heart; for the Nuer, like other Africans, seek to concentrate increasingly their attention on the lesser spirits, the spirits of the air, such as *deng*. The fact that these spirits "may be regarded as hypostases, representations, or refractions of God"[103] and that they are recent introductions into Nuer theology[104] only fortify the conclusion regarding the inadequacy of the Nuer explanation of the paradox. As is true of all peoples, the Nuer face the problems of life. They fear illness and death; and since "these troubles are manifestations of Spirit, they fear Spirit and wish to be rid of it."[105]

Prenatal Destiny

Another answer for the paradox, almost diametrically opposed to that of the Nuer, is found among the Tallensi people. The Tallensi take the concept of destiny, which is common to most African people but receives a particularly strong emphasis in West Africa,[106] and make it not only central to the problem of life but to its solution as well. The unusual twist which they give

to the idea, making it ultimately a non-theistic solution as contrasted with that of the Nuer, is that they blame man himself for
his destiny.

Fortes translates the term *Nuor-Yin* as Prenatal Destiny.[107]
The words literally mean "Spoken Destiny." In the Tallensi view
"Heaven" (*Naawun*) is the final source of all that takes place on
earth. Fortes avoids calling Naawun God and refuses to speculate
as to whether this Final Cause of all things should be identified
as "he" or "it." The Tallensi have no creation myth and no
shrines for the worship of Naawun.[108]

Before birth a child is "with Heaven," not literally but sym-
bolically in the sense of its coming into being. In this prenatal state
the child makes its desires known to Heaven, that is, it speaks its
destiny.[109] Sometimes the child affirms that it has no desire for
parents, children or wealth, thus rejecting the life of a normal
human being. The child cannot escape birth, but its evil Prenatal
Destiny can be expressed so strongly that its owner suffers misfortune and death or causes trouble for others.[110]

It often happens that a woman loses children one after another
resulting in despair for herself and her husband. In such a case
they suspect an evil Prenatal Destiny and seek confirmation from
a diviner. However, all is not lost, for it is possible to exorcise the
Prenatal Destiny in such cases. Sacrifices are made to the ancestors
who are urged to remove the offending fate.[111]

Even as there is an evil Prenatal Destiny, there is also a Good
Destiny. Once again the prenatal desires and wishes manifest
themselves in fixing the pattern of an individual's life, and this is
not uncommonly referred to as a manifestation of the universal
Heaven. Although the possible elements of life are limited and
stereotyped—illness or health, fecundity or sterility, success or
failure—the pattern of their combination is different for every
person. The way the various elements are put together depends on
the person's destiny.[112]

Fortes notes the value of the concept not only for social relations but also for its contribution to the psychological stability
of the individual himself:

> It seems that in these circumstances the notion of Prenatal
> Destiny serves as a legitimate alibi. It relieves the sufferer's kin,
> and therefore society at large, of responsibility and guilt for his
> troubles and, indeed, exonerates him in his own eyes. For he

is not aware that he is the victim of his Prenatal Destiny until this is revealed by a diviner.[113]

Fortes is not interested in the theological significance of the belief,[114] but there are deep theological implications, for the concept of Prenatal Destiny exonerates not only society but also God for the problems of life. God does not choose one's destiny; the person chooses his own destiny.

Whether the system speaks adequately to the paradox may be seriously questioned. Although the individual has presumably chosen his own destiny, he has no recollection of having done so. Indeed, it is inconceivable that he could have really chosen such an evil destiny. Moreover, the Tallensi retain alongside this belief the conviction that Naawun is the Final Cause of everything.[115] In the end, the person is not satisfied to rest in his chosen destiny but seeks to alter it by recourse to the exorcism of the ancestors.

Dualism

The Lugbara conception of God in the sky and God in the streams has been examined. The transcendent aspect of God, God remote in the sky and absent from men, is good. God in His immanence, close to men and manifest in the streams, is bad.[116]

An interesting feature is the Lugbara belief that death is caused by God in His transcendence. This phrase is used to describe it: "*Adroa 'ba o' dupiri*, 'God the taker away of men'." Witches or sorcerers, for example, may cause sickness ending in death, but they do not kill. Since God alone can cause death even as He alone can create, the most that witches or spirits can do is bring a man to God's attention.[117] The difficulty of this belief is self-evident: How can God's good aspect be responsible for fulfilling the evil designs of the witches?

In the case of the Lugbara the tendency toward dualism as an explanation for the ambiguity of life is evident, but the idea is not pushed further. The Lugbara retain the belief in God's unity. They do not separate their conception into a good and bad deity but insist on conceiving God with good and bad "aspects."

Parrinder calls attention to the belief of the Congo Kuta in two gods, Nzambi above and Nzambi below; but he mentions no identification of the earthly Nzambi with evil.[118] Andersson, on the other hand, observes that the Kuta dualism is a means of resolving the difficulty of Nzambi's relationship to death: "Belief in two gods affords a possibility of escaping from this dilemma. It is said that Nzambi *watanda* (above) is good, whilst Nzambi *wamutsele* (below) is wicked; the latter thus becomes almost a sort of Satan."[119] Nevertheless, it does not appear that the Kuta idea is greatly different from the Lugbara. Andersson concludes that it is a way of explaining the two sides of goodness and wickedness in God's nature as they are manifested in the reality of life itself.[120]

Another tendency[121] toward dualism is that found among the Vugusu,[122] and it is carried through more thoroughly than the Lugbara or Kuta conceptions. As Wagner makes clear, the Vugusu conceive of two gods to explain the good and evil of life. The "black god" (*wele gumali* or *wele evimbi*) is ultimately responsible for all the evil of life while the one responsible for good—the Creator—is identified as the "White God" (*Wele ómuwanga*).[123] In the Vugusu view, the black god does not serve the White God, nor are the two equal in power. They are independent in activity, and the black god is apparently of lesser force. In their prayers the Vugusu implore the White God to rid them of the influence of the black god:

> Wele, you who made us walk in your country,
> You who made the cattle and the things which are in it,
> You may spit the medicine on your person,
> He may recover and walk well,
> He may plant his gardens.
> Drive away the black god,
> He may leave your person,
> He may move into the snake
> And into the abandoned homestead;
> He may leave our home.[124]

Wagner confesses that among the other clans of the Abaluyia, he has not found a similar conception of a clear evil counterpart to the Creator God, although in all there is "a very pronounced belief in a dichotomy of good and evil forces."[125]

Yet even among the Vugusu God's responsibility for the ambiguity of life is not extinguished, as evidenced by this saying attributed to God: " 'It is I who made the people; whom I love he will thrive, and whom I refuse he will die'."[126]

Divine Capriciousness

The Ba-ila and Ashanti approach to God may also be placed in this schema, although the conclusions suggested here are not discussed by Smith. Among the Ashanti and the Ba-ila, there are some examples of lesser spirits who seem to epitomize evil, but the tendency toward a dualistic explanation is minimal and is never carried far enough to act as an exoneration of the Creator from the ultimate ambiguity. Since God controls the fate of all, He is also responsible for good and evil, which is to say that in the final analysis He is capricious.

Yet the thought is extremely complicated, for it is no easy task to define the African God as capricious. The Ashanti insist that He is in fact *Tweaduampon*, the Dependable One.[127] One is impressed in all of this at the difficulty of separating the elements of the paradox which is so all-embracing in the African view.

The paradox is precisely the fact that the Dependable One is undependable and the Capricious One is not capricious. He is responsible for evil although they call Him good, and He is capricious although they insist that He is dependable. A God who is so inscrutable is best left on the periphery of life. It is better to focus one's attention on such entities as the ancestors who, while also retaining characteristics of undependability and inscrutability, are nevertheless more understanding and understandable than the Supreme Being.

But God is not so easily pushed to the periphery, for the mystery of life cannot be explained or controlled by the ancestors; and sooner or later man is forced back to deal with the Creator and Determiner of all things. There is obviously no stereotyped way to "bring Him back" as is seen in the very different approaches of the Ashanti and Ba-ila to God. For both, as contrasted with the Nuer for example, the ancestors are clearly the dominant elements in their thought and religious experience.[128] Yet to their "worship" of the ancestors, the Ashanti also add daily offerings to God. It would seem that these are added perfunctorily, as a kind of amplified thought or extra insurance, to allow for whatever contingencies life might have to offer. This conclusion seems justified from the affirmation of the old Ashanti priest, quoted by Rattray and Smith,[129] that it is necessary to keep on good terms with all the spirits, including the High God.

The Bantu approach, as exemplified in the Ba-ila, concentrates the attention of the individual on the ancestors and lesser divinities until such time as one has reached an impasse in his life and there is no recourse other than God Himself. Kenyatta emphasizes that if all goes well, there is no need of prayers to God. He goes on to say: "Indeed they are inadvisable, for Ngai must not needlessly be bothered."[130] Other African peoples apparently never seek God's intervention. Gelfand affirmes: "I have not seen an occasion on which the MaKorekore have called on God, even as a last resort in times of crisis or calamity."[131]

It would seem that the view of God as responsible for all things good and bad, and therefore ultimately capricious, is more prevalent and possibly even a more fundamental expression of the African sentiment than the ideas noted among the Nuer, Tallensi and Vugusu. These latter explanations may perhaps be seen as secondary attempts to free God from the full responsibility for the ambiguity of life. However, it is important to note that, if they are meant to do so, in order to pave the way for His reentry into the mainstream of African life, they do not succeed. In the final analysis, for the Nuer, Tallensi and Vugusu, as for the Ashanti and Ba-ila (indeed for most Africans), God is still far away and the myths of His departure remain valid. To bring near again the God who went away, it took a new action: the introduction of Christianity.

9

Critical Analysis: Christian Contribution

MISUNDERSTANDING OF CHRISTIAN TASK

Christianity has made an extraordinary contribution to African life, especially to thought and belief regarding God. In this context Edwin Smith merits special praise as an early and prophetic interpreter of the Christian faith on the African scene. In saying this, however, one ought not to overlook the weaknesses of either Smith or the general Christian witness in Africa. Those weaknesses are directly traceable to a misunderstanding of the fundamental paradox of God's relationship to the ambiguity of life, as seen in African Traditional Religion.

Appeal of Christianity

There is no denying the appeal of Christianity in Africa. It is simply not possible to understand its impact or the very large acceptance of it by Africans without acknowledging that fact.

The African espousal of Christianity cannot be treated exhaustively in this study. Suffice it to say that the dynamics of that acceptance are extremely complex. Undoubtedly the political power of the colonial invaders was a factor, but one cannot explain the African adoption of the Christian faith simply as a political imposition.[1] There is something in the Christian message itself which speaks to a deep need in the African soul.

As has been seen, Edwin Smith believes that the kernel of special relevance for the African situation is the Christian conception of God. Smith's understanding of the influence which the idea of God has had on the diverse aspects of African religious experience has been noted throughout.

In African thought, God is far away and remote, but the African longs for a different view. The deepest yearning of his heart is to bring back into the consciousness of daily life and experience the God who has gone away; and it is this which Christianity effects. Christianity brings near the High God who has been lost sight of and pushes Him into the center of African consciousness. Under Christian influence, the Creator God becomes the focal point of African religious experience.

Moreover, God is brought back, under Christian aegis, not against the will of the African but with his warm embrace and consent. It is his own wish and desire which opens the door to a sincere acceptance of the Christian message. In a sense he is waiting precisely for that message. He knows in the deepest recesses of his heart that there must be a God like that—a God who is present, who loves and cares. When the Christians proclaim their message of God's nearness, as seen by His coming to men in Jesus, the African eagerly accepts that message.

Numerous illustrations could be given to show that Smith has correctly understood this aspect of the Christian appeal. Two will perhaps suffice: the Akan and the Ganda.

Williamson notes that some Akan see Christianity as a more satisfying expression of their traditional world-view than that afforded by their own religion. The need to qualify that statement will be apparent in due course, but it needs to be affirmed here. One informant calls attention to the fact that Africans not uncommonly offer thanks in the Church for healing received from a fetish. Another states that Christianity is more personally oriented than traditional belief. Still a third credits it to the fact that the Church calls for direct worship of the Supreme Being.[2] Williamson draws from this two conclusions.

In the first place, it is manifest that the attention which Christians give to the High God appeals directly to the Akan religious sense. The Christian idea of God is in fact the central attraction and has profound implications for every phase of Akan life. In agreement with Rattray and Smith,[3] Williamson affirms that Akan traditional belief has always retained a place for the worship of

God, but he does not see this as in any way diminishing the Christian appeal.[4]

Williamson's second conclusion alludes to the appeal of the Christian emphasis on the importance of the individual. Yet here again the thought is dependent on the concept of God, for it is God's love revealed in Christ which creates the possibility of a new attitude toward men:

> Just as the Christian faith appealed to the Akan because it accorded worship to the Supreme Being alone, so by application of its doctrine and worship it expressed Akan belief about the individual in his right of approach to the Creator in a detailed and meaningful manner.[5]

Another example is that found among the Ganda. Taylor calls attention to the difference between the gospel preached by the missionaries and the gospel heard by the people.[6] That which was proclaimed was man's sinfulness, Christ's atonement, individual conversion and the sanctification of the person; but the message which was heard and which formed the cornerstone for the building of the Church in Buganda was news about the transcendent God. The Ganda had a belief in Katonda, but He was remote and played little part in the daily round of their existence. Yet it was this God whom the Christians propelled into the center of life. Taylor affirms that the shock of the Christian message was so great that it was grasped as a new teaching. Using a biblical analogy, he pictures the missionaries as preaching Paul's Corinthian message, with the Africans hearing a mixture of the Athenian discourse and Isaiah's warning to Jerusalem. Taylor insists that it was this Word of God, almost in spite of the words of men, which formed the basis for the revivals on which the Ganda church was founded.[7]

Weakness of Christianity

Taylor's astute observation regarding the difference between the messages preached and heard by the Ganda shows not only Christianity's strength but also its weakness in Africa. For while it is true that the Ganda hear the message that the remote God is near, almost as a by-product of the missionary preaching, they receive virtually no guidance as to how this new concept can be integrated into their world view. Indeed, as Taylor shows so well, the missionaries are not concerned with that question at all. They are anxious that the Ganda should acknowledge their sin and the sufficiency of Jesus to cover it.

It is always dangerous to generalize regarding missionaries. Edwin Smith well remarks that there are differences between them and that the approach they take to their work is not uniform.[8] Nevertheless, it is not a misrepresentation to say that Taylor's observations regarding the situation in Buganda have a validity which goes beyond that country.

Missionary work reflects by and large the ambivalence of the sacred-secular dichotomy of Western culture. While in *practice* missionaries address themselves to the needs of this world—through education, agriculture, medical and social service, their *message* is principally oriented in an other-worldly direction. It is true that at some points the message and practice tend toward convergence. Missionaries do in fact call for prayer in time of need, and the religious emotion generated in Christian revivals is of profound significance for the daily lives of many Africans.[9] Undoubtedly the combination of prayer to God and medical service impresses the African as important to his situation. Nevertheless, it is not an exaggeration to suggest that the this-worldly emphasis is in general too divorced from the spiritual concerns of African thought and that Christian prayer is often so intellectualized that it does not speak to the deep needs of the African heart.

It is impossible to deny the dominant stress on other-worldliness in the Christian message preached in Africa.[10] The main problem of this life is to prepare for the life to come. The preparation is to be effected by the acknowledgment of sin, the recognition of Jesus' atoning sacrifice, the individual acceptance of God's offer of salvation and the dedication to live a good life in the power of the Holy Spirit. The missionaries reflect Western anxiety regarding the afterlife, and they want to make sure that the African is not excluded.

The ironic thing is that, although the African has many problems, uncertainty regarding the after-life is not one of them. His belief in the survival of the personality after death is his *a priori*.[11]

Andersson illustrates well the difference between the African and missionary point of view, comparing the African understanding of "salvation" with what he calls the biblical conception. For the African, salvation means help in time of trouble: healing, fertility and success in life's ventures. It is not a salvation of the soul but happiness and prosperity in this life. The "biblical view" by the same token is directed toward the afterlife: "Having arrived at greater maturity, the Congolese plainly understand that salvation means above all entry into heaven."[12]

The African's main difficulty is how to deal with evil and misfortune. This is central to his religious experience, and his whole life is oriented toward it. The missionaries are not entirely oblivious to it. Those who interpret the Bible in a more literal fashion sometimes make reference to "demons," and the concept of Satan is not completely ignored; but often missionaries gloss over the very passages which are of greatest interest to the African in the fear that any discussion of them as "realities" will take him back in the direction from which he is supposedly coming.[13] If these passages are taken seriously at all, it is not unusually in the context of the affirmation that Christ has gotten rid of the "evil spirits" once and for all. The emphasis is not placed on the continual role of exorcism by Christ and his disciples but on Jesus' role in their elimination during the first century. They are no longer realities, meaning that Christians now know that there simply are no such things.[14] Needless to say, this is perplexing to the African because he is as a matter of fact encountering them every day.

Some missionaries suggest that these biblical references reflect an outmoded world-view no longer tenable for modern man.[15] But this "outmoded view no longer tenable for modern man" is precisely the African world-view. Nor is it only the world-view of simple village people. It also reflects by and large the sentiment of the elite African who has completed many years of scientific study in Western universities.[16]

The Christian message as preached is too often an intellectual exercise of limited significance to the African who listens to it. He not uncommonly fails to understand it or see its validity.[17] One might even argue that if it had been better understood, it might have been rejected out of hand as unimportant to the African situation.[18] Be that as it may, there is no denial that the missionary and African dialogue is a classic example of a communications failure.[19] What the missionaries believe to be relevant, the Africans consider irrelevant and vice versa. At one point the two interests converge: on the question of the nearness of the remote God. However, because their interests in the concept are different, the missionaries are limited in their ability to help their converts see the implications of the new faith for the enigma of life which is their constant preoccupation. The missionaries are in fact largely oblivious to it.

The African's problem involves his whole life, his every experience.[20] The missionary message is largely aimed at providing knowledge of how to obtain something for which the African has never felt any great need. To be sure, the missionary insists that Christianity is also concerned with the whole of life, but the African soon comes to the conclusion that this cannot really be true.[21] It is quite clear to him that the missionary is not interested in his daily misfortunes, and in fact Christianity as presented rarely offers either an intellectual explanation or an adequate procedure by which the emotion generated by them can be dealt with on the practical level.[22]

Little wonder that the African, including the African Christian, returns to the traditional methods of dealing with his real problems. [23] Yet alongside this he retains the Christian emphasis on the Supreme God who is now no longer far but near. He does not know quite what to do with that new teaching, but he is reluctant to lose it. He feels its truth so much that he cannot renounce it. By remaining in the Church and continuing to follow the practices of African Traditional Religion, he believes that he can have the best of two worlds. However, this is an illusion, for the missionaries and African pastors make it clear that his charms and his reliance on the ancestors is really a contradiction of his faith in God, ending in a feeling of guilt.[24] The result is that he often finds himself in a bifurcated world, affirming what seem to be two contradictory truths which can neither be relinquished nor reconciled.[25]

Smith and Paradox

Edwin Smith obviously shares an orthodox understanding of the Christian faith including interest in the problems of sin, forgiveness through Christ's atonement and the significance of the Christian understanding of the afterlife. Nevertheless, it would be a mistake to suggest that he places great stress on these elements in his presentation of the Christian faith. As a matter of fact he does not do so. He says clearly that in evangelistic work in Africa, the Christian should not begin with the Bible or sin:

> How is one to begin? What point of contact can one establish with the people in order to win them for Christ? You cannot be-

gin with the Bible—they know nothing of it. It is futile to start by demonstrating to them the sinfulness of their life; mere denunciation of evil customs is more likely than not to arouse resentment. There must be a basis for your preaching—some common ground which you and the people occupy, some jumping-off place, something about which you agree. Well, you can always find it here in their awareness of God.[26]

Smith explicitly states that one must begin where the African leaves off, that is, with the concept of God.[27] It is necessary to develop his own rich heritage and to speak to the African question. For Smith the African question is: Why did God go away? The Christian answer is that God is not far away but near, which is proven by His coming among men in Jesus.

Smith believes that it is enough for Christians to preach God's nearness in Christ. It is this word which speaks to the African heart. This is the message to which he will respond. When the significance of that fact penetrates his consciousness, the African will recognize the meaning of sin and atonement and see their significance for every aspect of his life.[28]

Smith sees the essential problem of the African conception of God as its emphasis on God's remoteness. The solution therefore is to bring near the High God. Because of the Incarnation, Christianity is able to proclaim that God is not far away and uninterested but near and concerned. God showed His love for men by coming among them and sharing their life. As has been seen, Smith pursues this position in each phase of his understanding of the conception of God.

However, it is clear that, even as Smith misses the full paradox of African Religion, he also fails to see the fullness of the Christian answer to it. For him the problem is that God went away and now must be brought back. But in reality the issue is more complex. It is not merely that God went away. He was pushed away, and He was pushed away for good reasons. Therefore, He cannot merely be brought back. He must be brought back within a context.

If He is to be brought back to stay and to take His rightful place in the religious consciousness of His people, the context of His original departure cannot be ignored. Any attempt to bring near the High God without dealing at the same time with the fundamental reasons for His absenteeism, without taking into consideration the beliefs which prompted Him to be pushed away in the first place, cannot hope to achieve complete success.

Smith's principal failure is his misunderstanding of this dynamic. To be sure, he is well aware of the fact that the Christian God cannot be presented or appropriated entirely in Western garb. Few of his contemporaries saw this so clearly as he did. His early and poignant appeal for the expression of the Christian gospel in indigenous forms was prophetic. One is impressed, in reading many modern books on Africa, at how they emphasize today the need to take seriously the very things which Edwin Smith called for fifty years ago. Furthermore, very few go beyond Smith in their vision of the present need of the Church.[29] Little wonder that he is looked upon as such a significant figure in the history of African Christianity. Nor is it the purpose of this study to detract in any way from the enormous contribution which he made. Yet it is essential to see his weaknesses. His call for indigenization was extremely important. One might say for his day it was extraordinary, but it did not go far enough; nor is it adequate for the needs of the Church today. To the extent which he fails to see the African problem, he fails also to address himself to the Christian solution in its fullness.

As to the African preoccupation with the ambiguity of life, Edwin Smith is too much a son of his own day. He is overly enamoured with the ability of the education and science of Western culture to convince the African of the need to approach his problems as a Westerner does himself.

Smith and Fulfillment

The statement has been made at several points in this critique that Smith's major problem is a failure to address himself to the paradox of African Traditional Religion. However, it may well be that a more fundamental question is at issue: his understanding of the relationship of the two religions in terms of a "fulfillment" theology.

As has been noted, Edwin Smith constantly uses the word "fulfillment" to describe the relationship of African Traditional Religion and Christianity. Unfortunately at no point does he define precisely what he means by that expression. He seems to assume that it is either self-evident or its meaning so well known that a definition is unnecessary. This is by no means the case.[30]

The term "fulfillment" has had perhaps its greatest influence in the Hindu-Christian dialogue[31] and is seen most clearly in the writings of J. N. Farquhar in the early part of this century.[32] Farquhar distinguishes three aspects of the concept which may serve fruitfully as a foundation for understanding the thought of Edwin Smith:

> First, Hinduism is "fulfilled" by being replaced by Christianity: "fulfilment" therefore means "replacement." Secondly, the truths in Hinduism are "fulfilled" by reappearing in a "higher" form in Christianity. And thirdly, Christ "fulfills" the quests of Hinduism, by providing an answer to its questions, a resolution of its problems, a goal for its religious strivings.[33]

It is manifest that the concept of evolution plays an important part in "fulfillment" theologies.[34] Nevertheless, the exact role of evolution in the conception is not always the same. Sharpe insists that, for Farquhar, "a 'lower' stage does not merely *develop into* 'a higher:' it is *replaced by* a 'higher,' in a conscious choice of will."[35]

Such a distinction is not clear in Smith's writings. In his book *African Beliefs and Christian Faith*, Smith uses the analogy of the school to describe God's revelation.[36] God is the great Teacher, and history is the arena of His education of the nations. The different nations are at different stages, in a process of development which corresponds to God's progressive revelation. God would like to reveal Himself completely to all men, but it cannot be done at once. The way must be prepared for a higher grade. Only after the time is fully prepared can God reveal Himself by means of His Son.

The analogy is a dangerous one and of dubious value as a characterization of either African Traditional Religion in itself or the relationship of Christianity to it. There is no evidence that African Religion is in process of development from "lower" to "higher" expression, nor does the theory make allowances for wrong turns on the way. Error tends to be pictured not as sin but as a lack of sufficient "light," more of which will presumably make its appearance at the next stage.

There is no place here for "paradox" for paradox simply does not fit into an evolutionary scheme of fulfillment. The theology of fulfillment rather prefers to describe the situation in terms of "unclarity" becoming clarified, the half-light of dawn becoming the full light of midday.

By this logic, Jesus Christ does not come to turn things around or to set in motion a new movement. He comes to put the finishing touches on God's progressive revelation. Kraemer rightly criticizes the concept of fulfillment as giving the erroneous impression that "the lines of the so-called highest developments point naturally in the direction of Christ, and would end in Him if produced further."[37] Smith is not fully consistent, for he not uncommonly does present Jesus as the one who turns things around.

Farquhar's second category, the reappearance of truth in a "higher" form in Christianity, also has a place in Smith's thought. This is what Smith means by "sublimation," one of his fundamental terms in discussing the relationship of Christianity to African Traditional Religion.

In fulfillment theologies, an important distinction is whether Christ fulfills only the "good" or both the "good" and the "bad" of traditional religions. Sharpe observes that in the Indian debate and at Edinburgh 1910 it is often stated that Christ fulfills the best and destroys the worst, although the line between "best" and "worst" is not always easy to determine. Farquhar alters this slightly by looking for the "quest" behind all Hindu practices.[38] Smith too is concerned with the quest, but he sees sublimation principally as a seeking for the "good kernel" in African customs and beliefs:

> Applied to our missionary work, the word [sublimation] may be used analogously of the process of utilizing for Christian ends the experiences registered in African practices and beliefs. The customs have grown up out of some felt need and represent something of value to the people. Not all of them are unclean and false; very often in the heart of a false and unclean custom there is something admirable, and Africans will admit that many of the repugnant elements are not really essential. To sublimate means not to transplant the whole of any custom, good or bad, but to seek out the good kernel in things evil and to make it serve the interests of a higher moral and spiritual life. All that is best in the African's past experience should be enlisted into the service of Christ and His Church.[39]

As a general missionary *method*, it would be difficult to fault Smith's understanding of sublimation as the proper approach of Christians to the religion and culture of Africa; but as an aspect of the *theology* of fulfillment, the term is of questionable value, mainly because it is not universally applicable.

The essential problem is that not all the elements which go to

make up the life and religion of Africa lend themselves to sublimation. Hence the search for the "good kernel" is an arduous
one and, when finally discovered, often turns out to be far-fetched
and unconvincing.

It is not by any means an easy task to criticize Smith on his
understanding of sublimation, since there is no one all-embracing
definition to govern its use in different contexts. The matter seems
to depend principally on his subjective mood in making the interpretation. Although Smith insists that Christianity sublimates African Religion, his argument at many points leads one to believe that
Christianity does in fact radically alter, and even destroy many
traditional beliefs and practices. Smith opposes for example fu-
nereal murder and the killing of twins as incompatible with Christianity without listing the good elements enshrined in these practices.[40] In fact he states at one point that it is possible to spend so
much time looking for the good that one fails to resent the evil
as sin.[41] In all of this it may be seriously questioned whether Smith
is able to maintain a consistent position.

The third aspect of Farquhar's definition of fulfillment—Christianity as an answer to the Hindu question and search—also has a
parallel in Smith. Indeed Smith is at this point on stronger ground
than Farquhar.

Hogg criticizes the theology of fulfillment as applied to the Indian situation precisely because it presents Christianity as an answer to a question which the Hindu does not raise and a solution
to a problem the Hindu does not feel. He concedes that the need,
which Christianity is designed to satisfy, can be induced, but he
denies that the need is self-evident to the Hindu who has not heard
the gospel.[42] Kraemer emphasizes this also.[43]

Fulfillment theologies are often criticized in that they tend to
present traditional religion as "searching" and Christianity as
"finding."[44] Kraemer quotes Chenchiah to the effect that "in Hinduism many people have found salvation, with deep satisfaction."[45]

In the African situation also it would be a serious mistake to
suppose that African Traditional Religion encompasses only a
search without any satisfying solutions. Nevertheless, African Religion does differ from Hinduism in that it leaves unanswered the
most fundamental question of all, a question which Christianity is
uniquely able to answer: Why did God go away? If Edwin Smith
had confined his attention to this question, his use of the word
"fulfillment" would be easier to defend. But, as has been seen, he

confuses matters by including within the term an ambiguous concept of sublimation and an evolutionary understanding of revelation.

Although at several points Kraemer has been cited with approval, this is not meant to sanction his position in its entirety. The Achilles' heel of Kraemer's study is his vacillation regarding the existence of revelation in traditional religions.

In general Kraemer sees the religions as man's attempt to work out his own salvation, and thus they are manifestations of man's desire to escape God. Yet God's revelation also plays a part. Kraemer often asks the question: What is the place of revelation in the religions? But he never gives a clear answer.[46]

He notes that Soderblöm's demand for an answer is perfectly valid and concludes that "here it is still very difficult to find the right way."[47] He criticizes Witte for being too condemnatory of the religions,[48] whereas Farmer tries too hard to be fair.[49] He is willing to concede with Reichelt that Buddhism has something to do with God, but he does not define how.[50]

In discussing the weakness of the idea of *praeparatio evangelica*, Kraemer insists that the "best and highest elements" of the religions should not be despised as error. That, he says, "would be contrary to our former conclusion that somehow in these elements a continuous wrestling of God with men and men's answer to this in the manifestations of their religious consciousness is reflected."[51] But again he fails to explain what he means by "somehow" or the "wrestling of God with men."

Kraemer maintains that Barth is wrong when he says "that the Bible knows no other mode of revelation than Christ,"[52] and at another point he says: "Within the domain of the religions there are evidences of God's revealing activity."[53] However, he never tries to relate the revelation in the religions to the revelation in Christ. He keeps returning to the idea that there is only relevation in Christ. In fact he states the same openly:

> As we have already once hinted, in the strict sense there is only one revelation, that is God's self-disclosure in Christ, the Saviour, as the righteousness and the wrath of God.
>
> . . . .
>
> Therefore, the revelation in Israel is the only one which, properly speaking, can be called *praeparatio*, and in regard to which one can legitimately speak of the revelation of Christ in the terms "fulfillment" and "continuity."[54]

The ambiguity of these various quotations is obvious. Is there or is there not revelation in the non-Christian religions? And if so, what is the relationship of the revelation in the religions to the revelation in Christ? These are the fundamental questions. Because Kraemer gives a yes-and-no answer to the first, he feels no obligation to speak to the second at all.

Against Smith, Kraemer, along with Barth and Brunner, is justified in placing the Old Testament in the category of special revelation, principally because Jesus is incomprehensible apart from Jewish history. At the same time, Smith acts as a valuable corrective to Kraemer, for it is not possible to study African Traditional Religion and still insist that it is devoid of revelation or that the revelation is unknowable or that it contains no points of contact with Christianity. If nothing else, the African belief in the Creator God makes this impossible. Therefore any insistence that the relationship of Christianity to African Traditional Religion is to be characterized by the word "discontinuity" is untenable.

MISINTERPRETATION OF RATIONALISTIC APPEAL

Few Westerners have had such a profound understanding and appreciation for African life and thought as Edwin Smith. Born in Africa, he lives close to the African people for many years. He studies, loves and esteems them. Yet he is also the product of Western culture. He grows up in the colonial era when the West is politically and ideologically expansive. He does not share by any means the full sense of "superiority" of Westerners regarding Africa, but he is nevertheless influenced by that sentiment. He does not seriously doubt the ability of science to alter the traditional world-view of Africa.

Dynamism

Edwin Smith is convinced that the traditional beliefs regarding dynamism cannot stand competition with the ideas of Western education and science.[55] The former must therefore ultimately give way to the latter.

He is fearful for the future of Africa precisely because of the inevitability of this transformation. The African is bound to recognize the fallaciousness of his traditional world-view with its emphasis on magic, manipulative medicine, taboo and charms. He will come to see that these are largely figments of the imagination with no real basis in fact.

The problem then will be that the African will throw over his traditional morality, leaving him without restraints and a moral basis for life. Part of the urgency with which Smith writes is his vision of the role of Christianity in preventing an African holocaust. In making this assessment, he seems to have underestimated the resiliency of Africa's traditional world-view.

One is forced to ask once again whether Smith's understanding of the situation, and how it must inevitably develop, is not a product of his evolutionary orientation. It is perhaps no mere coincidence that his mentor, Sir James Frazer, saw the evolutionary progression as going from magic to religion to science. Smith differs with Frazer on his assessment of the place of religion in life, but he does seem to accept the inevitability of the replacement of dynamism by science. Since that is what happened in the West, everything seems to suggest to him that it will be true of Africa as well.

Smith does not entertain the possibility that dynamism may not necessarily be antithetical to science. Rather he assumes that it is.[56] In reality dynamism deals with a different level of experience. They concern themselves with different questions. Science tries to answer the "what" and "how" questions, whereas dynamism speaks to the "why" question.[57] Smith knows this, but he fails to see its full significance.

Science treats of the things that can be seen and touched, empirical phenomena. Dynamism addresses itself to a deeper level—the realm of mysticism, the explanation for sensory objects and events.

The Westerner may well believe that science answers his questions, but this is only because he has accustomed himself to be satisfied with explanations which do not probe too far beyond sight phenomena. If pushed a step further to answer the "why" question, the Westerner must also enter the realm of the mystical, either by a religious explanation (God, Satan, etc.) or a dynamistic explanation (good luck, bad luck, etc.). If he resorts to "coincidence" as an explanation, he is really saying that it is luck or that he simply does not know. The point is that the Westerner has by and large conditioned himself to avoid this deeper question, although there are times when even he has difficulty in avoiding it.

It is clear that the African can appropiate science just as well as a Westerner without altering his basic world-view. Even in his traditional society, the African used empirical data.[58] He learned how to cultivate, hunt, fish, use herbs to treat diseases, etc. Western science has broadened his ability to do all these things and has opened up new avenues for him, but science cannot be credited with teaching the African to observe or to act on the basis of his observation.

This does not mean that the African is traditionally a "scientist." As a method, science is a product of Western thought which can be historically dated. The point at issue here is whether scientific and traditional conceptions arc contradictory. As Foté's discussion of the "determinisme scientifique" displayed in the traditional technology of iron smelting suggests, the two cannot be placed in opposition.[59]

In the traditional culture, the African knew that although he followed all the rules that experience had taught him, there were still contingencies; and it was precisely because of these contingencies that he resorted to dynamistic practices. Although science has reduced in some cases the depth of uncertainty regarding certain actions, it has not eliminated the variabilities and uncertainties of life. In fact, in some cases, especially in urban Africa, it has succeeded in increasing them.[60]

The African concern with the deeper "why" question is not any more illogical than the Western position, but it is manifest that the two philosophies stop at different points in the explanations which they require for any given phenomenon. This explains how it is that Africans can accept both science and Christianity without altering their traditional world-view, a phenomenon which has not gone unnoticed by Western writers.[61]

M. Wilson calls attention to the problem created in the minds of Africans who, although serious about their Christian faith, are nevertheless confused by the inequities of life, the "natural" explanations (which seem so unnatural) given by Westerners to explain life and the bewildering assortment of medicines, some of which are permitted for Christians while others are prohibited.[62]

The intermingling of "Christian" and "non-Christian" elements in any given tribe is extremely complex. Pauw for example divides the Tswana into three groups: church members, church adherents and "pagans." Given Christianity's strong influence in altering the traditional conception of God, he wonders whether it is possible any longer to talk of "pagans." As an example he tells of a native doctor who insisted that the local Roman Catholic priest had offered prayers to make his doctoring more successful. Pauw himself doubted that the priest had actually made such a prayer, concluding that the "pagan" doctor considered the regular church prayers as efficacious for his vocation.[63]

Exactly what the percentage is of Christians who would eschew all dynamistic practices is difficult to determine. Pauw believes that, of committed church members, a "substantial core" have no private dealings with traditional magical practices. However, he admits in the same paragraph that, in spite of the opposition of their churches, "many church members" do in fact frequent native doctors when they are in trouble.[64] Schapera is more skeptical. He indicates that almost everybody, Christian and non-Christian, uses magic and that it is also used at Christian feasts.[65]

Messenger agrees with Schapera from his experience in Nigeria. He suggests that among Christians there are few true believers by mission standards.[66] He notes that many people regard the European doctor as a dispenser of magic and that those who are sick often go to both European and native doctors.

Hayley quotes a Lango Christian to the effect that the people are sometimes cured by English doctors and sometimes not, just as with their own traditional doctors. Significantly he adds that they are more likely to be cured by the traditional doctor.[67]

Diviners now pray for power to the Christian God and not uncommonly make use of Christian symbols: "Some diviners throw the cross on the ground after a question is posed and if the figure of Jesus faces up the answer is 'yes,' if down, 'no'. Another method involves opening the Bible at random and reading the advice contained on that page."[68] Nor is the problem merely that of the old or uneducated. Messenger insists that youth, while accepting Christian dogma, retain their beliefs in evil powers in the face of all attempts by missionaries to deny their existence. Magical practices are used in romance and in securing work, even in passing examinations in the very schools which presumably are teaching the invalidity of such practices.[69]

In that Christianity has provided no real alternative for dealing with the African's practical problems—evil and misfortune—it has provided him no alternative to his old solutions. The African needs to deal with the intellectual aspects of the problem, but even more he requires a spiritual means for coping with the emotion that fluctuating experiences of life create for him. Neither the Christian conception of God nor Western science has succeeded in detaching the African from his traditional world-view. Smith greatly underestimates the strength of the African traditional world-view and at the same time greatly overestimates the ability of the Western interpretation of Christianity and Western culture to alter it.

Witchcraft

For most Westerners there is no "reality" behind witchcraft. Nothing actually happens to men as a result of "witchcraft activity." There are no real witches. It is rather a way of explaining the problems of life and can be understood entirely as a social phenomenon. Evans-Pritchard says, for example:

> It is an inevitable conclusion from Zande descriptions of witchcraft that it is not an objective reality. The physiological condition which is said to be the seat of witchcraft, and which I believe to be nothing more than food passing through the small intestine, is an objective condition, but the qualities they attribute to it and the rest of their beliefs about it are mystical. Witches, as Azande conceive them, cannot exist.
>
> The concept of witchcraft nevertheless provides them with a natural philosophy by which the relations between men and unfortunate events are explained and a ready and stereotyped means of reacting to such events.[70]

As has been noted,[71] Smith takes a different view. For him there is a reality to witchcraft. Witchcraft does in fact exist. It is explained by the modern concept of telepathy in which the mind, by means of auto-suggestion, accomplishes psychologically the evil design.

Smith remarks on the logic of the African position. To outlaw the "witch doctors," those who identify the witches, is like trying to legislate against detectives. Since there is something to be said in support of their belief in witchcraft, they can hardly be blamed for finding it out and destroying it. Some laws may be required for the interim, but the ultimate solution does not lie in the promulgation of laws; rather one must go to the heart of the matter and correct the belief which causes such action. To resolve the problem, it is necessary to replace their beliefs with better beliefs. Here Christianity has a role to play.[72]

Yet the more one probes into the question, the more difficult becomes the task of understanding Smith's position. What are these beliefs which Christianity must correct?

It is important to recognize that Smith stakes his opposition to witchcraft on its belief, not its practice. Opposition to the practice of witchcraft would receive a ready assent everywhere in Africa. African society does not support the practice of witchcraft.[73] When he opposes the belief, on the other hand, the question is raised as to just what he means, especially in the light of his affirmation that witchcraft does in fact exist.

Most Westerners and missionaries have interpreted the "correction of the belief" to mean the denial of the reality of witchcraft.[74] Smith clearly does not mean that, for he insists that witchcraft exists.

Unfortunately he never explains his position. He does not spell out what is involved in altering the belief. A possible interpretation of his thought might perhaps emphasize that the only harm is that which a person does to himself by auto-suggestion. Presumably then the evil effects of the belief would be mitigated once the African understands the psychological mechanisms involved. But Smith himself never provides such an explanation. In fact in *The Ila-Speaking Peoples of Northern Rhodesia*, where he talks about auto-suggestion, he does not oppose the belief but merely tries to understand it. In *The Golden Stool* and *The Religion of Lower Races*, where he emphasizes the need to counteract the belief, he never mentions the term "auto-suggestion." It is precisely this confusion of thought which makes it so difficult to interpret his view. Needless to say, his lack of clarity has not shed much light on this difficult problem for the Church.

Africans have been much perplexed regarding the Church's attitude toward witchcraft, and they have not uncommonly believed that the Church harbors witches. Some have looked upon the missionaries as sorcerers.[75] To deny the existence of witchcraft is to them sheer nonsense. M. Wilson affirms that most African Christians are still fearful of it, and they often think that missionaries are only pretending not to believe in it. Those who are in close contact with the missionaries sometimes deny its reality, but they usually confess to a fear of "poisoning" which on analysis is little more than sorcery. An African is quoted as follows: "We all believe in witchcraft; it really exists."[76]

The views of Edwin Smith are more congenial to African ears

than those of most missionaries or Western anthropologists,[77] but he confounds the issue by opposing the belief, or some aspect of it, without explaining just what it is that he opposes.

The major difficulty is that Smith does not address himself to a careful consideration of the concept in all its ramifications. This is unfortunate and somewhat surprising in light of his affirmation that witchcraft is "a greater curse to Africa than ever the slave trade was."[78] He devotes only a few pages to the discussion in all his writings and never addresses himself to the fundamental question.[79] The impression he leaves is that education and science will ultimately resolve the problem for Africa as it did for the West.[80]

The truth of the matter is that the belief in witchcraft has not been reduced by missionary influence or contact with the West.[81] On the contrary, it is possible to argue that belief in witchcraft has never been greater and that it is in fact growing rapidly in present-day Africa.[82]

"Ancestor Worship"

The proper understanding of the place of the ancestors in African worship is still being debated. As in Smith's time, arguments are advanced stating that "worship" is the wrong term since the essential question is one of the relations of an extended family. J. V. Taylor is a contemporary interpreter who represents that view, and significantly he quotes Driberg as support for his position.[83]

The problem of Driberg's argument[84] is that it tends to make the African largely a "non-religious" person. It is not possible to have it both ways. Either the African is very religious, almost too religious, or he is not very religious at all, almost non-religious. If his relationship to the ancestors is "secular," then he is by and large a secular individual.

Furthermore, to say that his relations with the ancestors are "secular" and his relations with God are "religious" is to make a distinction between the two acts which the African does not himself make. As has been seen,[85] sometimes the same entreaty for help includes mention of the ancestors, the lesser divinities and the Supreme Being. To suggest that a portion of the supplication should be classified as a "secular request" and the other portion as "prayer" is to confuse the situation completely.

Smith understands well the complications involved in the use of the term "ancestor worship." That explains his insistence on keeping the phrase in quotations and his continual questioning of its appropriateness to describe African belief and practice.[86]

Unfortunately, Smith does not discuss the wider implications of the belief, specifically the place of God, the ancestors and the living kin as their relationship to each other is seen in the context of dependence of an African in need. He does not, for example, consider the possibility that the relations of a man with the living members of his family might also be "religious" relationships. This is precisely what is implied in the oneness of reality discussed at another point in this study.[87]

To be sure, the African makes no fundamental distinction between his relations with the "living" and the "living-dead"; but it is also true that he does not distinguish radically his relationship to the ancestors from his relationship to God. There are differences between each, but the distinctions are relative, not absolute, since they are in fact differences of position in the hierarchical web of life. Undoubtedly the ancestors are part of the "extended family" of African life, but God is also a part of that extended family. Of significance in this context is Danquah's insistence that God is conceived as the Great Ancestor,[88] an idea which is supported by Sawyerr. Indeed Sawyerr insists that God is both Creator and Ancestor.[89] The family then includes not only the living and the living-dead, but it is stretched hierarchically to its apex in the Creator God.[90]

It would seem that Christianity, with its emphasis on the importance of the distinction between Creator and creature, must temper this understanding of reality, but it would be a tragedy of enormous proportions if the price to be paid were a separation of life into the "sacred" and "secular" categories which have proven to be so barren in the West. This is a subject for future study and debate by African theologians and churchmen. It is not impossible that new biblical insights will emerge from such a study to enrich the understanding of the Christian faith in its totality. Although nothing can be done to compromise the Christian conception that the Supreme God alone is worthy of worship,[91] the African Church must address itself to a rethinking of traditional "ancestor worship" along lines which will breathe new life into the Christian concept of the communion of the saints.[92]

Edwin Smith is not oblivious to the need to utilize the old ancestral ties in reformulating Christian doctrine.[93] However, alongside this he expresses the conviction that the ancestral cult is a transitory phenomenon which cannot stand the competition of Western ideas and must inevitably wither on the vine of African thought.

The greatest hindrance to the durability of the ancestors in the new Africa, according to Smith, is that they do not travel. He is of the opinion that they are bound to the land and cannot therefore accompany the African on his present-day migrations from place to place and especially from village to city.[94]

In stating this Smith seems to have misread the ancestor cult, for other interpreters take issue with him. In noting Smith's remark that the ancestors do not travel, van der Merwe rejoins: "Some of my African informants do not agree with this statement of Dr. Smith."[95]

Van der Merwe agrees with Smith that urbanization has contributed to the decline of the ancestor cult. He suggests as explanations for that phenomenon the difficulty in arranging a real *bira* in the city where all the relatives, living and dead, can gather together and the lack of appropriate mediators to officiate.[96]

Schapera also calls attention to the decline in "ancestor worship" among the Tswana, going so far as to say that it has virtually disappeared.[97] He proceeds to emphasize that the practice of magic persists just as strongly as ever. Van der Merwe takes the argument further, stating that the decline in "ancestor worship" is actually accompanied by an increase in dynamism.[98]

It appears to be true that the impact of Western culture and Christianity had an initial effect in reducing the reliance of Africans on the ancestors, and this was in most cases accompanied by a corresponding increase in the belief in witchcraft and the value of charms. There now appear to be signs on the horizon of a return to the ancestors as well.

Mitchell calls attention to this new emphasis on the ancestors at the expense of beliefs in witchcraft, explaining it on the basis of the inadequacy of witchcraft beliefs to satisfy the socio-psychological needs of the African in the urban situation, especially since "the judicial processes in the town are part of an administrative system which does not countenance witchcraft beliefs."

> There are, after all, time-honoured methods of adjusting the relationships of a man to his ancestor spirits, but none of dealing with a witch in the alien circumstances of the town. A man takes his ancestor spirits to town with him and if he sees their hand in the

misfortunes that befall him he has the satisfaction of knowing that at least there is something he can do about it.[99]

Some commentators, on the other hand, insist that "ancestor worship" has never been seriously affected by the introduction of Western culture and Christianity.[100]

Whatever the explanation, and Africa is a big enough continent to embody different reactions, it is clearly necessary to reassess Smith's view of the ancestor cult and the strength of its position in the African world-view.

TOWARD A SOLUTION

It is not possible to suggest solutions until problems are defined. The fundamental problem of Christianity's approach to the African conception of God is increasingly apparent: how to relate the Christian God to the ambiguity of African life. Edwin Smith fails to see the full dimensions of the African paradox and consequently does not address himself to the fullness of the Christian answer.

One ought not to suppose that the following discussion is a solution in any definitive sense. There has not been enough reflection by a sufficient number of scholars to provide the background for such a claim. In any case it is highly doubtful that a "solution" is likely to come from the pen of a Westerner. The best hope for the future is the increasing preoccupation and study by African theologians and scholars of the relationship of Christianity to African Traditional Religion.[101] The most that can be anticipated here is a presentation of some suggestions pointing "toward a solution."

Whole of Life Approach

It is now clear what has happened and is happening in the Christian churches of Africa. The churches have tried to foster a substitution of Africa's traditional world-view by that of the West.[102]

The Supreme God is brought near through Christian teaching, but belief in Him is not integrated meaningfully into African thought. Hence He remains a "Foreigner" although He is warmly embraced. He belongs to Africa and the Africans. He is their own and they long to have Him back. Yet they do not know what to do with Him when He is returned to them. As a matter of fact, they seem to have managed to get along amazingly well without Him.[103]

Because so many missionaries and African Christians fail to see the full implications of the African question, they also fail to grasp the full significance of the Christian answer.

There is a sense in which the Christian God was not really brought near to African life and thought in the first place. There has been considerable talk of His nearness, and undoubtedly this has had a profound influence on African thought; but at the crucial points of life, He has remained largely transcendent, for He has not been pictured as interested in man's mundane problems.

Taylor calls attention to this with telling effect. He notes "how essentially this-worldly" is the African world-view and "how little it needs a transcendent God."[104] He suggests that Christianity does not differ radically from Islam in championing the cause of the transcendent God. To be sure, Jesus Christ has broken through the circle, but this has not bridged the separation: "The Incarnation has been presented as an isolated crossing over rather than as the closing of a gulf."[105] Taylor warns that "if God remains 'outside' much longer, Africa's this-worldliness will turn to materialism."[106]

All of this means that Christianity is in grave danger of irrelevance in Africa. It also means that Christianity is in danger of fostering a sacred-secular dichotomy equivalent to that which characterizes its expression in the West.[107] God is not looked to as the source of help and concern for all the problems of life. Rather He is relegated to a part of life. His major concern is the "soul" and the "after-life." Man takes care of his own "this-worldly" problems by means of his increasing knowledge and his scientific expertise.[108]

It is not too much to say that the first Africans to attempt an integration of the Christian conception of God into African traditional life were the "independent" churches. This is not the place to attempt an extensive analysis of them. This has been done very ably by others. But the significance of the "independents" for this study cannot be overlooked.

The central issue can be well illustrated by C. G. Baëta's assessment of the problems involved in accepting African independent churches for membership in national Christian councils. Baëta recognizes that both the historical and separatist churches identify themselves as Christian, but he suggests that "the substance of the religion taught by each" is radically different, so much so that the question is raised whether they are "even basically engaged upon the same business." The message of historical Christianity is presented in these words:

> The Christianity taught by the historical churches is a message calling men to repentence to their sin and to a life of faith. If sin is in essence rebellion against God, faith is complete trust in Him through our Lord Jesus Christ, and absolute dependence upon him [sic] in all one's affairs, both for this world and for the hereafter. This faith expresses itself in a life lived in God's forgiveness and grace (which are made available to man through the atoning work of Christ) and dedicated to the performing of God's will.[109]

Addressing himself to a description of Christianity as understood by the separatist churches, Baëta says:

> The Christianity offered by the separatist churches may be described as a power for overcoming the ills of the secular aspect of life. Human need is conceived almost entirely in terms of these ills. While such terms as "sin," "grace," "the precious blood of our Lord and Saviour Jesus Christ," and other Christian themes are constantly spoken about, the central preoccupation is and remains how to cope effectively with the ills of worldly life. For instance, "sin" is really relevant only in so far as it is a potent cause of bodily, mental, and social disorders; the significance of "the blood of Christ" resides in the fact that, by doing away with sin, it prepares the way for, or itself directly effects, bodily healing; "faith" is to entertain no inward doubt whatsoever that the particular help sought will be received.[110]

Baëta goes on to quote from the public invitation of a "typical" independent church to the effect that men are to bring their fears about witches, bad luck, poverty, illness, misfortune, barrenness (in short all their problems) to Jesus who will save those who come in faith. He notes that the requests are the same as those in African Traditional Religion and indicates that this explains their great attraction. Personally he questions whether they express the essence of the Christian faith since they confuse the "beneficial by-products" with the whole of Christianity. He calls attention to the special ceremonies which are an integral part of the separatist ritual. If these were "mere aids to worship," they could be baptized into the Christian faith. However, they are more than this. They are indispensable methods to secure the desired blessings. Failure is usually attributed to the individual's lack of faith. To be sure, the separatists call on the Christian God and this is a significant difference, although it is the only one evident.[111]

Baëta's views are extremely important. He is an African scholar of first rank and a committed churchman. He is one of the few African Christians to address himself to a thorough study of the African independence movement.[112] Throughout his life he has been deeply concerned about the indigenization of the Church.[113] Yet all of this only serves to illustrate the depths of the problem.

Significantly, Baëta feels obliged to suggest that the Christianity offered by the separatist churches is seen as "a power for over-coming the ills of the secular aspect of life."[114] Yet it is precisely this separation of life into "religious" and "secular" categories that Africans generally criticize. Busia is not alone in saying: "Religion and life are inseparable, and life is not comparted into sacred and secular."[115]

All of this is not meant to negate the significance of Baëta's emphasis on sin, forgiveness, grace and faith. Although these may not have been in the forefront of African thought, that is not in itself a negation of their significance. Nor is it to sanction all the techniques used by the "separatists" or to say that, by addressing themselves entirely to the problems created by the ambiguity of life, they exhaust the meaning of the Christian message about God.[116] It is merely to suggest that the two emphases need not necessarily be placed in opposition to one another as Baëta does. There seems no good reason to indicate that the God who is concerned about man's sin is not also interested in his poverty and unemployment, and not merely in a secularized Western sense which strips these of their spiritual implications. Faith relates not only to the life to come but to this life as well. Surely the God who forgives can also heal.

The Christian God was probably never brought so near to African life and thought as Edwin Smith supposed. Neverthe-less, there are signs that following the preaching of the early missionaries, He was taken more seriously than He is today. This is partially a reflection of the difference in the missionaries them-selves. Many younger missionaries are manifestly less dependent upon God than their predecessors. They are not nearly so prone to pray on every occasion and to take their cares to God and often have serious reservations regarding emotional revivals. The tend-ency of Christianity in the course of its history in Africa has been increasingly to separate God from the life of men, in spite of its protestations to the contrary. The consequence is a new absenteeism, which differs from African Traditional Religion mainly in that it affirms God's theoretical presence while denying the practical effects of that belief.

The Christian God is increasingly remote in Africa because He is unconcerned with man's everyday problems. The "independent" churches have seen this more clearly than their counterparts, both missionary and African, in the historical churches. Although not particularly sympathetic to independent Christianity, Oosthuizen notes their insight:

> It has been clear so far that the main emphasis of many of the nativistic movements is on man's destiny. They are interested not in the creation of the universe, but in divine involvement. The God of the mission is too remote for a system in which men's "gods" belonged to their lineage, and although far removed, could be approached through their ancestors. The God in the Christianity with which they came in contact had much to do with their souls, and with certain individuals, but not with them in all spheres of life and as a whole community.[117]

The future of Christianity in Africa is contingent on its willingness to assess realistically God's present position. His growing remoteness, because of Christianity's failure to integrate its belief into the whole of life, can no longer be ignored. Ironically the most hopeful sign on the horizon is that of the independent churches, not because they have attained to an adequate expression of Christianity, but because they have prophetically pointed in the direction toward which Christianity must move if it is to speak meaningfully and relevantly to the African situation.[118] There are signs that their challenge may be taken seriously by the "historical" churches.[119]

Centrality of Problem of Evil

If Christianity is to speak meaningfully to Africa today, it must take seriously the challenge of addressing itself to the problems created by the existence of evil and the ambiguity of life. It is Edwin Smith's failure to perceive this and to do it which constitutes his greatest weakness.

There are two important issues involved: the intellectual problem of God's relationship to evil and the emotional problem of how men can deal with misfortune in the context of their faith in God.

As to the intellectual side, it is apparent that Christianity also has difficulty in providing a fully satisfactory explanation for the problem of evil. Judaism and Christianity have in fact experimented with different solutions.

The Deuteronomic explanation, which was dominant in the early history of the Israelite nation, understood evil as guilt. Both as a nation and individually the Israelites prospered when they did right and suffered calamity when they did wrong.

That the idea is not ultimately satisfactory is apparent from the Book of Job. That book leaves the hint that Job's misfortune is a "testing of faith," which is a hard saying, but undoubtedly the book's keenest insight is Job's recognition that there is no satisfactory intellectual solution.

In late Judaism and at the time of the New Testament, there is an increasing emphasis on dualism as an explanation, which is important in that it makes possible a center for evil divorced completely from God. Nevertheless, dualism does not resolve all the intellectual problems in that it leaves unanswered the questions of the origin of Satan and the relationship of the Creator and the Adversary.

The task of the African Christian Church is perhaps in the long run not so much to provide a fully satisfactory intellectual answer as it is to recognize the reality of the problem and to open the door to a discussion of it in all its fullness in the Christian context. Too often in the past missionaries and African pastors have refused to concern themselves with the "reality" of evil. They have either ignored the problem entirely or suggested that it can be explained satisfactorily from the context of human sin. A climate must be created in which Africans are free to express their real feelings and sentiments and to explore in all its fullness Christianity's implications for those sentiments. Nothing whatsoever is to be gained by African Christians being fearful to express their conviction that witches exist and dynamistic practices are useful if in fact these are their real sentiments.[120]

Welbourn perceptively calls attention to the ironic fact that Christians now are made to feel guilty for sharing in many cases the beliefs of the New Testament.[121]

It is to be hoped that African theologians, because of their own grounding in traditional thought-forms, may provide a deeper

understanding of the question as they increasingly address themselves to it. It is not too much to anticipate that new insights will
emerge from that examination which will enrich the total witness
of Christianity throughout the world. Nevertheless, one should
not be surprised if in the final analysis the intellectual solution
to the problem of evil and the ambiguity of life remains as
intractable to the African theologian as to the European.[122]

Christianity does not stand or fall on its ability to provide a
fully satisfactory intellectual answer for the problem of evil.
Even if its answers fail to resolve all the intellectual problems
involved in dealing with evil, its solutions are not intrinsically
less satisfying than those of African Traditional Religion. The
key to Christian success in the matter will not be gauged on its
intellectual answer but on its practical ability to satisfy the
emotional need of Africans to deal with the problem of evil in
the context of their worship of the Creator God.[123]

The full significance of this remains for African theologians
and churchmen to say, but some insights are already available from
the experience of the independent churches.[124] For one thing it
is clear that Christianity must take more seriously than it ever
has to date the challenge of healing[125] and exorcism.[126]

This does not mean that there are any stereotyped answers as
to how this may be expressed. What is most essential is that
the people be given the assurance that their real problems are
taken seriously and that God is *really* near and concerned with
them.[127] This cannot be done ultimately by means of intellectual
affirmations but must be felt and experienced in an emotional and
ritual fashion.[128]

The experience of Simon Kimbangu and the movement which
he established in the lower Congo during the 1920's serves as a
good illustration. Although after his exile syncretistic elements[129]
made their appearance, Kimbangu himself was orthodox in dogma
and biblical orientation.[130] He insisted that the people abandon
their *minkisi* fetishes, their drums and polygamy which were
the very foundations of their traditional life, and he had extraordinary results in persuading them actually to do it.[131] The key
to his success was that he provided a spiritual substitute for the
fetish as an aid in illness. This was accomplished in the first place
by taking seriously the New Testament mandate for healing, in
spite of the fact that the evidence of his ability in this regard
is mixed.[132] Furthermore, the baptismal ritual became the sign of

entry into the community of the elect where the power of witch-craft could no longer molest them.[133] It is easy to criticize elements of Kimbanguist belief and practice,[134] but such an endeavor will only be useful if the Christians of the historical churches also take seriously the prophetic challenge of Kimbanguism.

The Kimbanguists have grappled not only with the emotional but also with the intellectual aspects of the problem of evil. In the beginning the popular sentiment tended to identify Kimbangu with the native *nganga* who purified and protected his people from witchcraft. At the present time there is a tendency to identify the witch with the figure of Satan in the Book of Job.[135] Perhaps even more significant is the Kimbanguist teaching that "religion does not automatically give protection from sickness and calamities, as the people would so readily like to believe."[136] This clearly is an African modification of Job's affirmation that there is a mystery involved in the problem which defies final explanation.

The important element to note is that the strength of the Kimbanguists does not reside in this or any other intellectual affirmation but in the serious consideration which they give to the problem and their attempt to relate it ritually and emotionally to the Christian concept of God.

Christian Answer

It has been stated above that the intellectual solution of Christianity for the problem of evil may not be more satisfactory than that of African Traditional Religion, but that it is no less satisfactory. That is to understate the fullness of the Christian answer.

In spite of the problem of evil, the Christian insists that God is near and concerned and completely good. Smith sees this. This is his great contribution. That he fails to see it in the context of the centrality of the problem of evil is his weakness.

In other words, Christianity does not resolve the paradox of God's relationship to the ambiguity of life, but the Christian faith does refocus that paradox. While not giving an incontrovertible intellectual answer, Christianity insists, against African Traditional Religion, on maintaining faith in God's love and goodness in the face of evil.

This does not mean that there are no fatalistic elements in the New Testament. Clearly there are. But they are dominated by three elements: (1) Jesus' sense of God's nearness and goodness as exemplified in his phrase *Abba*, Father; (2) the Christian recognition of God's nearness and goodness as seen in His coming to men in Jesus; and (3) the development of the concept of Satan as the source of evil.

Sin and evil are not God's will but the very opposite. God is not both good and bad; He is entirely good. He is not both dependable and capricious; He is entirely dependable. As Sawyerr says:

> The Christian attitude, firmly anchored in the implications of the Incarnation, should also reject any suggestions that both 'good' and 'bad' actions, i.e., acts, both socially constructive and morally destructive, can be equaly sponsored by God. To the Christian, God is holy and no evil resides in Him. . . . He is neither fickle nor capricious.[137]

Christians may also talk of the transcendence and immanence of God, but they mean something quite different from the thought of African Traditional Religion. God is not good in His transcendence and evil in His immanence. He is only good.[138] In African Religion God is most fearful in His immanence. Christianity insists that the most profound expression of God's love and goodness is His coming among men in Jesus Christ.

The Christians take the Fall seriously, but this does not provoke God's departure. Rather it provides the occasion for a new venture in search of man, which has its culmination in the Incarnation.

All of this comes to focus at the Cross. Here is God willing to suffer for men, indeed to suffer with men. Here is God's ultimate identification with evil through which He shows His goodness and love.[139]

Nevertheless, Christians must make the Incarnation and Cross continual realities in their own experience, through the power of the Holy Spirit, if they are to convince others of the unity of God's transcendence and immanence. Otherwise the Incarnation will continue to be looked upon, as Taylor remarks, merely as an isolated crossing and not a bridging of the gap.[140]

Jesus both healed and forgave sins. He exorcised the evil spirits and demonstrated God's grace. He was concerned about this life and the life to come. Why then must present-day Christians confine their attention to forgiveness, faith and the after-life merely because African Traditional Religion tends to confine its attention to healing, exorcism and the present life? Cannot grace relate to man's present life as well as his future?

Space does not permit a full analysis of all that is involved in bringing the Christian conception of God to bear on the totality of man's problems in Africa. Clearly the task must be accomplished in such a way that man does not become a mere manipulator of God.[141] This is the weakness of many of the independent churches, about which Baëta utters a valuable warning. Nevertheless, the danger cannot be prevented by ignoring the relationship of God to man's calamities, as the Christian Church in Africa has tended to do to date.

Moreover, while addressing itself in a fresh and vital way to the individual ills of man in Africa, Christianity must also speak anew to his social ills. Christianity needs to take seriously man's individual problems, but also thought regarding the problem of evil must be pushed beyond the individual to the great social forces which increasingly determine man's destiny. It is in this area that the concerns of the African and Western Christian increasingly coalesce. Jesus was interested in both, and the Church cannot act otherwise.

The insight of Africa—that life is a totality, that there can be no ultimate separation between the sacred and secular, and that religion must be brought to bear on all of man's problems—is Africa's great contribution to the West, a belief and faith which the West desperately needs. When this is coupled with the Christian recognition that "religion" relates to the Creator God who is near in Jesus or it is nothing, there is achieved the fulfillment not only of religion but life itself.

10

Conclusion

The weaknesses of Edwin Smith's presentation have been noted. They are real and significant. One stands out as predominant, the fundamental flaw of his scholarly edifice: Smith's evolutionary orientation. It is this aspect of his thought which distorts his understanding of both African Traditional Religion and the relationship of Christianity to it. It impels him to orient his study toward an elusive quest for the origin of religion and obscures from his view the paradox which lies at the center of the African conception of God. It leads him to an inadequate grasp of revelation and a dubious perception of Christianity as the fulfillment of African Traditional Religion.

As real as these weaknesses are, however, the last word in this assessment dare not be negative. The values inherent in Smith's study are enormous and must not be lost sight of. His recognition of the significance of *ubwanga*, his description of the triangle of dynamism-spiritism-theism, his grasp of the relationship of the worlds of the seen and unseen, the role of diviner and prophet, the significance of dreams, the place of taboo and the importance of the belief in God are lasting contributions to the understanding of African Traditional Religion. His perception of the Christian contribution is no less significant: the Church as the new trans-tribal clan, the morality of the heart as a corrective for taboo morality, the broadening of the petitionary element in worship and most important of all God as the Seeker of men.

Edwin Smith played his part in the great debate, and it now becomes the turn of others—especially African scholars and theologians—to carry on where he left off, to recognize his weaknesses and build on his strengths.

That the Christian message has an appeal in Africa is apparent from its past and present success. But there are also danger signs on the horizon. Some years ago Roland Oliver warned of the possibility that Christianity might disintegrate at the center while expanding at the circumference.[1] That danger is still a reality. Much depends on the Church's willingness to assess the present position of God in African Christianity and its ability to reorient its message; so that the God who revealed Himself fully in Jesus Christ will be able to speak in a new way to the deepest needs of the African heart.

Glossary of Foreign Terms

Abba—Aramaic word used by Jesus for God, meaning "Father."

Adonay—Hebrew name for God.

Adroa or *Adronga*—Lugbara terms for God in His transcendence.

Adroa 'ba o' dupiri—Lugbara phrase meaning "God the taker away of men."

Adro—Lugbara term for God in His immanence.

Amosu—Ashanti praise title for God, meaning "Giver of rain."

Amovwa—Ashanti praise title for God, meaning "Giver of sunshine."

Asase Ya—Ashanti name for Old Mother Earth.

Assista—Nandi name for God.

balubare—Ganda word for the departmental gods.

bara—Ashanti term meaning "puberty."

baraka—Arabic word for *mana*.

bira—Shona term referring to "ancestor worship" ceremonies.

buditazhi—Ila word referring to a misdeed for which a fine is levied but not so serious as to cause automatic retribution.

bwalo—open circular meeting place common to many African peoples.

Chaba—Ila praise title for God, meaning "the Giver."

Chaba-wakeaba-ocitadiwa—Ila term for God, meaning "the Giver who gives also what cannot be eaten."

chifundo—Ila word referring to a line on the ground which cannot be passed. The phrases *shifundo shaka Leza* and *chifundo chaka Leza* have moral connotations and have to do with actions prohibited by God.

Chilenga—Ila praise title for God, meaning "the Creator."

Chilenge—Batwa praise title for God, meaning "the Creator."

chipa—a type of divining-rod found among the Ba-ila.

chisapi—Ila word meaning "indecorum."

Chirazamauya—Shona epithet for God, meaning "the one who provides for good and bad."

Chirozva-mauva—Shona epithet for God, meaning "the one who has power to destroy the good and the bad."

chisondo—Ila noun meaning "divining instrument."

Deng—Nuer name for the greatest of the spirits of the air; also a Dinka divinity.

Elohim—Hebrew term for God.

Engai nanyokye—Massai red god who is bad.

Engai narok—Massai black god who is good.

funku owetwe—Ila phrase meaning "beer of the ash," forming part of the funeral ceremonies. Other ceremonies include: *funku owa nsako*, "beer of the shafts"; *funku owa kuzhola munganda*, "beer to bring back the deceased into the house"; *funku owa madidila*, "beer of the final weeping."

igabade—Banda word for "pumpkin" in common use.

Ihuwa—Pare word meaning both "God and "the sun."

ikintu—Banyarwanda term for "being who does not have intelligence."

Imana—Banyarwanda name for God.

impindo, shinda, insambwe—African words for mana, not identified by tribe.

inzuikizi—Ila word meaning "witchcraft medicine."

Ipaokubozha—Ila epithet for God, meaning "He who gives and causes to rot."

Juok—Shilluk name for God.

Kabaka—Ganda title for the king.

Kamona—Barotse name for the first man.

karma—Hindu term for retributive justice in which a person's life is determined by his deeds in a previous incarnation.

kasambi—a type of divining rod found among the Ba-ila.

kashia mumbo—Ila expression meaning "it is no concern of yours."

Katonda—Ganda name for God.

Kemba—Ila epithet for God, meaning "the Rain-Giver."

Kibuka—Ganda god of war, brother of Mukasa, God's chief minister.

Kiriamagi—Pare name for the first man.

kukomba—Ila verb meaning "to worship."

Kurios—Greek word for Lord.

kusonda—Ila verb meaning "to divine."

kutalabala—Ila verb meaning "to be age-lasting, to be everywhere at all times."

kutula and *kupaila*—Ila words used of presents given by one person to another and especially of gifts to a superior, including the divinities.

Kyala—Konde and Nyakyusa name for God.

Kyumbi—Pare name for God.

Leza—Ila name for God.

Leza wakombola mungo wakwe—Ila phrase meaning "God has snapped off his pumpkin," referring to a person's death.

Lobwe—Ila praise title for Shimunenga, meaning "Gatherer of men."

lubambo—Ila word meaning "an arranged thing," signifying a publicly recognized extra-marital relationship.

lubeta—Ila juridical term referring to a law case. The phrase *kudi lubeta kwizeulu*, "today there is a lubeta above" is a reference to God's judgment.

Lubumba—Ila epithet for God meaning "the Moulder."

lufwa Nzambi—Bacongo phrase meaning "a death from God" or "a bad death."

luloa—Ila term for the blood offering used as propitiation in cases of murder.

lunyensu—Congo-Fioti word for *mana*.

Luvhunabaumba—Ila praise title for God, meaning "Deliverer of those in trouble."

lwembe—Ila word for "weregild."

lwanga—Ila word for a public altar.

mampuba—Ila word to describe the emotion of fear, reverence and affection.

mana—The Melanesian term for the universal "power" inherent in all things. Smith compares it to "electricity" and "luck."

Mangwe—Ila epithet for God meaning "the Flooder."

mayembe—Ganda term for "fetishes."

Mawu—Ewe name for God.

minkisi—Bacongo word meaning "fetish" or "charm."

Modimo—Tswana name for God.

Mukasa—God's chief minister in the Ganda pantheon.

mulabile Leza—Ila phrase "one upon whom God has looked," used to describe those bereft of children.

mulozhi—Ila word meaning "witch" or "warlock."

munganga—Ila noun meaning "doctor"; the one who manipulates *ubwanga*.

Muninde—Ila praise title for God meaning "the Guardian."

muntu—common word for "man" among the Bantu-speaking Africans.

musediakwe—Ila word for "guardian spirit," "namesake" or "tutelary genius."

musonzhi—Ila noun meaning "diviner."

Mususi—Ganda god of earthquakes, father of Mukasa, God's chief minister.

Mutalabala—Ila epithet for God, meaning "the one who is age-lasting and everywhere at the same time."

muzhimo—Ila word for ancestral spirit or divinity. *Muzimo* (plural *mizimu*) is the Ganda term for the ghosts and is common among Bantu-speaking peoples.

mwazhi—A poison shrub in Zambia; Ila term for the "poison oracle."

Mwari—Karanga name for God.

Naawun—Tallensi name for "God" or "Heaven."

Nalwanga—Ganda goddess, wife of Mukasa, God's chief minister.

Namakungwe—Ila praise title for God, meaning "the one from whom all things come."

Namulenga—Ila praise title for God, meaning "the Creator."

namenze—An Ila beverage, the only drink permitted during smelting operations.

Namesi—Ila praise title for God, meaning "the Water-Giver."

Nasilele—Barotse name for God's wife.

Natamaukilwa—Ila word applied to God, meaning "the one who constantly changes his mind."

ndufu lwaka Leza—Ila phrase meaning "it is a death which comes from God."

Ngai—Gikuyu name for God.

nganga—Bacongo word meaning "doctor."

Ngwale nkolo—Karanga name for the oracle of God.

Nhialic—Dinka word for God, translated by Lienhardt as "Divinity."

nkondo mi Nzambi—Bacongo phrase meaning "the laws of God."

notangala Leza udikubwene—Ila phrase "when you are filled with joy, God sees you," meaning that disaster will soon strike.

nsiriba—Ganda term for "amulets."

ntoro—Ashanti word meaning "breath" or "familiar spirit."

Nuor-Yin—Tallensi phrase meaning "prenatal destiny" or "predestined fate."

Nyambe—Barotse and Luyi name for God.

Nyame dua—Ashanti term meaning "God's tree," a family altar dedicated to the Sky God.

Nyankopon—Ashanti name for God.

Nzambi—Ndembu and Bacongo name for God.

Nzambi watanda—Bacongo term for the transcendent God (God above).

Nzambi wamutsele—Bacongo term for the immanent God (God below).

obosom—Ashanti term for the lesser gods.

ogun—Yoruba word for *mana*.

Olódùmarè—Yoruba name for God.

Onyame—Ashanti name for God.

onyiru—Lugbara word meaning "good."

onzi—Lugbara word meaning "bad."

orenda, manitou, wakonda—North American Indian words for *mana*.

Raluvimbi—Venda word meaning both "Creator" and "earthquake."

Ruremakwaci—Banyarwanda name for God when He does not create successfully.

Ruwa—Chagga name for God.

samanfo—Ashanti word meaning "ancestors."

senohi—Makololo term for "seer" or "prophet."

Shakapanga—Ila epithet for God, meaning "the Constructor."

Shakatabwa—Ila epithet for God, meaning "the Faller."

Shichenchemenwa—Ila epithet for God, meaning "the Good-Natured One." Also the one who takes advantage of a person's good nature by asking for unwarranted favors.

shikisapi—Ila word for a rude person who commonly breaks tribal etiquette.

shimubi—A type of divining rod found among the Ba-ila.

shimubi mwaniche—A type of divining rod found among the Ba-ila.

Shimunenga—The principal communal divinity of the Ba-ila at Kasenga.

Shikakunamo—Ila epithet for God, meaning "the Besetting One."

Shintemwe—Ila praise title for God; meaning "the Compassionate."

suman—Ashanti word for *mana;* also used for "charms."

sumu ku Nzambi—Bacongo phrase meaning "an act against God."

Sungwasungwa—Ila word applied to God, meaning "the one who stirs up another to do good and bad things."

σώζω, Σιατώζω—Greek verbs meaning "to save, rescue."

tanga—Banda word for "pumpkin" but not commonly used.

Tetereboensu—Ashanti praise title for God, meaning "widespread Creator of water."

Theos—Greek word for God.

Tilo—Tonga word meaning both "God" and "the sky."

tonda—Adjectival form of the verb *kutonda* and the noun *mutondo*, meaning "taboo."

Tweaduampon—Ashanti epithet for God, meaning "the one who is dependable."

ubwanga or *bwanga*—Ila words for *mana.*

Udimbabachembe—Ila praise title for Shimunenga, meaning "Giver of virility to males."

uina ng'aela—Ila phrase applied to God, meaning "He has nowhere or nowhen that he comes to an end."

ula or *ukaho*—Forbidden fruit of the banana garden of Chagga mythology.

umuntu—Banyarwanda term for "being who has intelligence."

Unkulunkulu—Zulu name for God, meaning either "the old, old one" or "the great, great one."

Ushatwakwe—Ila epithet for God, meaning "the one who is Master and Owner of his things."

Voortrekkers—South African Dutch who migrated from Cape Province to the Transvaal in the 1830s.

Wanga—Oldest of the Ganda gods, grandfather of Mukasa, God's chief minister.

Wele gumali or *Wele evimbi*—Vugusu name for "the black god" who is responsible for the evil of life.

Wele ómuwanga—Vugusu name for "the White God" who is responsible for the good of life.

Yahwe—Hebrew name for God.

Bibliography

A. Books by Edwin W. Smith

A Handbook of the Ila Language. London: Oxford University Press, 1907.

Ila Made Easy. Kasenga, Northern Rhodesia: Book Room of Baila-Batonga Mission, 1914.

The Religion of Lower Races, as Illustrated by the African Bantu. New York: The Macmillan Company, 1923.

Robert Moffat, One of God's Gardeners. London: C.M.S. Press, 1925.

The Christian Mission in Africa: A Study Based on the Work of the International Conference at Le Zoute, Belgium, September 14th to 21st, 1926. London: The International Missionary Council, 1926.

The Golden Stool: Some Aspects of the Conflict of Cultures in Modern Africa. London: Church Missionary Society, 1927.

Tales of God's Packmen. London: British and Foreign Bible Society, 1928.

The Way of the White Fields in Rhodesia: A Survey of Christian Enterprise in Northern and Southern Rhodesia. London: World Dominion Press, 1928.

The Secret of the African. London: Student Christian Movement, 1929.

Aggrey of Africa: A Study in Black and White. London: Student Christian Movement, 1929.

Exploration in Africa. London: J. M. Dent and Sons, 1929.

The Shrine of a People's Soul. London: C.M.S. Press, 1929.

The Story of the B.F.B.S. London: S.P.C.K., 1930.

The Impossible. London: British and Foreign Bible Society, 1932.
African Beliefs and Christian Faith. London: Lutterworth Press, 1936.
The Basic St. John. London: Trench, Trubner and Co., 1938.
The Mabilles of Basutoland. London: Hodder and Stoughton, 1939.
Events in African History. New York: The Committee on Africa, the War, and Peace Aims, 1942.
Knowing the African. London: Lutterworth Press, 1946.
Plans and People: A Dynamic Science of Man in the Service of Africa. London: Lutterworth Press, 1948.
The Life and Times of Daniel Lindley. London: Epworth Press, 1949.
African Ideas of God: A Symposium. London: Edinburgh House Press, 1950.
The Blessed Missionaries. London: Oxford University Press, 1950.
Great Lion of Bechuanaland: The Life and Times of Roger Price, Missionary. London: Independent Press, 1957.
Smith, Edwin W. and Dale, Andrew M. *The Ila-Speaking Peoples of Northern Rhodesia.* 2 vols. 2nd ed. New Hyde Park, N.Y.: University Books, 1968.

B. ARTICLES BY EDWIN W. SMITH*

"The Ila-Speaking People of Northern Rhodesia." *Journal of the African Society,* XX (January, 1921), 89–94.
"The Sublimation of Bantu Life and Thought." *International Review of Missions,* XI (January, 1922), 83–95.
"An Unbroken Fellowship: the Story of 120 Years' Close Co-operation." *Church Missionary Review,* LXXIV (December, 1923), 212–220.
"The Bible in the Empire." *The Native Races of the Empire.* Edited by Godfrey Lagden. London: W. Collins Sons and Co., 1924.
"An Unbroken Fellowship: the Story of 120 Years' Close Cooperation." *Church Missionary Review,* LXXV (March, 1924), 18–26.
"The Disintegration of African Society." *The East and the West,* XXII (April, 1924), 143–160.
"Social Anthropology and Missionary Work." *International Review of Missions,* XIII (October, 1924), 518–531.
"These Fifty Years in Africa: 1875–1925." *Church Missionary Review,* LXXVI (December, 1925), 296–308.
"Some Periodical Literature Concerning Africa." *International Review of Missions,* XV (July, 1926), 602–607.
"Exploring the African's Soul." *The Missionary Review of the World* (o.s.), LI (October, 1928), 793–798.

* The Bibliography does not include Smith's "Editorial Notes" in the *Journal of the African Society* and the *Journal of the Royal African Society,* 1923–1940 or his "Notes and News" in *Africa,* 1944–1948.

"La Langue Indigène et l'Education Africaine." *Le Monde non-Chrétien*, II (March, 1938), 21–28.

"Indigenous Education in Africa." *Essays Presented to C. G. Seligman*. Edited by E. E. Evans-Pritchard, *et al.* London: Kegan Paul, Trench, Trubner and Co., 1934.

"The Story of the Institute: A Survey of Seven Years." *Africa*, VII (January, 1934), 1–27.

"Presidential Address: Anthropology and the Practical Man." *Journal of the Royal Anthropological Institute of Great Britain and Ireland*, LXIV (January-June, 1934), xiii–xxxvii.

"Obituary Notice of H. A. Junod." *Man*, XXXIV (July, 1934), 111.

"Sectional Proceedings of the International Congress, Ethnography, Africa." *Man*, XXXIV (September, 1934), 148–149.

"Presidential Address: Africa: What do we know of it?" *Journal of the Royal Anthropological Institute of Great Britain and Ireland*, LXV (January-June, 1935), 1–81.

"Inzuikizi." *Africa*, VIII (October, 1935), 471–480.

"Land in Kenya." *Journal of the Royal African Society*, XXXV (July, 1936), 246–250.

"The South African Protectorates." *Journal of the Royal African Society*, XXXVII (April, 1938), 199–205.

"Obituary: Robert Sutherland Rattray: 1881–14th May, 1938." *Man*, XXXVIII (July, 1938), 107–108.

"The Language of Pygmies of the Ituri." *Journal of the Royal African Society*, XXXVII (October, 1938), 464–470.

"Polygamy and African Marriage Customs." Paper presented to a missionary conference on Africa, called to follow up the recommendations of the Tambaram Conference, New York, N.Y., December 9, 1939, 1–6. (Mimeographed.)

"The Function of Folk Tales." *Journal of the Royal African Society*, XXXIX (January, 1940), 64–83.

"Association and Assimilation in the Christian Mission." *International Review of Missions*, XXX (July, 1941), 324–336.

Smith, Edwin W., *et al.* "The Indigenous African Church." *The Church Conference on African Affairs*. Westerville, Ohio: Otterbein College, 1942, pp. 1–32.

"Lord Lugard, the Man." *Africa*, XV (July, 1945), 112–113.

"A School for Translators." *International Review of Missions*, XXXIV (July, 1945), 243–252.

"African Symbolism: Henry Myers Lecture, 1952." *Journal of the Royal Anthropological Institute of Great Britain and Ireland*, LXXXII (January-June, 1952), 13–37.

"Foreword." *West African Religion* by Geoffrey Parrinder. 2nd ed. London: The Epworth Press, 1961.

C. A Selection of Book Reviews by Edwin W. Smith*

"The Organization of 'Primitive' Society." Review of *Primitive Society*, by Robert H. Lowie. *International Review of Missions*, XI (April, 1922), 300–302.

"African Ethnography." Reviews of *The Bakitara or Banyoro*, by John Roscoe; *The Banyankole*, by John Roscoe; *In Witch-Bound Africa*, by Frank H. Melland; and *Equatoria: The Lado Enclave*, by Major C. H. Stigand. *International Review of Missions*, XIII (January, 1924), 128–129.

Review of *Ashanti*, by Captain R. S. Rattray. *Journal of the African Society*, XXIII (July, 1924), 317–318.

Review of *Bibliothèque-Congo. Vol. IX La Poésie chez les Primitifs, ou Contes, Fables, Récits et Proverbes du Rwanda*, by Eugene Hurel; *Vols. X and XI Mayombsch Idioticon*, by Leo Bittremieux; *Vol. XIV La Langue Kisonge*, by A. Samain. *Journal of the African Society*, XXIII (July, 1924), 326–327.

Review of *The Lango*, by J. H. Driberg. *Journal of the African Society*, XXIII (July, 1924), 329–331.

Review of *Principi di Diritto consuetudinario della Somalia Italiana meridionale*, by Massimo Colucci. *Journal of the African Society*, XXIV (October, 1924), 73–74.

Review of *The Language-Families of Africa*, by A. Werner. *Church Missionary Review*, LXXVI (June, 1925), 179.

Review of *The Mythology of All Races, Vol. VII. Armenian*, by Mardiros H. Ananikian; *African*, by Alice Werner. *Journal of the African Society*, XXV (April, 1926), 298–299.

Review of *The Peoples of Southern Nigeria*, by P. Amaury Talbot. *Journal of the African Society*, XXV (July, 1926), 378–381.

" 'Primitive' Psychology." Review of *How Natives Think*, by Lucien Lévy-Bruhl. *International Review of Missions*, XV (October, 1926), 760–763.

Review of *Religion and Art in Ashanti*, by Capt. R. S. Rattray. *Journal of the African Society*, XXVI (July, 1927), 404–406.

Review of *Arabic Literature*, by H. A. R. Gibb. *Journal of the African Society*, XXVI (July, 1927), 408–409.

Review of *Rissalat al Tawhid: exposé de la religion musulmane*, traduite de l'Arabe du Cheikh Moustaphia Abdou par B. Michel et le Cheikh Moustapha Abdel Razik. *Journal of the African Society*, XXVII (October, 1927), 93.

Review of *A History of South Africa*, by Eric A. Walker. *Journal of the African Society*, XXVIII (July, 1928), 419–420.

Review of *The Life of a South Arican Tribe*, by Henri A. Junod. *Africa*, I (July, 1928), 391–392.

* Edwin W. Smith wrote more than 300 book reviews.

Review of *Kirk on the Zambesi, A Chapter of African History*, by R. Coupland, *Africa*, 11 (April, 1929), 213.

"The Root of Primitive Belief." Reviews of *The Soul of the Bantu*, by W. C. Willoughby and *The 'Soul' of the Primitive*, by Lucien Lévy-Bruhl. *International Review of Missions*, XVIII (April, 1929), 284–287.

"A Batch of Biographies." Reviews of *Livingstone*, by R. J. Campbell; *The Story of David Livingstone*, by W. P. Livingstone; *Thomas Birch Freeman: The Son of an African*, by F. Deaville Walker; *Tucker of Uganda: Artist and Apostle*, by Arthur P. Shepherd; and *The Life of Titus Mtembu*, by James Mtembu. *International Review of Missions*, XIX (January, 1930), 127–129.

Review of *The South-Eastern Bantu*, by J. H. Soga. *Man*, XXXI (March, 1931), 51–52.

Review of *The Khoisan Peoples of South Africa*, by I. Schapera. *Man*, XXXI (May, 1931), 91–93.

"Fresh Light Upon African Religion." Reviews of *Nuer Customs and Folklore*, by Ray Huffman: *The Bavenda*, by H. A. Stayt; and *Tales Told in Togoland*, by A. W. Cardinall. *International Review of Missions*, XX (October, 1931), 596–589.

"The Lambas." Review of *The Lambas of Northern Rhodesia: A Study of their Customs and Beliefs*, by Clement M. Doke. *International Review of Missions*, XXI (July, 1932), 429–431.

"Some Books about Africans." Reviews of *Nature-Worship and Taboo*, by W. C. Willoughby; *Geistesleben Afrikanischer Völker im Lichte des Evangeliums*, by Ernst Johannsen; *Hunger and Work in a Savage Tribe*, by Audrey I. Richards; *The Ama-Xosa; Life and Customs*, by John H. Soga; *Notes on the History of the Tumbuka-Kamanga Peoples. Notes on the Speech of the Tumbuka-Kamanga Peoples*, by T. Cullen Young; and *Die Stammeslehren der Dschagga. Band I*, by Bruno Gutmann. *International Review of Missions*, XXII (January, 1933), 120–123.

Review of *Notes on the History of the Tumbuka-Kamanga Peoples. Notes on the Speech of the Tumbuka-Kamanga Peoples*, by T. Cullen Young. *Man*, XXXIII (January, 1933), 19–20.

Review of *Bantu Beliefs and Magic*, by C. W. Hobley. *Journal of the Royal African Society*, XXXVII (October, 1938), 520–521.

"Law and Custom in West and South Africa." Reviews of *Niger Ibos*, by G. T. Basden, and *A Handbook of Tswana Law and Custom*, by I. Schapera. *International Review of Missions*, XXVII (October, 1938), 680–682.

"The Book of the Quarter: The Exploitation of East Africa." Review of *The Exploitation of East Africa, 1856–1890: The Slave Trade and the Scramble*, by R. Coupland. *Journal of the Royal African Society*, XXXVIII (October, 1939), 483–489.

"Primitive Peoples." Review of *The Economic Life of Primitive Peoples*, by Melville J. Herskovits. *International Review of Missions*, XXIX (July, 1940), 406–408.

"David Livingstone." Reviews of *Some Letters from Livingstone*, by R. Coupland, and *Livingstone the Liberator*, by James I. Macnair. *International Review of Missions*, XXIX (October, 1940), 553–556.

"Religious Beliefs of the Akan." Review of *The Akan Doctrine of God*, by J. B. Danquah. *African*, XV (January, 1945), 23–29.

Review of *Essays on Lozi Land and Royal Property*, by Max Gluckman. *Africa*, XV (April, 1945), 99–101.

Review of *Livingstone's Last Journey*, by Reginald Coupland. *Africa*, XVI (April, 1946), 129–131.

Review of *La Philosophie Bantoue*, by Placide Tempels. *Africa*, XVI (July, 1946), 199–203.

Review of *The Matebele Journals of Robert Moffat 1829–1860*, edited by J. P. R. Wallis. *African Affairs*, XLV (July, 1946), 157–158.

Review of *Contribuicão para o estuda da antropologia de Mocambique*, by J. R. Dos Santos junior. *Africa*, XVI (October, 1946), 276.

Review of *The Planting of Christianity in Africa Vol. I*, by C. P. Groves. *Africa*, XX (January, 1950), 84–85.

"Nilotic Conceptions of God." Review of *Der Ursprung der Gottesidee. Band VIII*, by Wilhelm Schmidt. *International Review of Missions*, XXXIX (October, 1950), 469–472.

Review of *The Christian Church and Missions in Ethiopia (including Eritrea and the Somalilands)*, by J. Spencer Trimingham. *Africa*, XXII (January, 1952), 88–89.

Review of *Apprenticeship at Kuruman*, edited by I. Schapera. *Africa*, XXII (April, 1952), 186–187.

Review of *The Missionary Factor in East Africa*, by Roland Oliver. *African Affairs*, LII (April, 1953), 163–165.

Review of *The Zambesi Journal of James Stewart 1862–1863 with a selection from his correspondence*, edited by J. P. R. Wallis. *Africa*, XXIII (July, 1953), 255–256.

Review of *Religion in an African City*, by Geoffrey Parrinder. *Africa*, XXIV (January, 1954), 69–70.

Review of *The Planting of Christianity in Africa, Vol. II*, by C. P. Groves. *Africa*, XXV (July, 1955), 297–298.

Review of *The Planting of Christianity in Africa, Vol. III*, by C. P. Groves. *African Affairs*, LIV (October, 1955), 327–328.

"A European Doctor on His African Counterpart." Review of *Medicine and Magic of the Mashona*, by Michael Gelfand. *International Review of Missions*, XLVI (April, 1957), 212–214.

"African Symbolism." Review of *Rituals of Kinship among the Nyakyusa*, by Monica Wilson. *International Review of Missions*, XLVI (July, 1957), 337–339.

Review of *An African Survey revised 1956. A Study of Problems arising in Africa South of the Sahara*, by Lord Hailey. *Africa*, XXVIII (April, 1958), 168–170.

D. SOME REVIEWS OF SMITH'S BOOKS

Baker, R. H. "South African Missionaries." Reviews of *The Blessed Missionaries*, by Edwin W. Smith, and *An Introduction to South African Methodists*, by Leslie A. Hewson. *International Review of Missions*, XLI (January, 1952), 103–104.

Beach, Harlan P. Review of *The Golden Stool. The Missionary Review of the World* (o.s.), LI (July, 1928), 606–607.

Booth, Newell S. "Mission Priorities in Africa." Review of *Knowing the African. International Review of Missions*, XXXVII (January, 1948), 93–98.

———. "The Supreme Being in Africa." Review of *African Ideas of God*, edited by Edwin W. Smith. *International Review of Missions*, XL (January, 1951), 112–115.

Crowfoot, J. W. Review of *The Christian Mission in Africa. Man*, XXVII (July, 1927), 137–138.

Dougall, J. W. C. "African Beliefs." Review of *African Beliefs and Christian Faith. International Review of Missions*, XXVI (January, 1937), 129–130.

———. "Africa and the Issues of the War." Review of *Events in African History: A Supplement to "The Atlantic Charter and Africa from an American Standpoint*," compiled by Edwin W. Smith and others. *International Review of Missions*, XXXII (January, 1943), 100–102.

Durand, Ralph. Review of *A Handbook of the Ila Language. Man*, VII (August, 1907), 127–128.

Evans-Pritchard, E. E. Review of *Knowing the African. Africa*, XVII (July, 1947), 217–218.

Gluckman, H. M. Review of *Plans and—People! A Dynamic Science of Man in the Service of Africa. Man*, IL (March, 1949), 34.

Gollock, Georgina A. Review of *Aggrey of Africa: A Study in Black and White. The Church Overseas*, II (July, 1929), 279–280.

Groves, C. P. Review of *African Beliefs and Christian Faith. The East and West Review*, III (January, 1937), 85–86.

Hobley, C. W. Review of *The Religion of Lower Races as Illustrated by the African Bantu. Journal of the African Society*, XXIII (April, 1924), 251–253.

———. Review of *The Golden Stool. Man,* XXVII (April, 1927), 48.

Hooper, H. D. Review of *The Golden Stool. Church Missionary Review,* LXXVII (September, 1926), 281–282.

Jacka, H. T. "Some Biographies of Pioneers." Review of *Robert Moffat: One of God's Gardeners,* by Edwin W. Smith and others. *International Review of Missions,* XV (April, 1926), 290–294.

Jackson, Bernard C. Review of *Robert Moffat: One of God's Gardeners. Church Missionary Review,* LXXVI (December, 1925), 359.

James, E. O. "The Religion of Bantu Peoples." Review of *The Religion of Lower Races as Illustrated by the African Bantu. International Review of Missions,* XII (October, 1923), 595–596.

Jones, T. J. "Aggrey of Africa." Review of *Aggrey of Africa: A Study in Black and White. International Review of Missions,* XVIII (October, 1929), 616–618.

Junod, Henri A. "A Study of the Ba-ila." Review of *The Ila-Speaking Peoples of Northern Rhodesia,* by Edwin W. Smith and Andrew M. Dale. *International Review of Missions,* X (April, 1921), 278–280.

———. "The Conflict of Cultures in Africa." Review of *The Golden Stool. International Review of Missions,* XV (July, 1926), 607–610.

Kaberry, Phyllis M. Review of *African Ideas of God: A Symposium,* edited by Edwin W. Smith. *Africa,* XXI (January, 1951), 76.

Lerrigo, P. H. J. Review of *The Christian Mission in Africa. The Missionary Review of the World* (o.s.), L (October, 1927, 798–799.

Lienhardt, R. G. Review of *African Ideas of God: A Symposium,* edited by Edwin W. Smith. *Man,* L (December, 1950), 164–165.

Longland, F. Review of *The Blessed Missionaries. Africa,* XXI (October, 1951), 340–341.

Macmillan, W. M. "The Book of the Quarter." Review of *The Mabilles of Basutoland. Journal of the Royal African Society,* XXXIX (April, 1940), 154–159.

———. "An American Pioneer in South Africa." Review of *The Life and Times of Daniel Lindley. International Review of Missions,* XXXIX (April, 1950), 221–223.

———. "Critical Years of Bechuana History." Review of *Great Lion of Bechuanaland: The Life and Times of Roger Price, Missionary. International Review of Missions,* XLVI (October, 1957), 465–467.

Meuron, Abel de. "The Mabilles of Basutoland." Review of *The Mabilles of Basutoland. International Review of Missions,* XXIX (July, 1940), 395–397.

Morgan, E. R. Review of *The Secret of the African. The East and West Review,* IV (July, 1938), 285.

Parrinder, Geoffrey. Review of *African Ideas of God,* edited by Edwin W. Smith. *The East and West Review,* XVI (October, 1950), 128.

Rowling, F. Review of *The Religion of Lower Races. Church Missionary Review,* LXXV (September, 1924), 269.

Schapera, Isaac. Review of *Great Lion of Bechuanaland: The Life and Times of Roger Price, Missionary. Africa,* XXVIII (April, 1958), 170–171.

Schlunk, M. Review of *The Secret of the African. Africa,* III (January, 1930), 128–129.

———. Review of *The Shrine of a People's Soul. Africa,* III (January, 1930), 129.

Spier, Leslie. Review of *The Ila-Speaking Peoples of Northern Rhodesia,* by Edwin W. Smith and Andrew M. Dale. *American Anthropologist,* XXIII (July-September, 1921), 372–374.

Underhill, M. M. "Short Notices." Reviews of *The Shrine of a People's Soul,* and *The Secret of the African: Lectures on African Religion. International Review of Missions,* XVIII (October, 1929), 626.

Vischer, H. Review of *Aggrey of Africa: A Study in Black and White. Africa,* II (July, 1929), 322.

Welch, James. Review of *African Ideas of God,* edited by Edwin W. Smith. *African Affairs,* XLIX (October, 1950), 350–352.

Werner, Alice. Review of *The Ila-Speaking Peoples of Northern Rhodesia,* by Edwin W. Smith and Andrew M. Dale. *Man,* XXI (August, 1921), 125-126.

———. Review of *Robert Moffat: One of God's Gardeners. Journal of the African Society,* XXV (October, 1925), 100.

———. Review of *The Golden Stool: Some Aspects of the Conflict in Modern Africa. Journal of the African Society,* XXV (April, 1926), 284–285.

———. Review of *The Christian Mission in Africa: A Study based on the Proceedings of the International Conference at Le Zoute, Belgium, September 14th to 21st, 1926. Journal of the African Society,* XXVI (April, 1927), 298–299.

———. Review of *The Shrine of a People's Soul. Journal of the African Society,* XXVIII (July, 1929), 419–420.

———. Review of *The Secret of the African. Journal of the African Society,* XXVIII (July, 1929), 429–430.

Westermann, D. Review of *Exploration in Africa,* edited by Edwin W. Smith. *Africa,* III (January, 1930), 127–128.

Willoughby, W. C. Review of *The Religion of Lower Races: As Illustrated by the African Bantu. The Missionary Review of the World,* (o.s.) XLVII (January, 1924), 79.

Young, R. R. Reviews of *Knowing the African,* by Edwin W. Smith, and *Distinguished Negroes Abroad,* by Beatrice Jackson Flemming and Marion Jackson Pryde. *The East and West Review,* XIII (January, 1948), 31–32.

Young, T. Cullen. Review of *The Life and Times of Daniel Lindley 1801–1880. Africa,* XX (October, 1950), 351–352.

———. Review of *The Blessed Missionaries. African Affairs,* L (July, 1951), 254–255.

Review of *A Handbook of the Ila Language. Journal of the African Society,* VI (July, 1907), 438–439.

Review of *The Ila-Speaking Peoples of Northern Rhodesia,* by Edwin W. Smith and Andrew M. Dale. *Journal of the African Society,* XX (January, 1921), 150–152.

Review of *The Ila-Speaking Peoples of Northern Rhodesia,* by Edwin W. Smith and Andrew M. Dale. *The East and the West,* XIX (January, 1921), 80.

Review of *The Religion of Lower Races as Illustrated by the African Bantu. The East and the West,* XXII (January, 1924), 96.

Review of *Robert Moffat. The East and the West,* XXIII (July, 1925), 278–279.

Review of *The Golden Stool. The East and the West,* XXIV (October, 1926), 371–372.

Review of *Aggrey of Africa. The Missionary Review of the World,* (o.s.) LII (December, 1929), 978–979.

Review of *The Way of the White Fields in Rhodesia—A Survey of Christian Enterprise in Northern and Southern Rhodesia. The Church Overseas,* II (July, 1929), 285.

E. Selected Other Works

Andersson, Efraim. *Messianic Popular Movements in the Lower Congo.* Uppsala: Almquist-Wilkells, 1958.

———. *Church at the Grass Roots.* London: Lutterworth Press, 1968.

Baëta, Christian G. "The Challenge of African Culture to the Church, and the Message of the Church to African Culture." *Christianity and African Culture.* Accra: Christian Council of the Gold Coast, 1955, pp. 51–61.

———. "Conflict in Mission: Historical and Separatist Churches." *The Theology of the Christian Mission.* Edited by Gerald H. Anderson. Nashville: Abingdon Press, 1961.

———. *Prophetism in Ghana.* London: S. C. M. Press, 1962.

————, ed. *Christianity in Tropical Africa*. London: Oxford University Press, 1968.

Barrett, David B. "AD 2000: 350 Million Christians in Africa." *International Review of Mission*, LIX (January, 1970), 39–54.

Bartsch, H. W., ed. *Kerygma and Myth*. London: S.P.C.K., 1953.

Baumann, Hermann. *Schöpfung und Urzeit des Menschen im Mythus der Afrikanischen Völker*. Berlin: Verlag von Dietrich Reimer, 1936.

Beetham, T. A. *Christianity and the New Africa*. London: Pall Mall Press, 1967.

Beyerhaus, Peter. "The Christian Approach to Ancestor Worship." *Ministry*, VI (July, 1966), 137–145.

Busia, K. A. *The Position of the Chief in the Modern Political System of Ashanti*. London: International African Institute, 1951.

————. "The African World View." *Christianity and African Culture*. Accra: Christian Council of the Gold Coast, 1955, pp. 1–6.

————. "Ancestor Worship." *Practical Anthropology*, VI (January-February, 1959), 23–28.

————. *Africa in Search of Democracy*. London: Routledge and Kegan Paul, 1967.

Colson, Elizabeth and Gluckman, Max, eds. *Seven Tribes of British Central Africa*. 2nd ed. Manchester: Manchester University Press, 1959.

Colson, Elizabeth. "Introduction." *The Ila-Speaking Peoples of Northern Phodesia*, by Edwin W. Smith and Andrew M. Dale. 2nd ed. New Hyde Park, N.Y.: University Books, 1968.

Dammann, Ernst. *Die Religionen Afrikas*. Stuttgart: W. Kohlhammer Verlag, 1963.

————. *Das Christentum in Afrika*. München: Siebenstern Taschenbuch Verlag, 1968.

Danquah, J. B. *The Akan Doctrine of God*. London: Lutterworth Press, 1944.

Debrunner, Hans W. *Witchcraft in Ghana*. Accra: Presbyterian Book Depot, 1959.

————. *A Church Between Colonial Powers: A Study of the Church in Togo*. London: Lutterworth Press, 1965.

Dickson, Kwesi A. and Ellingworth, Paul, eds., *Biblical Revelation and African Beliefs*. London: Lutterworth Press, 1969.

Driberg, J. H. "The Secular Aspect of Ancestor Worship in Africa." *Supplement to the Journal of the Royal African Society*, XXV (January, 1936), 1–22.

Evans-Pritchard, E. E. *Witchcraft, Oracles and Magic among the Azande*. Oxford: The Clarendon Press, 1937.

————. Review of *Knowing the African*, by Edwin W. Smith. *Africa*, XVII (July, 1947), 217–218.

————. *Nuer Religion*. Oxford: The Clarendon Press, 1956.

————. *Theories of Primitive Religion*. Oxford: The Clarendon Press, 1965.

Farquhar, J. N. *The Crown of Hinduism*. London: Oxford University Press, 1920.

Fehderau, Harold W. "Kimbanguism: Prophetic Christianity in Congo." *Practical Anthropology*, IX (July-August, 1962), 157–178.

Field, Margaret J. *Religion and Medicine of the Gã People*. London: Oxford University Press, 1937.

————. *Search for Security: An Ethno-Psychiatric Study of Rural Ghana*. Evanston, Ill.: Northwestern University Press, 1960.

Foerster, Werner. "σώζω und σωτηρία im Neuen Testament." *Theologisches Wörterbuch zum Neuen Testament. Band VII*. Herausgegeben von Gerhard Friedrich. Stuttgart: W. Kohlhammer Verlag, 1964.

Forde, Daryll, ed. *African Worlds*. London: Oxford University Press, 1954.

————. "Obituary: Edwin Williams Smith." *Africa*, XXVIII (April, 1958), 93–94.

Fortes, Meyer. *The Web of Kinship among the Tallensi*. London: Oxford University Press, 1949.

————. *Oedipus and Job in West African Religion*. Cambridge: The University Press, 1959.

———— and Dieterlen, G., eds. *African Systems of Thought*. London: Oxford University Press, 1965.

Foté, Memel. "Rapport sur la civilisation animiste." *Colloque sur les Religions Abidjan, Avril 1961*. Edited by Alioune Diop. Paris: Présence Africaine, 1962.

Gelfand, Michael. *Shona Religion*. Cape Town: Juta and Company, 1962.

————. *An African's Religion: The Spirit of Nyajena*. Capetown: Juta and Company, 1966.

Gilis, Charles-André. *Kimbangu: Fondateur d'Eglise*. Bruxelles: Editions de la Libraire Encyclopédique, 1960.

Gluckman, Max. *Custom and Conflict in Africa*. Oxford: Basil Blackwell, 1963.

Groves, C. P. *The Planting of Christianity in Africa, I-IV*. London: Lutterworth Press, 1948–58.

————. Letter to Malcolm J. McVeigh, December 24, 1970.

Harjula, Raimo. *God and the Sun in Meru Thought*. Helsinki: Finnish Society for Missiology and Ecumenics, 1969.

Harris, W. T. and Sawyerr, Harry. *The Springs of Mende Belief and Conduct*. Freetown: Sierra Leone University Press, 1968.

Hastings, Adrian. *Church and Mission in Modern Africa*. London: Burns and Oates, 1967.

Hayley, T. T. S. *The Anatomy of Lango Religion and Groups*. Cambridge: The University Press, 1947.

Herskovits, Melville J. *Dahomey: An Ancient West African Kingdom*. New York: J. J. Augustin, 1938.

————. *Cultural Anthropology*. An abridged and revised edition of *Man and His Works*. New York: Alfred A. Knopf, 1955.

Hogg, A. G. " 'The Crown of Hinduism,' and Other Volumes." Reviews of *The Crown of Hinduism*, by J. N. Farquhar; *The Soul of India: An Introduction to the Study of Hinduism, in its Historical Setting and Development, and in its Internal and Historical Relations to Christianity*, by George Howells; and *Hinduism, Ancient and Modern, Viewed in the Light of the Incarnation*, by John A. Sharrock. *International Review of Missions*, III (January, 1914), 172–173.

————. *The Christian Message to the Hindu*. London: S.C.M. Press, 1947.

Hollis, A. C. *The Masai: Their Language and Folklore*. Oxford: The Clarendon Press, 1905.

Horton, Robin. "African Traditional Thought and Western Science." *Africa*, XXXVII (January, 1967), 50–71.

————. "African Traditional Thought and Western Science." *Africa*, XXXVII (April, 1967), 155–187.

Idowu, E. Bolaji. *Olódùmarè: God in Yoruba Belief*. London: Longmans, Green and Co., 1962.

————. *Towards an Indigenous Church*. London: Oxford University Press, 1965.

Ilogu, Edmund. "The Problem of Indigenization in Nigeria." *International Review of Missions*, XLIX (April, 1960), 167–182.

Isichei, Elizabeth. "Ibo and Christian Beliefs: Some Aspects of a Theological Encounter." *African Affairs*, LXVIII (April, 1969), 121–134.

Jahn, Janheinz. *Muntu: umrisse der neoafrikanischen Kultur*. Düsseldorf-Köln: Eugen Diederichs Verlag, 1958.

Kagame, Alexis. *La Philosophie bantu-rwandaise de l'Être*. Bruxelles: Académie Royale des Sciences Coloniales, 1956.

Kaberry, Phyllis M. Review of *African Ideas of God: A Symposium*, ed. by Edwin W. Smith. *Africa*, XXI (January, 1951), 76.

Kenyatta, Jomo. *Facing Mount Kenya: The Tribal Life of the Gikuyu*. London: Martin Secker and Warburg, 1938.

King, Noel Q. *Religions in Africa*. New York: Harper and Row, 1970.

Kraemer, Hendrik. *The Christian Message in a non-Christian World*. New York: Harper and Brothers, 1938.

————. *Religion and the Christian Faith*. Philadelphia: The Westminster Press, 1956.

Lerrigo, P. H. J. "The 'Prophet' Movement in Congo." *International Review of Missions*, XI (April, 1922), 270–277.

Lienhardt, Godfrey. *Divinity and Experience: The Religion of the Dinka*. London: Oxford University Press, 1961.

Macmillan, W. M. "The Book of the Quarter." Review of *The Mabilles of Basutoland*, by Edwin W. Smith. *Journal of the Royal African Society*, XXXIX (April, 1940), 154–159.

————. "An American Pioneer in South Africa." Review of *The Life and Times of Daniel Lindley*, by Edwin W. Smith. *International Review of Missions*, XLVI (October, 1957), 221–223.

————. "Critical Years of Bechuana History." Review of *Great Lion of Bechuanaland: The Life and Times of Roger Price, Missionary*, by Edwin W. Smith, *International Review of Missions*, XLVI (October, 1957), 465–467.

Maurier, H. *Religion et Développement: Traditions Africaines et Catéchèses*. Tours: Maison Mame, 1965.

Messenger, John C. Jr. "The Christian Concept of Forgiveness and Anang Morality." *Practical Anthropology*, VI (May-June, 1959), 97–103.

————. "Religious Acculturation among the Anang Ibibio." *Continuity and Change in African Culture*. Edited by William R. Bascom and Melville J. Herskovits. Chicago: The University Press, 1959.

Mbiti, John S. *African Religions and Philosophy*. New York: Frederick A. Praeger, 1969.

————. *Concepts of God in Africa*. London: S.P.C.K., 1970.

Middleton, John. *Lugbara Religion*. London: Oxford University Press, 1960.

Murphree, Marshall W. *Christianity and the Shona*. New York: The Athlone Press, 1969.

Nadel, S. F. *Nupe Religion*. London: Routledge and Kegan Paul, 1954.

Nketia, J. H. *Funeral Dirges of the Akan People*. 2nd ed. New York: Negro Universities Press, 1969.

O'Connell, James. "The Withdrawal of the High God in West African Religion: An Essay in Interpretation." *Man*, LXII (May, 1962), 67–69.

Ogot, Bethwell A. "The Concept of Jok." *African Studies*. XX, No. 2 (1961). 123–130.

Oliver, Roland. *The Missionary Factor in East Africa*. London: Longmans, Green and Co., 1952.

Oosthuizen, Gerhardus C. *Post-Christianity in Africa*. London: C. Hurst and Co., 1968.

Ottenberg, Simon and Phoebe, eds. *Cultures and Societies of Africa*. New York: Random House, 1960.

Parrinder, Geoffrey. *West African Psychology*. London: Lutterworth Press, 1951.

———. *West African Religion*. 2nd ed. London: The Epworth Press, 1961.

———. *Religion in Africa*. Harmondsworth, Middlesex: Penguin Books, 1969.

Pauw, B. A. *Religion in a Tswana Chiefdom*. London: Oxford University Press, 1960.

p'Bitek, Okot. *African Religions in Western Scholarship*. Nairobi: East African Literature Bureau, 1970.

———. *Religion of the Central Luo*. Nairobi: East African Literature Bureau, 1971.

Phillips, Godfrey E. *The Old Testament in the World Church*. London: Lutterworth Press, 1942.

Raymaekers, Paul. "L'Eglise de Jesus Christ sur la Terre par le prophète Simon Kimbangu." *Zaïre: Belgian African Review*, XIII, No. 7 (1959), 677–756.

Roe, James M. *A History of the British and Foreign Bible Society 1905–1954*. London: The British and Foreign Bible Society, 1965.

Rotberg, Robert I. *Christian Missionaries and the Creation of Northern Rhodesia 1880–1924*. Princeton, N.J.: Princeton University Press, 1965.

Sawyerr, Harry. *Creative Evangelism: Towards a New Christian Encounter with Africa*. London: Lutterworth Press, 1968.

———. *God: Ancestor or Creator?* London: Logman Group, 1970.

Schapera, Isaac. "Obituary: Edwin Williams Smith: 1876–1957." *Man*, LIX (December, 1959), 213.

Sharpe, Eric J. *Not to Destroy but to Fulfill: The Contribution of J. N. Farquhar to Protestant Missionary Thought in India before 1914*. Uppsala: Almqvist & Wiksells Boktryckeri AB, 1965.

Sheldon, Austin J. "On Recent Interpretations of Deus Otiosus: The Withdrawn God in West African Psychology." *Man*, LXIV (March-April, 1964), 53–54.

Smith, John. *Christ and Missions*. London: Robert Bryant Primitive Methodist Publishing House, 1900.

Smith, Julia A. *Sunshine and Shade in Central Africa*. London: W. A. Hammond, 1911.

Smith, Noel. *The Presbyterian Church in Ghana, 1835–1960*. Accra: Ghana University Press, 1966.

Sundkler, Bengt G. M. *Bantu Prophets in South Africa*. 2nd ed. London: Oxford University Press, 1961.

Swanzy, H. V. L. "Quarterly Notes." *African Affairs*, XLIV (January, 1945), 1–9.

Taylor, John V. *The Growth of the Church in Buganda*. London: S.C.M. Press, 1958.

————. *The Primal Vision.* London: S.C.M. Press, 1963.

————. *CMS News-Letter.* No. 338, May 1970.

Tempels, Placide. *La Philosophie Bantoue.* Paris: Présence Africaine, 1949.

Thiam, Joseph. "Du clan tribal à la communauté chrétienne." *Des prêtres noirs s'interrogent.* Paris: Les Editions du Cerf, 1957.

Thompson, P. E. S. "Reflections Upon the African Idea of God." *The Sierra Leone Bulletin of Religion,* VII (December, 1965), 56–61.

Turner, Victor W. *The Drums of Affliction: A Study of Religious Processes among the Ndembu of Zambia.* Oxford: The Clarendon Press, 1968.

van der Merwe, W. J. *The Shona Idea of God.* Fort Victoria: Morgenster Mission Press, 1957.

van Wing, J. *Études Bakongo.* Louvain: Imprimerie M. and L. Symons, 1959.

————. "Le Kibangisme vu par un témoin." *Zaïre: Belgian African Review,* XII, No. 6 (1958), 563–618.

Wagner, Günther. *The Bantu of North Kavirondo, I-II.* London: Oxford University Press, 1949, 1956.

Welbourn, F. B. *East African Christian.* London: Oxford University Press, 1965.

Werner, Alice. "African Mythology." *The Mythology of All Races VII.* Edited by John A. MacCulloch. Boston: Marshall Jones Co., 1925.

————. *Myths and Legends of the Bantu.* 2nd ed. London: Frank Cass and Co., 1968.

Williamson, Sidney G. *Akan Religion and the Christian Faith.* Accra: Ghana Universities Press, 1965.

Wilson, Monica. *Communal Rituals of the Nyakyusa.* London: Oxford University Press, 1959.

Wyatt, B. E. "Notes and News: The Royal African Society's Silver Medal." *Africa,* XV (April, 1945), 88–90.

Zoa, Jean B. "Der Christliche Beitrag zum Gestaltwandel Afrikas." *Theologie und Kirke in Africa.* Herausgegeben von Horst Burkle. Stuttgart: Evangelisches Verlagswerk, 1968.

"Obituary: Rev. Dr. Edwin Smith." *African Affairs,* LVII (January, 1958), 62.

Who Was Who, Vol. V 1951–1960. London: Adam and Charles Black, 1961.

Notes

Foreword

A See Father Placide Tempels, *Bantu Philosophy* (Paris: Présence Africaine, 1952). Cf. the concept of *Shakti* in Hinduism, another understanding of God as Power.

B The Divine Suzerainty concept of God in Biblical thought as set forth by G. Ernest Wright in *The Old Testament and Theology* (New York: Harper & Row, 1969) is compatible with the Bantu view of hierarchy of forces.

C See Harold K. Schilling, *The New Consciousness in Science and Religion* (Philadelphia: Pilgrim Press, 1973).

1. Introduction

1 David B. Barrett, "AD 2000: 350 Million Christians in Africa," *International Review of Mission*, LIX (January, 1970), pp. 39–54.

2 The biographical sketch presented here is a composite from many sources: Julia A. Smith, *Sunshine and Shade in Central Africa* (London: W. A. Hammond, 1911); Edwin W. Smith, "Editorial Notes," *Journal of the Royal African Society*, XXXVII (July, 1938), p. 271; B. E. Wyatt, "Notes and News: The Royal African Society's Silver Medal," *Africa*, XV (April, 1945), pp. 88–90; H. V. L. Swanzy, "Quarterly Notes," *African Affairs*, XLIV (January, 1945), p. 8; Daryll Forde, "Obituary: Edwin Williams Smith," *Africa*, XXVIII (April, 1958), pp. 93–94; "Obituary: Rev. Dr. Edwin Smith," *African Affairs*, LVII (January, 1958), p. 62; Isaac Schapera, "Obituary: Edwin Williams Smith: 1876–1957," *Man*, LIX (December, 1959), p. 213; *Who Was Who, Vol. V, 1951–1960* (London: Adam and Charles Black, 1961), p. 1013; Robert I. Rotberg, *Christian Missionaries and the Creation of Northern Rhodesia 1880–1924* (Princeton, New Jersey: Princeton University Press, 1965), p. 190; letter from C. P. Groves to Malcolm J. McVeigh, December 24, 1970; and numerous other references in Smith's published works. These sources do not always agree.

Rotberg claims, for example, that Smith received his honorary D.D. from the University of Toronto while Forde, Schapera and *Who Was Who* list Wesley College, Winnipeg as the donor. That the latter is correct is confirmed by a search of the records of the University of Toronto and its related colleges. Rotberg inaccurately calls Elmfield College Enfield College and also states that Smith was awarded the Silver Medal from the Royal Anthropological Society in 1939. Schapera may have led Rotberg astray on the date which Swanzy and Wyatt identify as 1944. All agree against Rotberg that the award was made by the Royal African Society. A definitive biography of Edwin W. Smith has yet to be written.

3 John Smith, *Christ and Missions* (London: Robert Bryant Primitive Methodist Publishing House, 1900).

4 Roe characterizes his service with the Bible Society as one of "great distinction." James M. Roe, *A History of the British and Foreign Bible Society 1905–1954* (London: The British and Foreign Bible Society, 1965), p. 202.

5 E. E. Evans-Pritchard, review of *Knowing the African* by Edwin W. Smith, *Africa*, XVII (July, 1947), p. 217.

6 In making the presentation Lord Hailey said: "Edwin Smith has made a contribution to Africa which few can equal; and in presenting him with this medal the Society may feel that in honouring him it has honoured the Society." Swanzy, "Quarterly Notes," p. 8.

7 Smith wrote by far the largest and most significant part of the book.

8 "We have dedicated our essay with respect and admiration to Dr. Edwin W. Smith, in tribute to the book which he and the late Captain Andrew Dale wrote over thirty years ago: *The Ila-Speaking Peoples of Northern Rhodesia.*" Elizabeth Colson and Max Gluckman, eds., *Seven Tribes of British Central Africa* (2nd ed.; Manchester: Manchester University Press, 1959), p. ix.

9 Bibliographical references listing publisher and date of publication for books written by Edwin Smith are not given in the introduction but are included as an integral part of the presentation of his position in Chapters II–VII and in the bibliography at the back of the dissertation.

10 Forde, "Obituary: Edwin Williams Smith," p. 93.

11 In addition to some devotional works in Ila and the Ila New Testament he wrote one article in French: Edwin W. Smith, "La Langue Indigène et l'Education Africaine," *Le Monde non-Chrétien*, II (March, 1932), pp. 21–28.

12 W. M. Macmillan, "The Book of the Quarter," review of *The Mabilles of Basutoland* by Edwin W. Smith, *Journal of the Royal African Society*, XXXIX (April, 1940), pp. 154–159; W. M. Macmillan, "American Pioneer in South Africa," review of *The Life and Times of Daniel Lindley*, by Edwin W. Smith, *International Review of Missions*, XXXIX (April, 1950), pp. 221–223; W. M. Macmillan, "Critical Years of Bechuana History," review of *Great Lion of Bechuanaland: The Life and Times of Roger Price, Missionary* by Edwin W. Smith, *International Review of Missions*, XLVI (October, 1957), pp. 465–467; I. Schapera, review of *Great Lion of Bechuanaland: The Life and Times of Roger Price, Missionary* by Edwin W. Smith, *Africa*, XXVIII (April, 1958), pp. 170–171.

13 Geoffrey Parrinder, *West African Religion* (2nd ed.; London: The Epworth Press, 1961), p. 12.

14 M. Fortes and G. Dieterlen, "Christianity in Africa," *African Systems of Thought*, ed. by M. Fortes and G. Dieterlen (London: Oxford University Press, 1965), p. 31.

[15] Phyllis M. Kaberry, review of *African Ideas of God: A Symposium*, ed. by Edwin W. Smith, *Africa*, XXI (January, 1951), p. 76.

[16] Geoffrey Parrinder, *Religion in Africa* (Harmondsworth, Middlesex: Penguin Books, 1969), p. 39.

[17] See Chapter IX.

[18] See Chapter VII.

[19] See Chapter VIII.

[20] See Chapter IX.

[21] John S. Mbiti, *Concepts of God in Africa* (London: S.P.C.K., 1970), pp. 327–336.

[22] Smith did not choose this title and apologized for it. See Chapter II, note 52.

2. Personality: Is God a Person?

[1] Edwin W. Smith, *The Secret of the African* (London: Student Christian Movement, 1929), p. 21. See also Edwin W. Smith, *African Beliefs and Christian Faith* (London: Lutterworth Press, 1936), pp. 29–30.

[2] "I believe myself that, among the many who have attempted to define religion, Schleiermacher comes nearest the truth: 'The essence of religious emotion,' he said, 'consists in the feeling of an absolute dependence'." Edwin W. Smith, *Knowing the African* (London: Lutterworth Press, 1946), p. 105.

[3] Smith, *Secret of the African*, pp. 22–25.

[4] *Ibid.*, p. 22.

[5] *Ibid.*, p. 25.

[6] *Ibid.*, pp. 20, 27.

[7] *Ibid.*, p. 20.

[8] Here Smith quotes from Malinowski. He is critical of Levy-Bruhl's idea that Africans do not act rationally. *Ibid.*, pp. 27–28.

[9] Smith prefers to follow Marett and retain the term "magic" only for "the black or anti-social branch of occultism." Edwin W. Smith, "The Whole Subject in Perspective: An Introductory Survey," in *African Ideas of God: A Symposium*, ed. by Edwin W. Smith (London: Edinburgh House Press, 1950), p. 16. See also Edwin W. Smith and Andrew M. Dale, *The Ila-Speaking Peoples of Northern Rhodesia*, Vol. II (2nd ed.; New Hyde Park, New York: University Books, 1968), p. 80.

[10] Smith, *Secret of the African*, p. 29.

[11] *Ibid.*, p. 44.

[12] *Ibid.*, p. 46.

[13] *Ibid.*, pp. 45–46.

[14] *Ibid.*, p. 45. Smith, *African Beliefs and Christian Faith*, p. 35.

[15] Smith, *African Beliefs and Christian Faith*, p. 35. See also Smith, *Ila-Speaking Peoples*, II, p. 89.

[16] Smith, *Ila-Speaking Peoples*, II, pp. 82–83.

[17] Smith, *Knowing the African*, p. 113.

[18] Smith, *Ila-Speaking Peoples*, II, p. 83.

[19] Smith, *African Beliefs and Christian Faith*, p. 35.

[20] Smith, *Secret of the African*, pp. 29–30.

[21] *Ibid.*, p. 31.

[22] *Ibid.*, p. 32.

[23] *Ibid.*, p. 35.

[24] Smith, *African Beliefs and Christian Faith*, p. 36.

[25] Smith, *African Ideas of God*, p. 21.

26 *Ibid.*, pp. 23–24. Here the "other Something" is clearly conceived as *ubwanga.*
27 Smith, *African Ideas of God*, p. 59.
28 *Ibid.*, p. 58.
29 Smith, *African Beliefs and Christian Faith*, p. 41.
30 *Ibid.*, p. 42.
31 Smith, *Secret of the African*, p. 86.
32 Smith, *African Beliefs and Christian Faith*, pp. 42–44.
33 *Ibid.*, p. 44.
34 *Ibid.*, pp. 44–45.
35 Smith, *Ila-Speaking Peoples*, II, p. 202.
36 *Ibid.*, p. 204.
37 *Ibid.*
38 *Ibid.*, p. 206.
39 *Ibid.*, p. 202.
40 *Ibid.*, pp. 202, 209.
41 *Ibid.*, p. 304.
42 Smith, *African Beliefs and Christian Faith*, p. 43.
43 *Ibid.*, p. 38.
44 *Ibid.*, p. 35.
45 *Ibid.*, p. 38.
46 *Ibid.*, p. 37.
47 Smith, *African Ideas of God*, p. 15. See also Smith, *Secret of the African*, p. 83.
48 Smith, *Ila-Speaking Peoples*, II, p. 208.
49 Smith, *Secret of the African*, pp. 74–75.
50 Smith, *African Beliefs and Christian Faith*, p. 37.
51 Smith, *African Ideas of God*, p. 58.
52 Mulungu is really a class name, not a personal name. However, when referring to the Supreme Being, the term takes on the character of a personal name. *Ibid.*, p. 60. See also Edwin W. Smith, *The Religion of Lower Races as Illustrated by the African Bantu* (New York: The Macmillan Company, 1923), p. 61. Smith did not choose the title of the above-mentioned book (*The Religion of Lower Races*) and apologized for it. See Edwin W. Smith, *The Way of the White Fields in Rhodesia: A Survey of Christian Enterprise in Northern and Southern Rhodesia* (London: World Dominion Press, 1928), p. 23.
53 Smith, *Religion of Lower Races*, p. 61.
54 Smith, *African Beliefs and Christian Faith*, p. 45. Smith lists the following as criteria for a High God distinct from "Cosmic Mana": "1. He has personality, is in sharp distinction from everyone and everything else. He has a personal name. 2. He has a life and consciousness analogous to that of man . . . . 3. He is a Being who is not human, and never in the recollection of men was human. This rules out such divinities as the Nilotic Nyikang. 4. He is Creator, or Fashioner or Constructor, if not directly of all things, at least of some. 5. He is the ultimate power and authority behind the world and all life. 6. He is worshipped, i.e., men offer prayers and sacrifices to him, rarely though this may be. 7. He is regarded as Judge, or at least as being in an ethical relationship with mankind." Smith, *African Ideas of God*, pp. 21–22.
55 Edwin W. Smith, *The Golden Stool: Some Aspects of the Conflict of Cultures in Modern Africa* (London: Church Missionary Society, 1927), pp. 264–282. Edwin W. Smith, *Aggrey of Africa: A Study in Black and*

White (London: Student Christian Movement, 1929), pp. 132, 139. Smith, *Knowing the African,* p. 59.

56 Smith, *Golden Stool,* pp. 252, 257.

57 Edwin W. Smith, *The Christian Mission in Africa: A Study Based on the Work of the International Conference at Le Zoute, Belgium, September 14th to 21st, 1926* (London: The International Missionary Council, 1926), p. 104.

58 Smith, *Secret of the African,* p. 97.

59 Smith, *African Beliefs and Christian Faith,* p. 34. See also Smith, *Christian Mission in Africa,* p. 41.

60 This is a fundamental theme in all Smith's writings. See Smith, *Knowing the African,* p. 120; Smith, *Golden Stool,* p. 260; Smith, *Christian Mission in Africa,* pp. 40–41.

61 Smith, *Secret of the African,* p. 15.

62 Smith, *African Beliefs and Christian Faith,* p. 24.

63 *Ibid.,* pp. 79–80.

64 *Ibid.,* p. 24. See also Edwin W. Smith, *The Blessed Missionaries* (London: Oxford University Press, 1950), p. 127.

65 Smith, *African Beliefs and Christian Faith,* p. 23.

66 *Ibid.,* p. 24.

67 Smith considers these as different stages of thought. Smith, *Secret of the African,* pp. 100–101.

68 *Ibid.,* pp. 98–99.

69 Smith, *African Beliefs and Christian Faith,* pp. 153–154; 158–159.

70 Edwin W. Smith, "The Sublimation of Bantu Life and Thought," *International Review of Missions,* XI (January, 1922), p. 95.

71 *Ibid.,* p. 36.

72 Smith, *Knowing the African,* pp. 104–105.

73 Smith, *Ila-Speaking Peoples,* II, pp. 98–99. See also Smith, *Golden Stool,* pp. 210–211.

74 Smith, *Ila-Speaking Peoples,* II, p. 99.

75 *Ibid.*

76 Edwin W. Smith, "African Symbolism: Henry Myers Lecture, 1952," *Journal of The Royal Anthropological Institute of Great Britain and Ireland,* LXXXII (January-June, 1952), p. 34. Edwin W. Smith, *Great Lion of Bechuanaland: The Life and Times of Roger Price, Missionary* (London: Independent Press Ltd., 1957), p. 424.

77 Smith, *Religion of Lower Races,* p. 14.

78 *Ibid.,* pp. 16–17.

79 *Ibid.,* p. 17.

80 Smith, *Golden Stool,* p. 211.

81 Smith, *Ila-Speaking Peoples,* II, p. 89.

82 Smith, *Religion of Lower Races,* pp. 20–21; Smith, *Golden Stool,* p. 280.

83 Smith, *Ila-Speaking Peoples,* II, p. 89; Smith, *Golden Stool,* p. 189.

84 Smith, *Knowing the African,* p. 113.

85 Smith, *Secret of the African,* p. 48.

86 Smith, *Religion of Lower Races,* p. 69.

87 *Ibid.,* pp. 69–70.

88 *Ibid.,* p. 70. See also Smith, *Blessed Missionaries,* p. 18; Smith, *Golden Stool,* p. 90.

89 Smith, *African Beliefs and Christian Faith,* p. 178.

90 Smith, *African Ideas of God,* p. 1.

91 See as an example: Smith, *African Beliefs and Christian Faith,* pp. 56–59. See also Chapter IV.

[92] Smith, *Secret of the African*, p. 115. See also Smith, *Golden Stool*, p. 194. The subject of "fetishism," especially in its relationship to "spiritism," is also discussed in Chapter III.

[93] Smith, *Secret of the African*, pp. 126–127.

[94] Smith notes the parallel between the African myths of God's departure and the Fall in biblical literature. Smith, *African Ideas of God*, pp. 7–8.

[95] Smith, *Secret of the African*, p. 82.

[96] Smith, *Knowing the African*, p. 120.

[97] *Ibid.*, p. 101.

[98] *Ibid.*, p. 113.

[99] Smith, *Aggrey of Africa*, p. 132.

[100] Smith, *Secret of the African*, p. 79.

[101] See on this Smith's three short articles: "A Note on Mulungu," "A Note on Nyambe," and "A Note on Leza" in *African Ideas of God*, pp. 58–60; 76–77; 156–161.

[102] Smith, *African Beliefs and Christian Faith*, pp. 23–24.

3. Monotheism: Is God One?

[1] Edwin W. Smith, *et al.*, "The Indigenous African Church," in *The Church Conference on African Affairs* (Westerville, Ohio: Otterbein College, 1942), p. 4. Smith, *Way of White Fields*, p. 23. Smith, "African Symbolism," p. 35.

[2] Smith, "Indigenous African Church," p. 5. Smith, *Knowing the African*, p. 103.

[3] Smith, *Secret of the African*, p. 63; Smith, *African Ideas of God*, p. 84.

[4] Smith, *African Beliefs and Christian Faith*, p. 46.

[5] To provide an analysis of the African conception of the "soul" would take the discussion too far afield. Suffice it to say that the African view is very complex. See Smith, *Secret of the African*, pp. 57–59; *Religion of Lower Races*, pp. 22–27; *Ila-Speaking Peoples*, II, pp. 101–162.

[6] Smith admits that both Africans and Westerners would have great difficulty in arriving at a common definition of the term. Smith, *Secret of the African*, pp. 57–58.

[7] *Ibid.*, p. 57.

[8] Edwin W. Smith, *Robert Moffat: One of God's Gardeners* (London: CMS Press, 1925), p. 104. Smith, *Ila-Speaking Peoples*, II, p. 118; *Knowing the African*, p. 102; *Secret of the African*, p. 57; *Religion of Lower Races*, p. 28.

[9] Smith, *Religion of Lower Races*, pp. 28–32; *Secret of the African*, pp. 52–57; *Ila-Speaking Peoples*, II, 101–118.

[10] Smith, *Secret of the African*, pp. 55–56.

[11] *Ibid.*, p. 56. See also Smith, *Religion of Lower Races*, pp. 30–31; *Ila-Speaking Peoples*, II, p. 114.

[12] Smith, *Religion of Lower Races*, p. 29.

[13] *Ibid.*

[14] *Ibid.*, p. 31.

[15] Smith, *Secret of the African*, p. 60.

[16] *Ibid.*, pp. 60–61.

[17] Smith, *Ila-Speaking Peoples*, II, p. 152.

[18] *Ibid.* See also Smith, *Religion of Lower Races*, p. 26.

[19] Smith, *Ila-Speaking Peoples*, II, pp. 52–53; *Religion of Lower Races*, p. 26.

[20] Smith, *Ila-Speaking Peoples*, II, p. 156.

21 *Ibid.*, p. 157.
22 *Ibid.*, p. 155.
23 Edwin W. Smith, "Religious Beliefs of the Akan," review of *The Akan Doctrine of God* by J. B. Danquah, *Africa*, XV (January, 1945), 23–29.
24 *Ibid.*, p. 26.
25 *Ibid.*, p. 24.
26 *Ibid.*, p. 26.
27 *Ibid.*
28 *Ibid.*, p. 23.
29 Smith, *African Beliefs and Christian Faith*, p. 46.
30 Smith, *Religion of Lower Races*, p. 39.
31 *Ibid.*, p. 34.
32 *Ibid.*, pp. 34–35.
33 Smith, *Secret of the African*, p. 64.
34 Smith, *Ila-Speaking Peoples*, II, pp. 124–125.
35 Smith, *Religion of Lower Races*, pp. 39–40. See also Edwin W. Smith, review of *Serpent Worship in Africa* by W. D. Hambly, *Africa*, VI (July, 1933), p. 350.
36 Smith, *Religion of Lower Races*, p. 41.
37 *Ibid.*
38 As noted in Chapter II, Smith does not like the term "fetishism," but it is difficult to eradicate from the vocabulary of African Religion. See p. 43.
39 Smith, *Secret of the African*, p. 114.
40 Smith, *Religion of Lower Races*, pp. 49–50.
41 *Ibid.*, pp. 50–51. See also Smith, *African Ideas of God*, p. 84. See also Edwin W. Smith, "Some Books about Africans," reviews of *Nature-Worship and Taboo* by W. C. Willoughby, *Geistesleben Afrikanischen Volker im Lichte des Evangeliums* by Ernest Johannsen, *Hunger and Work in a Savage Tribe* by Audrey I. Richards, *The Ama-Xosa: Life and Customs* by John H. Soga, *Notes on the History of the Tumbuka-Kamanga Peoples. Notes on the Speech of the Tumbuka-Kamanga Peoples* by T. Cullen Young and *Die Stammeslehren der Dschagga. Band I* by Bruno Gutmann, *International Review of Missions*, XXII (January, 1933), p. 120.
42 Smith, *Religion of the Lower Races*, p. 51.
43 Smith, *African Ideas of God*, p. 23.
44 *Ibid.*
45 Smith, *Religion of Lower Races*, p. 36.
46 *Ibid.*
47 *Ibid.*, p. 52.
48 Smith, *Ila-Speaking Peoples*, II, pp. 180–196; *Secret of the African*, pp. 49–52; *Knowing the African*, pp. 106–107.
49 Smith, *Secret of the African*, p. 52.
50 *Muzhimo* is the Ila word for ancestor, divinity or spirit.
51 Smith, *Ila-Speaking Peoples*, II, p. 180.
52 *Ibid.*, p. 184.
53 *Ibid.*, p. 188.
54 *Ibid.*, pp. 180–196.
55 Smith, *African Beliefs and Christian Faith*, p. 48.
56 Smith, *Secret of the African*, p. 110.
57 *Ibid.*, p. 127.
58 This concept is also well developed among other West African peoples, especially the Jukun, Ibo and Ibibio, all of Nigeria. Smith, *African Beliefs and Christian Faith*, pp. 52–53.

[59] Smith, *Secret of the African*, pp. 128–129.

[60] *Ibid.*, p. 129.

[61] Smith, *Religion of Lower Races*, p. 44.

[62] Another example of the same phenomenon, taken from the experience of the Chagga people of Tanzania, is quoted in Smith, *African Beliefs and Christian Faith*, p. 55.

[63] *Ibid.*, p. 47.

[64] For Smith's view of the term "ancestor worship," see Chapter VII.

[65] Edwin W. Smith, "African Ethnography," reviews of *The Bakitara or Banyoro* by John Roscoe, *The Banyankole* by John Roscoe, *In Witch-Bound Africa* by Frank H. Melland and *Equatoria: The Lado Enclave* by Major C. H. Stigand, *International Review of Missions*, XIII (January, 1924), p. 129. Edwin W. Smith, "Fresh Light Upon African Religion," reviews of *Nuer Customs and Folklore* by Ray Huffman, *The Bavenda* by H. A. Stayt and *Tales Told in Togoland* by A. W. Cardinall, *International Review of Missions*, XX (October, 1931), p. 597. Edwin W. Smith, "The Lambas," review of *The Lambas of Northern Rhodesia* by Clement Doke, *International Review of Missions*, XXI (July, 1932), p. 430.

[66] Edwin W. Smith, "Nilotic Conceptions of God," review of *Der Ursprung der Gottesidee. Band VIII* by Wilhelm Schmidt, *International Review of Missions*, XXXIX (October, 1950), p. 470.

[67] Edwin W. Smith, "Foreword," *West African Religion* by Geoffrey Parrinder (2nd ed.; London: The Epworth Press, 1961), p. xi.

[68] Smith, *Secret of the African*, pp. 94–95. They are not exactly the same. See Smith, "Foreword," *op. cit.*

[69] Smith, "Foreword," p. xii.

[70] "As in the case of nature spirits, it is extremely difficult to draw a hard and fast line between discarnate spirits and gods, between spiritism and polytheism." Smith, *African Ideas of God*, pp. 23–24.

[71] Smith, *Secret of the African*, pp. 110–111.

[72] *Ibid.*, p. 82.

[73] Smith, *Religion of Lower Races*, p. 53.

[74] This is what Smith means by the word "sublimation." See Smith, *Golden Stool*, pp. 272–282. Edwin W. Smith, "The Sublimation of Bantu Life and Thought," *International Review of Missions*, XI (January, 1922), 83–95.

[75] Smith, *Knowing the African*, p. 109.

[76] Smith, *Religion of Lower Races*, p. 38.

[77] Smith, *Knowing the African*, p. 105.

[78] *Ibid.*, p. 106.

[79] Smith, *African Beliefs and Christian Faith*, p. 55.

[80] *Ibid.*, p. 54.

[81] Smith, *Secret of the African*, pp. 130–131.

[82] Smith, *Religion of Lower Races*, p. 54.

[83] *Ibid.*, p. 55.

[84] God's absenteeism is discussed in detail in Chapter IV.

[85] Smith, *Secret of the African*, p. 82.

[86] *Ibid.*, pp. 126–127.

[87] *Ibid.*, pp. 82–83.

[88] Smith, *African Beliefs and Christian Faith*, pp. 149–192.

[89] Smith, *Religion of Lower Races*, p. 30.

[90] *Ibid.*

[91] *Ibid.*, pp. 30–31.

92 *Ibid.*, p. 31.
93 Smith, *Ila-Speaking Peoples*, II, p. 114.
94 Smith records that if a stranger happened to be passing by at the moment, he was killed quickly and added to the pile! *Ibid.*
95 Edwin W. Smith, "Social Anthropology and Missionary Work," *International Review of Missions*, XIII (October, 1924), 525–528.
96 Smith, *Knowing the African*, p. 105.
97 Smith, *Religion of Lower Races*, p. 40.
98 *Ibid.*, pp. 34–35.
99 Smith, *African Beliefs and Christian Faith*, pp. 155–158.
100 Smith, *Religion of Lower Races*, p. 35.
101 *Ibid.* See also Smith, *Secret of the African*, p. 64.
102 Smith, *Secret of the African*, p. 64.
103 Smith, "Indigenous African Church," p. 5.
104 Smith, *Knowing the African*, p. 54. Edwin W. Smith, "Anthropology and the Practical Man," *Journal of the Royal Anthropological Institute of Great Britain and Ireland*, LXIV (January-June, 1934), p. xxxii.
105 Smith, *Secret of the African*, p. 65.
106 Smith, *Knowing the African*, p. 50. Smith, *Blessed Missionaries*, p. 15. Smith, *Christian Mission in Africa*, pp. 32–33.
107 Smith, *Golden Stool*, p. 213.
108 *Ibid.*, p. 214.
109 *Ibid.*
110 Smith, *Knowing the African*, pp. 25–27.
111 Edwin W. Smith, *Great Lion of Bechuanaland: The Life and Times of Roger Price, Missionary* (London: Independent Press, 1957), p. 180. Edwin W. Smith, *The Mabilles of Basutoland* (London: Hodder and Stoughton, 1939), p. 122.
112 Smith, *Golden Stool*, p. 256.
113 Smith believes that the encounter of Africa and the West was inevitable. Edwin W. Smith, "The Disintegration of African Society," *The East and the West*, XXII (April, 1924), p. 147.
114 Smith, *Golden Stool*, p. 257.
115 Smith, *Knowing the African*, p. 107.
116 Smith quotes Moshesh, the great chief of the Sotho: "You white people do not steal cattle, it's true, but you steal whole countries; and if you had your wish you would send us to pasture our cattle in the clouds." Smith, *Mabilles of Basutoland*, p. 42. See also Smith, *Blessed Missionaries*, pp. 64–65.
117 Smith, *Way of White Fields*, p. 133.
118 Smith, "Disintegration," p. 150.
119 *Ibid.*, p. 153.
120 Smith, *Secret of the African*, p. 139.
121 Smith, *Religion of Lower Races*, p. 69.
122 Smith, *Golden Stool*, p. 266.
123 Smith, *Religion of Lower Races*, p. 47.
124 Smith discusses the challenge of Islam but finds Christianity a more adequate answer to Africa's needs. Smith, *Golden Stool*, pp. 217–248.
125 Smith, "Sublimation," p. 88.
126 See again p. 85.
127 Smith, *Golden Stool*, pp. 268–269.
128 *Ibid.*, p. 268.
129 *Ibid.*, p. 271.

4. Disposition: Does God Love Man?

[1] Smith, *Secret of the African,* p. 106.

[2] *Ibid.,* pp. 106–107. For other accounts of the legend see Smith, *Ila-Speaking Peoples,* II, pp. 197–198; *African Beliefs and Christian Faith,* pp. 60–61; *Knowing the African,* p. 120; *African Ideas of God,* pp. 33–34; *Religion of Lower Races,* pp. 61–62.

[3] Smith, *Ila-Speaking Peoples,* II, p. 198.

[4] Smith, *African Beliefs and Christian Faith,* p. 62.

[5] Unfortunately Smith does not identify these people. Smith, *Secret of the African,* pp. 107–108.

[6] *Ibid.,* p. 107.

[7] Smith, *Golden Stool,* p. 85.

[8] Smith, *African Beliefs and Christian Faith,* p. 61.

[9] *Ibid.,* pp. 61–62.

[10] *Ibid.,* p. 62.

[11] *Ibid.,* p. 60.

[12] Smith, *Secret of the African,* p. 119.

[13] *Ibid.,* p. 97. See also Smith, *Ila-Speaking Peoples,* II, p. 202.

[14] Smith, *Ila-Speaking Peoples,* II, p. 203.

[15] *Ibid.,* p. 202.

[16] *Ibid.* See also Smith, *Secret of the African,* p. 105; *African Beliefs and Christian Faith,* p. 62.

[17] Smith, *Secret of the African,* pp. 101–102.

[18] *Ibid.,* p. 102.

[19] The Zulus replace "Hare" with "Lizard." *Ibid.,* p. 76.

[20] Smith, *Ila-Speaking Peoples,* II, pp. 100–101, 228.

[21] Smith, *Secret of the African,* p. 126.

[22] Smith, *African Beliefs and Christian Faith,* p. 63.

[23] *Ibid.*

[24] Smith, *Secret of the African,* p. 106.

[25] Smith, *Ila-Speaking Peoples,* II, p. 202.

[26] Smith, *Secret of the African,* p. 90.

[27] *Ibid.,* p. 107.

[28] Smith, *African Ideas of God,* p. 9; in *Secret of the African,* p. 71, Smith quotes from Rattray to similar effect.

[29] Smith, *Secret of the African,* pp. 126–127.

[30] Smith, *African Beliefs and Christian Faith,* p. 56.

[31] *Ibid.,* p. 57.

[32] *Ibid.,* p. 59.

[33] Smith, *Secret of the African,* pp. 110–111.

[34] "He [Onyame] is considered, says Captain Rattray, to be too remote to be concerned very directly in person with the affairs of men. He has delegated his powers to his lieutenants, the lesser gods, whom we shall describe presently." *Ibid.,* p. 121.

[35] Smith, *African Ideas of God,* p. 15.

[36] Smith, *African Beliefs and Christian Faith,* p. 58.

[37] Smith, *Ila-Speaking Peoples,* II, p. 198.

[38] Smith, *Secret of the African,* pp. 90–91.

[39] Smith, *African Ideas of God,* p. 33.

[40] *Ibid.,* pp. 8–9.

[41] Smith, *African Beliefs and Christian Faith,* p. 87.

[42] *Ibid.,* p. 95.

[43] *Ibid.,* pp. 168–169.

44 *Ibid.*, p. 152.
45 *Ibid.*, p. 189.
46 *Ibid.*, p. 46.
47 *Ibid.*, p. 192.
48 Smith, *Aggrey of Africa,* p. 133.
49 Smith, *African Beliefs and Christian Faith,* pp. 156–157.
50 *Ibid.*, p. 157.
51 Smith, *Christian Mission in Africa,* pp. 40–41. See also Smith, *Knowing the African,* p. 120; Smith, *Golden Stool,* p. 260; Smith, *Secret of the African,* p. 91.
52 Smith, *African Beliefs and Christian Faith,* p. 157.
53 *Ibid.*, p. 153.
54 Smith, *Secret of the African,* p. 84.
55 *Ibid.*
56 Smith, *African Beliefs and Christian Faith,* p. 153.
57 *Ibid.*, p. 154.
58 *Ibid.*, p. 159.
59 Smith, *African Ideas of God,* pp. 91, 122. Smith, *Aggrey of Africa,* p. 31.
60 Smith, *African Beliefs and Christian Faith,* p. 162.
61 *Ibid.*, p. 164.
62 *Ibid.*, p. 155.
63 *Ibid.*, p. 156.
64 *Ibid.*, p. 87.
65 *Ibid.*, pp. 117–119.
66 Smith, *Secret of the African,* p. 108.
67 *Ibid.*, p. 91.
68 "This is true love as it is in man—the love which was seen at its fullest and best in the Lord Jesus. And it is that love which is the heart of God. 'God had such love for all men that He gave up His only Son, so that every one who has belief in Him may have eternal life' (John 3:16)." Smith, *African Beliefs and Christian Faith,* p. 156.
69 Smith, *Ila-Speaking Peoples,* II, p. 198.
70 "The old woman never found God; and from her day to this nobody has ever had an answer to her question. So say the Ba-ila, and in this legend one seems to hear the questionings of all the millions of the Bantu. What answer is there but Christ?" Smith, *Religion of Lower Races,* p. 62.
71 Smith, *African Ideas of God,* p. 34.

5. Revelation: Does God Reveal Himself?

1 Smith, *Ila-Speaking Peoples,* I, p. 265.
2 *Ibid.*, pp. 265–266.
3 Smith says: "We use 'it' in refrence to *Shimubi;* a native would say 'he'." *Ibid.*, p. 267.
4 *Ibid.*, p. 266.
5 *Ibid.*, p. 267.
6 *Ibid.*, p. 268.
7 *Ibid.*
8 Smith, *Ila-Speaking Peoples,* I, pp. 270–272.
9 *Ibid.*, pp. 356–357.
10 *Ibid.*, p. 357.
11 *Ibid.*, p. 356.
12 *Ibid.*, p. 270.
13 *Ibid.*, p. 267.

[14] Smith, *Ila-Speaking Peoples*, II, p. 134.
[15] *Ibid.*, p. 135.
[16] *Ibid.*, p. 136.
[17] *Ibid.*, pp. 134–135.
[18] *Ibid.*, p. 134.
[19] *Ibid.*, pp. 134–135.
[20] Smith, *Religion of Lower Races*, p. 39.
[21] See again chapter III, p. 57.
[22] Smith, *Ila-Speaking Peoples*, II, p. 136.
[23] *Ibid.*, pp. 140–142.
[24] *Ibid.*, p. 142.
[25] *Ibid.*, pp. 142–143.
[26] *Ibid.*, p. 143.
[27] Smith, *Great Lion of Bechuanaland*, p. 401.
[28] Smith, *African Beliefs and Christian Faith*, p. 110.
[29] *Ibid.*, pp. 110–111. See also Edwin W. Smith, *Plans and People: A Dynamic Science of Man in the Service of Africa* (London: Lutterworth Press, 1948), p. 12.
[30] Smith, *Ila-Speaking Peoples*, II, p. 141.
[31] Smith, *African Beliefs and Christian Faith*, p. 111.
[32] Smith, *Ila-Speaking Peoples*, II, p. 342.
[33] *Ibid.*, pp. 143–144.
[34] Smith, *Great Lion of Bechuanaland*, p. 399.
[35] Smith, *Religion of Lower Races*, pp. 41–42.
[36] Smith, *Ila-Speaking Peoples*, II, pp. 147–152; *Secret of the African*, pp. 9–15.
[37] Smith, *Ila-Speaking Peoples*, II, p. 149.
[38] *Ibid.*, p. 150.
[39] Smith, *Secret of the African*, p. 13.
[40] *Ibid.*, p. 14.
[41] *Ibid.*, p. 15.
[42] Smith, *African Beliefs and Christian Faith*, p. 111.
[43] Smith, *African Ideas of God*, pp. 8–9; *Ila-Speaking Peoples*, II, pp. 311–417; *Knowing the African*, pp. 121–170. Edwin W. Smith, "Indigenous Education in Africa" in *Essays Presented to C. G. Seligman*, ed. by E. Evans-Pritchard *et al.* (London: Kegan Paul, Trench, Trubner and Co. Ltd., 1934), pp. 30–32. Edwin W. Smith, "The Function of Folk Tales," *Journal of the Royal African Society*, XXXIX (January, 1940), 64–83.
[44] An exception is the Vai people of Liberia. Smith, *Knowing the African*, p. 170.
[45] Smith, *Ila-Speaking Peoples*, II, p. 334.
[46] Smith, "Function of Folk Tales," pp. 64–76; *Knowing the African*, pp. 146–160.
[47] Smith, "Function of Folk Tales," p. 77.
[48] *Ibid.*, pp. 65–66.
[49] *Ibid.*, p. 79.
[50] Smith, "Indigenous Education in Africa," p. 322. See also Smith, "Function of Folk Tales," p. 77; *Knowing the African*, p. 160.
[51] Edwin W. Smith, "Social Anthropology and Missionary Work," *International Review of Missions*, XIII (October, 1924), p. 530.
[52] Edwin W. Smith, *The Shrine of a People's Soul* (London: Student Christian Movement, 1929), p. 150.
[53] "Archdeacon Owen said of those whom he has known for many years in Uganda and Kenya that it would be possible to construct out of their

traditions a book that might be called the African Old Testament—legends, histories and oracles that had been God's way of educating the people in the past." Smith, *Christian Mission in Africa*, p. 41.

54 *Ibid.*

55 Edwin W. Smith, "The Bible in the Empire," *The Native Races of the Empire*, ed. by Godfrey Lagden (London: W. Collins Sons and Co. Ltd., 1924), p. 339. On the importance of translation see also: Edwin W. Smith, "A School for Translators," *International Review of Missions*, XXXIV (July, 1945), pp. 243–252. In his book *The Impossible*, which is a story of the work of the British and Foreign Bible Society, he calls the Bible the "Forerunner" of the Lord and the most effective of missionary pioneers. Edwin W. Smith, *The Impossible* (London: The British and Foreign Bible Society, 1932), p. 15.

56 Smith, *Shrine of People's Soul*, p. 194.

57 Smith, *African Beliefs and Christian Faith*, pp. 111–112.

58 *Ibid.*, p. 125.

59 *Ibid.*, p. 126.

60 *Ibid.*, p. 18.

61 *Ibid.*, p. 19.

62 *Ibid.*, p. 20.

63 *Ibid.*, p. 22.

64 *Ibid.*, p. 23.

65 *Ibid.*

66 *Ibid.*, p. 24.

67 *Ibid.*, p. 25.

68 Smith, Secret of the African, p. 142.

69 Smith, African Beliefs and Christian Faith, p. 185.

70 *Ibid.*, p. 186.

71 Smith, *Blessed Missionaries*, p. 127; *Christian Mission in Africa*, p. 48; *Shrine of People's Soul*, p. 193.

72 Smith, *African Beliefs and Christian Faith*, p. 25.

73 *Ibid.*, p. 113.

74 *Ibid.*, p. 26.

75 Smith, *African Ideas of God*, p. 33.

76 *Ibid.*, p. 32.

77 Smith, *Shrine of People's Soul*, pp. 133–134.

78 Smith, *African Ideas of God*, pp. 34–35.

79 Smith specifically encourages missionaries to look for points of contact. Smith, *Religion of Lower Races*, p. 74.

80 Smith, *African Ideas of God*, p. 35.

81 Smith, *Secret of the African*, p. 141.

82 *Ibid.*, p. 90.

83 Smith, *Christian Mission in Africa*, p. 41.

84 Smith, *African Beliefs and Christian Faith*, p. 34.

85 Smith, *African Ideas of God*, p. 31.

86 This is a favorite text and is cited in several of Smith's writings. See for example Smith, *Secret of the African*, p. 100.

87 Smith, *African Ideas of God*, p. 32.

88 *Ibid.*

89 Smith, "Sublimation of Bantu Life and Thought," p. 83.

90 Smith, *African Beliefs and Christian Faith*, p. 24.

91 Smith, *Knowing the African*, p. 11.

92 Smith, "Sublimation of Bantu Life and Thought," p. 84.

93 Smith, *Christian Mission in Africa*, p. 43.

6. Ethics: Does God Require Righteousness?

[1] Smith recognizes a distinction between customs and laws. Smith, *African Beliefs and Christian Faith*, p. 65.

[2] Smith, "Disintegration of African Society," p. 144.

[3] Smith, *Ila-Speaking Peoples*, I, pp. 343–344.

[4] *Ibid.*, pp. 344–345.

[5] *Ibid.*, pp. 346–347.

[6] *Ibid.*, p. 346.

[7] Smith, *Secret of the African*, p. 137.

[8] See Chapter II, pp. 21, 40.

[9] Smith, *Ila-Speaking Peoples*, II, p. 83.

[10] Smith, "Disintegration of African Society," p. 146.

[11] Smith, *Ila-Speaking Peoples*, I, pp. 348–349.

[12] *Ibid.*, pp. 206–207.

[13] Smith, *Ila-Speaking Peoples*, II, pp. 43–44.

[14] A form of cicisbeism discussed later in this chapter. See *ibid.*, pp. 67–69.

[15] This is the real meaning. The literal rendering is: "As for us, our little axe is long; as for you the stump is short." *Ibid.*, p. 113.

[16] *Ibid.*, pp. 112–113.

[17] Smith, *Secret of the African*, p. 54.

[18] Smith, *Ila-Speaking Peoples*, II, p. 114.

[19] Smith, *Secret of the African*, p. 54.

[20] It should be noted that the kind of incest allowed in such cases is carefully prescribed. Smith, *Ila-Speaking Peoples*, I, p. 261; *Ila-Speaking Peoples*, II, pp. 41–44.

[21] Smith, *Ila-Speaking Peoples*, II, pp. 83–84.

[22] Smith, *Ila-Speaking Peoples*, I, p. 345.

[23] *Ibid.*

[24] Smith, *Ila-Speaking Peoples*, II, p. 189.

[25] *Ibid.*, p. 68.

[26] Smith, *Secret of the African*, p. 51.

[27] Smith, "Disintegration of African Society," pp. 145–146.

[28] Smith, *Ila-Speaking Peoples*, I, p. 345.

[29] Smith, "Disintegration of African Society," pp. 144–145.

[30] Smith, *Ila-Speaking Peoples*, I, pp. 345–346.

[31] *Ibid.*, p. 345.

[32] Smith, "Sublimation of Bantu Life and Thought," p. 95.

[33] Smith, "Disintegration of African Society," p. 145; *Golden Stool*, p. 191.

[34] Smith, *Ila-Speaking Peoples*, II, p. 211.

[35] *Ibid.*, p. 212.

[36] Smith, *Religion of Lower Races*, p. 60.

[37] Smith, *Secret of the African*, p. 140.

[38] Smith, *African Beliefs and Christian Faith*, p. 66.

[39] *Ibid.*, p. 65.

[40] *Ibid.*, p. 66.

[41] *Ibid.*, pp. 67–68.

[42] *Ibid.*, p. 66.

[43] *Ibid.*, p. 68.

[44] *Ibid.*, p. 65.

[45] See again Chapter IV.

[46] Smith, *African Beliefs and Christian Faith*, pp. 58–59.

[47] Smith, *Golden Stool*, p. 280.

[48] Smith, "Sublimation of Bantu Life and Thought," p. 93.

[49] *Ibid.*, p. 92.

[50] Smith, *Christian Mission in Africa*, p. 50. See also Smith, "Function of Folk Tales," p. 77.

[51] Edwin W. Smith, "Polygamy and African Marriage Customs" (paper presented to a missionary conference on Africa, called to follow up the recommendations of the Tambaram Conference, New York, N.Y., December 9, 1939), p. 2. (Mimeographed.) Smith, *Knowing the African*, pp. 81–82.

[52] Smith, *Golden Stool*, p. 263; *Christian Mission in Africa*, pp. 32–33; *Aggrey of Africa*, pp. 3–4.

[53] Smith, *Knowing the African*, p. 19. See also Smith, *Way of White Fields in Rhodesia*, p. 137; "Indigenous African Church," p. 21; *Aggrey of Africa*, p. 226; *Blessed Missionaries*, p. 115; *Golden Stool*, p. 97; "Association and Assimilation in the Christian Mission," *Internatonal Review of Missions*, XXX (July, 1941), 324–326; "Presidential Address: Anthropology and the Practical Man," *Journal of the Royal Anthropological Institute of Great Britain and Ireland*, LXIV (January–June, 1934), p. xxvii.

[54] Smith, *Christian Mission in Africa*, p. 21; *Aggrey of Africa*, p. 257; *Golden Stool*, p. 257; *Blessed Missionaries*, p. 115; *Knowing the African*, pp. 45, 192.

[55] Smith, *Christian Mission in Africa*, p. 104.

[56] Smith, *Golden Stool*, p. 282.

[57] Smith, *Way of White Fields in Rhodesia*, pp. 136–137; *Knowing the African*, p. 19; *Golden Stool*, pp. 97, 259–260, 282; *Christian Mission in Africa*, pp. 32–33, 54.

[58] Smith, "Indigenous African Church," p. 21.

[59] Smith, "Polygamy and African Marriage Customs," pp. 1–6; *Knowing the African*, pp. 91–95.

[60] Smith, "Polygamy and African Marriage Customs," pp. 3–4; *Knowing the African*, pp. 86–89; *Golden Stool*, p. 83; *Great Lion of Bechuanaland*, p. 277; *Mabilles of Basutoland*, pp. 188–189, 210–212; *The Life and Times of Daniel Lindley* (London: Epworth Press, 1949), pp. 365, 391.

[61] Smith, *Christian Mission in Africa*, pp. 50–51; *Knowing the African*, pp. 131–133.

[62] Smith, "Polygamy and African Marriage Customs," pp. 1–6; "Disintegration of African Society," p. 158; *Golden Stool*, pp. 135, 279; *Knowing the African*, pp. 90–92; *Life and Times of Daniel Lindley*, pp. 365, 391; *Christian Mission in Africa*, p. 51; *Aggrey of Africa*, p. 137.

[63] Smith, "Indigenous African Church," pp. 21–22.

[64] *Ibid.*, p. 21.

[65] Smith, *Ila-Speaking Peoples*, II, p. 87.

[66] Smith, "Indigenous African Church," p. 21.

[67] Smith, *Ila-Speaking Peoples*, I, p. 348.

[68] *Ibid.*

[69] Smith, *African Beliefs and Christian Faith*, p. 180.

[70] Smith, "Disintegration of African Society," pp. 153–154.

[71] *Ibid.*, p. 147.

[72] *Ibid.*, p. 157.

[73] Smith, *Secret of the African*, p. 137.

[74] Smith, "Disintegration of African Society," p. 157; *Religion of Lower Races*, p. 68.

[75] Smith, *Religion of Lower Races*, p. 69.

[76] Smith, *Secret of the African*, p. 137.

[77] Smith, "Sublimation of Bantu Life and Thought," pp. 93–94.

[78] Smith, *African Beliefs and Christian Faith*, p. 177.

[79] *Ibid.*

80 Smith, *Religion of Lower Races*, p. 47.
81 Smith, *African Beliefs and Christian Faith*, p. 182.
82 *Ibid.*, p. 178.
83 *Ibid.*
84 *Ibid.*, p. 190.

7. Worship: Is God Worshipped?

1 Smith, *Ila-Speaking Peoples*, II, p. 174.
2 Smith, *Religion of Lower Races*, p. 45.
3 Smith, *Secret of the African*, p. 117.
4 Smith, *Knowing the African*, pp. 108–109.
5 Smith, *African Ideas of God*, p. 26.
6 *Ibid.*, p. 85.
7 Smith, *African Beliefs and Christian Faith*, p. 70.
8 *Ibid.*, pp. 70–71.
9 Smith, *Religion of Lower Races*, p. 44.
10 Smith, *Ila-Speaking Peoples*, II, p. 174.
11 Smith, *Religion of Lower Races*, pp. 44–45.
12 Smith, *Ila-Speaking Peoples*, II, p. 174.
13 Smith, *Secret of the African*, p. 116.
14 See again Chapter VI.
15 Smith, *Ila-Speaking Peoples*, II, p. 187.
16 Smith, *Ila-Speaking Peoples*, I, p. 113.
17 *Ibid.*, p. 176.
18 *Ibid.*, p. 388.
19 Smith, *Ila-Speaking Peoples*, II, p. 156.
20 *Ibid.*, pp. 172–173.
21 *Ibid.*, p. 173.
22 Smith, *Ila-Speaking Peoples*, I, p. 293.
23 Smith, *Ila-Speaking Peoples*, II, p. 120.
24 *Ibid.*, pp. 174–175.
25 *Ibid.*, p. 176.
26 *Ibid.*
27 Smith, *Religion of Lower Races*, p. 45.
28 Smith, *African Beliefs and Christian Faith*, p. 70.
29 Smith, *Religion of Lower Races*, p. 45.
30 *Ibid.*
31 Smith, *Ila-Speaking Peoples*, I, p. 145.
32 Smith, *Religion of Lower Races*, p. 45.
33 Smith, *Ila-Speaking Peoples*, II, pp. 170–171.
34 Smith, *African Beliefs and Christian Faith*, pp. 69–71.
35 Smith, *Secret of the African*, p. 121.
36 Smith, *African Beliefs and Christian Faith*, p. 69.
37 *Ibid.*, p. 70.
38 *Ibid.*, pp. 71–73.
39 Smith, *Secret of the African*, pp. 122–125.
40 *Ibid.*, p. 122.
41 *Ibid.*, pp. 121–122.
42 Smith, *African Ideas of God*, p. 12.
43 Smith, *Secret of the African*, p. 122.
44 Smith, *African Beliefs and Christian Faith*, p. 74.
45 *Ibid.*, pp. 75–76.
46 Smith, *Secret of the African*, p. 125.

[47] Smith, *African Beliefs and Christian Faith*, p. 69. See also Smith, *African Ideas of God*, p. 159.

[48] Smith *African Beliefs and Christian Faith*, p. 72.

[49] *Ibid.*

[50] Smith, *Ila-Speaking Peoples*, II, p. 210.

[51] Smith, *African Beliefs and Christian Faith*, p. 74.

[52] Smith, *Ila-Speaking Peoples*, II, pp. 209–211.

[53] Smith, *African Beliefs and Christian Faith*, p. 74.

[54] Smith, *Ila-Speaking Peoples*, II, p. 209.

[55] Smith, *African Beliefs and Christian Faith*, p. 74.

[56] Smith, *Knowing the African*, p. 113.

[57] Smith, *African Ideas of God*, p. 26.

[58] Smith, *Secret of the African*, p. 110.

[59] *Ibid.*, p. 35.

[60] *Ibid.*, pp. 111, 121.

[61] Smith, *African Beliefs and Christian Faith*, p. 69.

[62] Smith, *Secret of the African*, p. 123.

[63] *Ibid.*, pp. 124–125.

[64] Smith, *African Beliefs and Christian Faith*, p. 54. See again Chapter III.

[65] Smith, *Secret of the African*, p. 63. See also Smith, *Ila-Speaking Peoples*, II, p. 208.

[66] Smith, *African Beliefs and Christian Faith*, p. 49. See also Smith, *African Ideas of God*, pp. 10, 15.

[67] Smith, *Aggrey of Africa*, p. 132.

[68] *Ibid.* See also Smith, *Secret of the African*, pp. 132–133.

[69] Smith, *Robert Moffat*, p. 101.

[70] *Ibid.*, p. 114.

[71] *Ibid.*, p. 103.

[72] *Ibid.*

[73] *Ibid.*, p. 106.

[74] *Ibid.*, p. 94.

[75] Smith, *Blessed Missionaries*, p. 18.

[76] Smith, *Secret of the African*, p. 128.

[77] *Ibid.*, pp. 129–130.

[78] *Ibid.*, p. 130.

[79] Smith, *African Beliefs and Christian Faith*, p. 190.

[80] See again Chapter VII.

[81] Smith, "Indigenous African Church," p. 9.

[82] *Ibid.*

[83] *Ibid.*

[84] Smith, *Golden Stool*, p. 280.

[85] Smith, "Indigenous African Church," p. 12.

[86] *Ibid.*, p. 13.

[87] Smith, "Sublimation of Bantu Life and Thought," p. 91.

[88] Smith, *Golden Stool*, pp. 274–275.

[89] Smith, "Indigenous African Church," p. 13.

[90] *Ibid.*, p. 14. See also Smith, *Golden Stool*, p. 280.

[91] Smith, *Golden Stool*, p. 273.

[92] *Ibid.*, p. 279; Smith, *Knowing the African*, p. 279.

[93] Smith, "Indigenous African Church," p. 10.

[94] *Ibid.*, p. 11.

[95] *Ibid.*, pp. 11–12.

[96] Smith, *Religion of Lower Races*, p. 45.

[97] Smith, *African Beliefs and Christian Faith*, p. 74. See again Chapter VII.

[98] Smith, *Ila-Speaking Peoples*, II, p. 211.

[99] See Chapter VI.

[100] Smith, *Ila-Speaking Peoples*, II, p. 176. See again Chapter VII.

[101] See especially Smith, *Aggrey of Africa; Blessed Missionaries; Golden Stool; Knowing the African; Way of the White Fields.*

[102] Smith, "Indigenous African Church," p. 8.

[103] *Ibid.*

[104] *Ibid.*, pp. 10–11.

[105] *Ibid.*, p. 10.

[106] *Ibid.*, pp. 10–11.

[107] *Ibid.*, pp. 5–6.

8. Critical Analysis: Traditional View

[1] Victor W. Turner, *The Drums of Affliction: A Study of Religious Processes among the Ndembu of Zambia* (Oxford: The Clarendon Press, 1968), pp. 14–15.

[2] J. B. Danquah, *The Akan Doctrine of God* (London: Lutterworth Press, 1944), p. 12, 79.

[3] *Ibid.*, p. 82.

[4] E. Bolaji Idowu, *Olódùmarè: God in Yoruba Belief* (London: Longmans, Green and Co., 1962), p. vii, 140, 143.

[5] K. A. Busia, *Africa in Search of Democracy* (London: Routledge and Kegan Paul, 1967), p. 5.

[6] K. A. Busia, "The Ashanti," *African Worlds*, ed. by Daryll Forde (London: Oxford University Press, 1954), pp. 192–193.

[7] Mbiti, *Concepts of God in Africa*, p. 12.

[8] John Middleton, *Lugbara Religion* (London: Oxford University Press, 1960), p. 27.

[9] *Ibid.*, p. 252.

[10] Godfrey Lienhardt, *Divinity and Experience: The Religion of the Dinka* (Oxford: The Clarendon Press, 1961), p. 38.

[11] E. E. Evans-Pritchard, *Nuer Religion* (Oxford: The Clarendon Press, 1956), p. 9.

[12] *Ibid.*, p. 2.

[13] *Ibid.*, pp. 9–10.

[14] *Ibid.*, p. 4.

[15] *Ibid.*

[16] Godfrey Lienhardt, "The Shilluk of the Upper Nile," *African Worlds, op. cit.*, pp. 160–161.

[17] *Ibid.*, p. 158.

[18] Lienhardt, *Divinity and Experience*, pp. 54–55.

[19] Middleton, *Lugbara Religion*, p. 27.

[20] J. van Wing, *Études Bakongo* (Louvain: Imprimerie M. and L. Symons, 1959), p. 299.

[21] W. J. van der Merwe, *The Shona Idea of God* (Fort Victoria: Morgenster Mission Press, 1957), p. 8. M. Murpree agrees: "He [God] is, possibly, the source of both good and evil." Marshall W. Murpree, *Christianity and the Shona* (New York: The Athlone Press, 1969), p. 49.

[22] J. J. Maquet, "The Kingdom of Ruanda," *African Worlds, op. cit.*, p. 169.

[23] *Ibid.*

[24] Monica Wilson, *Communal Rituals of the Nyakyusa* (London: Oxford University Press, 1959), p. 157.

25 Busia, *African Worlds*, pp. 200, 209.

26 Idowu, *Olódùmarè*, pp. 117, 120.

27 *Ibid.*, p. 173.

28 S. F. Nadel, *Nupe Religion* (London: Routledge and Kegan Paul, 1954), pp. 11–12.

29 Some Africans laugh at this suggestion, indicating that it is due to poor cultivation. Wilson, *Communal Rituals of Nyakyusa*, p. 158.

30 *Ibid.*

31 Mary Douglas, "The Lele of Kasai," *African Worlds, op. cit.,* p. 9.

32 Maquet, *African Worlds*, p. 169.

33 Evans-Pritchard, *Nuer Religion*, p. 12.

34 *Ibid.*, pp. 6–7.

35 See again Chapter IV.

36 Smith, *Ila-Speaking Peoples*, II, p. 200.

37 *Ibid.*, pp. 201–202.

38 *Ibid.*, p. 202.

39 *Ibid.* See also pp. 62, 322. Smith says: "The name Ushatwakwe indicates a more or less fatalistic belief, i.e. that God will do as He lists, apart from us: that we are in the hands of fate." Edwin W. Smith, *A Handbook of the Ila Language* (London: Oxford University Press, 1907), p. 300.

40 Smith, *Ila-Speaking Peoples*, II, p. 207.

41 Smith, *Secret of the African*, pp. 104–105.

42 Smith, *Religion of Lower Races*, p. 59.

43 Smith, *African Beliefs and Christian Faith*, pp. 60–64.

44 Smith, *Ila-Speaking Peoples*, II, pp. 199–200.

45 *Ibid.*, p. 199.

46 O'Connell suggests as an explanation for God's withdrawal man's inability to cope with God's righteousness, but he makes no attempt to prove God's "all-purity" in traditional thought. Shelton's criticism therefore seems well taken: "To claim that men shrank from God because of their sense of impurity by contrast with God's 'all-purity' is erroneous, a romanticization obscuring the simpler fact that people find One so powerful impossible to comprehend." However, Shelton himself adds little further light to the subject since his major preoccupation is to suggest that in the traditional view God is not in fact withdrawn. James O'Connell, "The Withdrawal of the High God in West African Religion: An Essay in Interpretation," *Man*, LXII (May, 1962), pp. 67–69. Austin J. Shelton, "On Recent Interpretations of Deus Otiosus: The Withdrawn God in West African Psychology," *Man*, LXIV (March–April, 1964), p. 53–54.

47 Wilson, *Communal Rituals of Nyakyusa*, p. 157.

48 *Ibid.*, p. 187.

49 van Wing, *Études Bakongo*, p. 300.

50 Evans-Pritchard, *Nuer Religion*, p. 312. See also p. 275.

51 Smith, *African Beliefs and Christian Faith*, p. 68. This example from the Konde adds some support to O'Connell's thesis, cited earlier, linking God's withdrawal to His "purity." However, the thesis is not thereby proven since many African peoples do not see God's part in life's tragedies as a punishment for man's wrongdoing.

52 John V. Taylor, *CMS News-Letter*, No. 338 (May, 1970), p. 2.

53 John V. Taylor, *The Primal Vision* (London: S.C.M. Press, 1963), pp. 86–87.

54 Smith, "Foreword," p. xiii.

55 Smith, "Anthropology and the Practical Man," p. xiv.

56 Smith, *Knowing the African*, p. 116.

[57] Smith, *Religion of Lower Races*, pp. 62–63.

[58] *Ibid.*, pp. 63–64; *Secret of the African*, p. 80.

[59] E. E. Evans-Pritchard, *Theories of Primitive Religion* (Oxford: The Clarendon Press, 1965), p. 15.

[60] Smith, *Religion of Lower Races*, pp. 63–64.

[61] Evans-Pritchard, *Theories of Primitive Religion*, pp. 100, 105.

[62] *Ibid.*, p. 121. See also Evans-Pritchard, *Nuer Religion*, p. 322.

[63] Melville J. Herskovits, *Cultural Anthropology*, an abridged and revised edition of *Man and His Works* (New York: Alfred A. Knopf, 1955), pp. 216–217.

[64] Elizabeth Colson, "Introduction," *The Ila-Speaking Peoples of Northern Rhodesia*, I, *op. cit.*, p. 4.

[65] When Smith and Rattray wrote, there was considerable direct worship of God among the Ashanti. See Smith, *Secret of the African*, p. 121; R. S. Rattray, *Ashanti* (London: Oxford University Press, 1923), pp. 141–142. For references to the fact that the Ashanti now offer God less direct worship than formerly, see Busia, *African Worlds*, p. 192; Noel Smith, *The Presbyterian Church of Ghana, 1835–1960* (Accra: Ghana Universities Press, 1966), p. 76.

[66] Baumann insists that "die missglückte Botschaft" is "ein echter Sündenfallmythus" although even he must admit "die passive Rolle der Menschen" in the process. Hermann Baumann, *Schöpfung und Urzeit des Menschen im Mythus der Afrikanischen Völker* (Berlin: Verlag von Dietrich Reimer, (1936), p. 268, 272. In discussing the role of Chameleon in the Zulu story of the origin of death, Werner says: "Here no reason is given for Unkulunkulu's sending the second messenger. I do not think any genuine native version suggests that he changed his mind on account of men's wickedness. Where this is said one suspects it to be a moralizing afterthought, due perhaps to European influence." Alice Werner, *Myths and Legends of the Bantu* (2nd ed.; London: Frank Cass and Co., 1968), p. 32. See also Alice Werner, "African Mythology," *The Mythology of All Races*, VII, ed. by John A. MacCulloch (Boston: Marshall Jones Co., 1925), p. 161.

[67] John S. Mbiti, *African Religions and Philosophy* (New York: Frederick A. Praeger, 1969), p. 98.

[68] Lienhardt, *Divinity and Experience*, p. 53.

[69] See especially Smith, *African Beliefs and Christian Faith*, pp. 34–36.

[70] Placide Tempels, *La Philosophie Bantoue* (Paris: Présence Africaine, 1949), pp. 33–38.

[71] *Ibid.*, p. 37.

[72] *Ibid.*, pp. 39–45.

[73] Edwin W. Smith, review of *La Philosophie Bantoue*, by Placide Tempels, *Africa*, XVI (July, 1946), p. 202.

[74] *Ibid.*, p. 200.

[75] Smith, *African Ideas of God*, p. 18.

[76] *Ibid.*

[77] *Ibid.*

[78] Mbiti, *African Religions and Philosophy*, p. 92.

[79] Busia says: "Animals and inanimate objects too have spirits, and are to be propitiated according as their spirits are conceived to be strong and potentially harmful or not." Busia, *African Worlds*, p. 205.

[80] Sawyerr states that, although sometimes latent, "all existent matter—human, animal, vegetable and mineral—possesses life." Harry Sawyerr, *Creative Evangelism: Towards a New Christian Encounter with Africa* (London: Lutterworth Press, 1968), p. 14.

81 Kagame distinguishes between "beings" which have intelligence and those which do not. He defines *umuntu* as "être qui a l'intelligence," and *ikintu* as "être qui n'a pas l'intelligence." Alexis Kagame, *La Philosophie bantu-rwandaise de l'Être* (Bruxelles: Académie Royale des Sciences Coloniales, 1956), p. 108. Surprisingly while quoting Kagame, Jahn feels the necessity of returning to the word "force" (*Kraft*) as a translation of the root *NTU*. Janheinz Jahn, *Muntu: Umrisse der neoafrikanischen Kultur* (Düsseldorf-Köln: Eugen Diederichs Verlag, 1958), pp. 104–105.

82 Sawyerr insists that "God is the symbol of cosmic totality of which man is a small part." Harry Sawyerr, *God: Ancestor or Creator?* (London: Logman Group, 1970), p. 30. See also pp. 46, 50. Taylor talks of the sense of cosmic oneness which characterizes African Religion: "No distinction can be made between sacred and secular, between natural and supernatural, for Nature, Man and the Unseen are inseparably involved in one another in a total community." Taylor, *Primal Vision*, p. 72. Griaule says: "The body of the first man having been created from the soil, a constant relationship exists between the actual human body and the earthly surroundings . . . Moreover, this matter [the earth] is not inert." Marcel Griaule, "The Idea of Person among the Dogon," *Cultures and Societies of Africa*, ed. by Simon and Phoebe Ottenberg (New York: Random House, 1960), p. 366.

83 Mbiti is both appreciative and critical of Tempels' study. He does not believe that Tempels' theory of "vital force" is characteristic of other African peoples. In this he may be thrown off by the term "vital force." It is clear that Mbiti's understanding of reality is very different from the Western view. See Mbiti, *African Religions and Philosophy*, pp. 10, 56–57. For a West African people illustrating Tempels' thesis, see L. V. Thomas, "Brève esquisse sur la pensée cosmologique du Diola," *African Systems of Thought, op. cit.*, pp. 366–381. Ogot insists that Tempels' ideas are also true of Nilotic peoples. Bethwell A. Ogot, "The Concept of Jok," *African Studies*, XX, No. 2 (1961), pp. 126–127.

84 This may be a partial explanation for the interest that Danquah shows in Spinoza and pantheism. Danquah, *Akan Doctrine of God*, pp. 173, 176. Parrinder also calls attention to the semi-pantheism of the African conception. Geoffrey Parrinder, *West African Psychology* (London: Lutterworth Press, 1951), p. 31; *Religion in Africa*, p. 28.

85 This is not meant to suggest that the word "person" should never be employed to describe African thought, but it does point up the ambiguities in its use and the necessity that it be carefully defined. Merely to talk of "person" is to conjure up in the Western mind an approach to reality which differs radically from that in Africa. Idowu also raises some questions about the word as applied to God and notes at the same time the importance of its definition. E. Bolaji Idowu, "God," *Biblical Revelation and African Beliefs*, ed. by Kwesi A. Dickson and Paul Ellingworth (London: Lutterworth Press, 1969), p. 21.

86 See on this Evans-Pritchard, *Nuer Religion*, pp. 123–125. Raimo Harjula, *God and the Sun in Meru Thought* (Helsinki: Finnish Society for Missiology and Eucumenics, 1969).

87 Edwin W. Smith, "Africa: What do we know of it?" *Journal of the Royal Anthropological Institute of Great Britain and Ireland*, LXV (January–June, 1935), p. 76.

88 Smith, "Foreword," p. xi.

89 Smith, *Knowing the African*, p. 99.

90 Gelfand is impressed by the similarities of African belief in different parts of the continent. Michael Gelfand, *An African's Religion: The Spirit*

of Nyajena (Capetown: Juta and Company, 1966), pp. 110–117. Thompson takes the opposite view: There is no African idea of God; there are as many ideas as there are tribes. He says: "Any particular African religion would have to be studied in its totality in all its manifestations; and all its myths and legends studied in great detail and in relation to each other before any valid conclusions can be drawn as to the nature and content of such religion." P. E. S. Thompson, "Reflections Upon the African Idea of God," *The Sierra Leone Bulletin of Religion,* VII (December, 1965), p. 58.

91 Busia, *Africa in Search of Democracy,* p. 4. Mbiti mentions specifically that each African people "has its own religious system." Nevertheless, his treatment of the whole of Africa in one book is a witness to his basic agreement with Busia. Mbiti, *African Religions and Philosophy,* p. 1.

92 This method is most noticeable in *African Beliefs and Christian Faith.*

93 Evans-Pritchard, *Nuer Religion,* p. 315.

94 *Ibid.,* pp. 315–316.

95 *Ibid.,* p. 315.

96 *Ibid.,* pp. 9–10.

97 *Ibid.,* pp. 16–21.

98 *Ibid.,* pp. 12–13.

99 *Ibid.,* p. 13.

100 *Ibid.,* p. 14.

101 *Ibid.,* p. 13.

102 *Ibid.,* pp. 316–317.

103 *Ibid.,* p. 200.

104 *Ibid.,* pp. 29, 317.

105 *Ibid.,* p. 312.

106 Danquah, *Akan Doctrine of God,* pp. 41, 113–114. Busia, *African Worlds,* p. 197. Idowu, *Olódùmarè,* pp. 116–117, 120, 173–174, 182, 209. W. T. Harris and Harry Sawyerr, *The Springs of Mende Belief and Conduct* (Freetown: Sierra Leone University Press, 1968), pp. 2–3. Melville J. Herskovits, *Dahomey: An Ancient West African Kingdom,* II (New York: J. J. Augustin, 1938), p. 206.

107 Meyer Fortes, *Oedipus and Job in West African Religion* (Cambridge: The University Press, 1959), pp. 36–38. Fortes also translates the term as "Predestined Fate." See Meyer Fortes, *The Web of Kinship among the Tallensi* (London: Oxford University Press, 1949), p. 90.

108 Fortes, *Oedipus and Job,* pp. 38–39.

109 The idea of an individual choosing his own destiny is also found among the Yoruba. Idowu, *Olódùmarè,* p. 173.

110 Fortes, *Oedipus and Job,* pp. 38–39; *Web of Kinship,* p. 228.

111 Fortes, *Oedipus and Job,* p. 37; *Web of Kinship,* pp. 90, 203.

112 Fortes, *Oedipus and Job,* p. 40.

113 *Ibid.*

114 *Ibid.,* p. 78.

115 *Ibid.,* pp. 38–39.

116 Middleton, *Lugbara Religion,* p. 27.

117 *Ibid.,* p. 193.

118 Parrinder, *Religion in Africa,* p. 43.

119 Efraim Andersson, *Churches at the Grass-Roots* (London: Lutterworth Press, 1968), p. 113.

120 *Ibid.*

121 Dammann notes the different tendencies in African dualism. Ernst Dammann, *Die Religionen Afrikas* (Stuttgart: W. Kohlhammer Verlag, 1963), pp. 25–26.

¹²² The accepted orthography in Western Kenya today is Bukusu, but Vugusu is retained in this study because of its use by Günther Wagner who carried on the early anthropological work among them. See Günther Wagner, *The Bantu of North Kavirondo*, I (London: Oxford University Press, 1949).

¹²³ *Ibid.*, p. 175. See also Wagner, 'The Abaluyia of Kavirondo," *African Worlds, op. cit.*, p. 44. Among the Maasai, the black God (*Engai narok*) is good, while the red god (*engai nanyokye*) is bad. A. C. Hollis, *The Masai: Their Language and Folklore* (Oxford: The Clarendon Press, 1905), pp. 264–65. However, it appears that Maasai ideas are closer to those of the Lugbara and Kuta than the Vugusu.

¹²⁴ Wagner, *African Worlds*, p. 44.

¹²⁵ *Ibid.*

¹²⁶ *Ibid.*, p. 43.

¹²⁷ Busia, *African Worlds*, p. 192; Rattray, *Ashanti*, p. 51.

¹²⁸ Busia says: "The religion of the Ashanti is mainly ancestor-worship; and the position of the chief gains significance within the organized ceremonies by which the people express their sense of dependence on the ancestors." K. A. Busia, *The Position of the Chief in the Modern Political System of Ashanti* (London: International African Institute, 1951), p. 23.

¹²⁹ Smith, *Secret of the African*, p. 130. Rattray, *Ashanti*, p. 150.

¹³⁰ Jomo Kenyatta, *Facing Mount Kenya: The Tribal Life of the Gikuyu* (London: Martin Secker and Warburg, 1938), p. 237.

¹³¹ Michael Gelfand, *Shona Religion* (Capetown: Juta and Company, 1962), pp. 143–144.

9. Critical Analysis: Christian Contribution

¹ See C. P. Groves, *The Planting of Christianity in Africa*, I–IV (London: Lutterworth Press, 1948–58). Roland Oliver, *The Missionary Factor in East Africa* (London: Longmans, Green and Co., 1952).

² Sidney G. Williamson, *Akan Religion and the Christian Faith* (Accra: Ghana Universities Press, 1965), p. 25.

³ Rattray, *Ashanti*, pp. 141–144; Smith, *Secret of the African*, pp. 121–122.

⁴ "None the less, as a monotheistic faith Christianity expresses in fuller and deeper manner this recognition of the existence and power of the Supreme Being. Christian worship, offered solely to God, attracts the Akan as supplementing in practice what theoretically Akan religion enunciates in its beliefs." Williamson, *Akan Religion and Christian Faith*, p. 26.

⁵ *Ibid.*

⁶ John V. Taylor, *The Growth of the Church in Buganda* (London: S.C.M. Press, 1958), p. 252.

⁷ *Ibid.*, pp. 252–253.

⁸ Smith, *Blessed Missionaries*, p. 8.

⁹ Andersson, *Churches at Grass-Roots*, pp. 158–159; Taylor, *Growth of Church in Buganda*, pp. 102–105.

¹⁰ Zoa complains that Christians are expected to be interested in heavenly rather than worldly realities. Jean B. Zoa, "Der Christliche Beitrag zum Gestaltwandel Afrikas," *Theologie und Kirke in Afrika*, Herausgegeben von Horst Bürkle (Stuttgart: Evangelisches Verlagswerk, 1968), p. 288. Debrunner laments the conception of Christianity as a "burial society" providing "burial insurance." Hans W. Debrunner, *A Church Between Colonial Powers: A Study of the Church in Togo* (London: Lutterworth Press, 1965), p. 277. Welbourn says: "For many Christ became a ticket to a 'happy

land, far, far away.' But for few did he have any relation to the important events of life." F. B. Welbourn, "Some Problems of African Christianity: Guilt and Shame," *Christianity in Tropical Africa*, ed. by C. G. Baëta (London: Oxford University Press, 1968), p. 191.

11 Mbiti remarks that very few African peoples picture the afterlife in terms of punishment or reward. For most the hereafter is a continuation of this life in the realm of spirit. Mbiti, *African Religions and Philosophy*, p. 161. Nketia says: "It is believed that there is a world of the dead built on much the same pattern as that of this world and that when a person dies he goes to the Ancestors." J. H. Nketia, *Funeral Dirges of the Akan People* (2nd ed.; New York: Negro Universities Press, 1969), p. 6.

12 Andersson, *Churches at Grass-Roots*, pp. 148–149. Andersson would be hard put to prove his case. Foerster lists eighteen places in the Synoptics where σώsω and διασώsω are used to describe Jesus' healing ministry. An example is Mark 3:4 where the term carries the double meaning of "making alive" and "making healthy." In most cases the reference is to the whole man, including his spiritual and bodily needs. Werner Foerster, "σώsω und σωτηεία im Neuen Testament," *Theologisches Wörterbuch zum Neuen Testament, Band VII*, Herausgegeben von Gerhard Friedrich (Stuttgart: W. Kohlhammer Verlag, 1964), p. 990.

13 Andersson calls attention to three such passages relating to sorcery: Deut. 18:10f., Rev. 21:8 and Rev. 22:15. He states that the translations are correct but often lead the African's thoughts in the wrong direction. He does not discuss how they are to be interpreted, but he does mention the accusation that the missionaries have concealed biblical truths from their African converts. Andersson, *Churches at Grass-Roots*, p. 143. Kenyatta also complains about the missionary refusal to discuss the problem of polygamy with the African from the biblical perspective. Kenyatta, *Facing Mount Kenya*, pp. 271–273.

14 "La catéchèse de la victoire du Christ sur toutes les Puissances contribue à mettre de côté tout l'animisme populaire: le Christ a débouté toutes les Puissances, il n'y a plus à s'en occuper; il n'y a pas à croire dans leur influence déterminante comme si nous étions encore leurs esclaves. Il n'y a plus à avoir peur ou à se méfier . . . L'homme est désormais, par le savoir scientifique, en présence des causalités naturelles . . ." Henri Maurier, *Religion et Développement: Traditions Africaines et Catéchèses* (Tours: Maison Mame, 1965), p. 91.

15 In this context, one thinks naturally of the influence of R. Bultmann, especially his famous 1941 essay, reproduced in *Kerygma and Myth*, ed. H. W. Bartsch (London: S.P.C.K., 1953). However, it is a mistake to suppose that Bultmann was the first one to propound such a thesis.

16 K. A. Busia, "The African World View," *Christianity and African Culture* (Accra: Christian Council of the Gold Coast, 1955). Idowu, "Introduction," *Biblical Revelation and African Beliefs*, p. 10. Edmund Ilogu, "The Problem of Indigenization in Nigeria," *International Review of Missions*, XLIX (April, 1960), pp. 170–174.

17 "The early missionaries brought with them not only the Christian gospel. They brought also an attitude which was characteristic more of nineteenth-century scientific rationalism than of Christian faith. They tended to deny the existence of such mystical forces as magic, curses, witchcraft or ancestral spirits." F. B. Welbourn, *East African Christian* (London: Oxford University Press, 1965), p. 37.

18 Andersson would probably deny this, but it is worthwhile noting his testimony to the effect that both pagan and Christian Africans "misunderstand" the meaning of salvation. Andersson, *Churches at Grass-Roots*, p. 148.

19 Taylor, *Growth of Church in Buganda*, p. 253.

20 E. Bolaji Idowu, "The Predicament of the Church in Africa," *Christianity in Tropical Africa*, pp. 434–435.

21 "It was, thus, a religion divorced from life which the missionaries brought to Africans." Welbourn, *East African Christian*, p. 189.

22 "Thus unless Christian worship can be made to satisfy the emotional and spiritual needs of the African, it is unlikely that he will ever have a full grasp of Christian teaching such that his whole life becomes hallowed by Christian truth. What these needs are can be seen in the various rites by which he seeks to give security to his life and to find a permanent basis for it." Thompson, "Reflections Upon African Idea of God," p. 61.

23 Idowu, *Christianity in Tropical Africa*, p. 433.

24 M. Field is overly optimistic in suggesting that African Christians can go to pagan shrines with "no conflict in their own minds." Margaret J. Field, *Search for Security: An Ethno-Psychiatric Study of Rural Ghana* (Evanston, Ill.: Northwestern University Press, 1960), p. 54.

25 Welbourn, *East African Christian*, p. 102.

26 Smith, *Secret of the African*, p. 97.

27 Smith, *Knowing the African*, p. 120.

28 Messenger advances the thesis that the Christian message of forgiveness has undermined traditional morality by giving the African the impression that he can sin with impunity. John C. Messenger, Jr., "The Christian Concept of Forgiveness and Anang Morality," *Practical Anthropology*, VI (May–June, 1959), pp. 100–101. John C. Messenger, Jr., "Religious Acculturation among the Anang Ibibio," *Continuity and Change in African Culture*, ed. by William R. Bascom and Melville J. Herskovits (Chicago: The University Press, 1959), p. 297. There is no doubt some truth to Messenger's contention, but a case can also be made for saying that missionaries brought a new legalism to Africa, with the present life of an individual determining his future destiny. In any case Edwin Smith maintains a healthy balance between the indicative and imperative of the gospel. See especially *African Beliefs and Christian Faith*, p. 159.

29 Indeed many are very far from understanding the issues as well as Smith. Taylor alludes to the fact that the enthusiasts for indigenization are often non-Africans. The reason for African reluctance is not always conservatism but a recognition that "the white 'indigenizers' are too superficial, and Africans know it." Taylor, *Primal Vision*, p. 23.

30 Sharpe points out that there are many different meanings for the concept and that not all those who use it are aware of its full implications. Erich J. Sharpe, *Not to Destroy but to Fulfill: The Contribution of J. N. Farquhar to Protestant Missionary Thought in India before 1914* (Uppsala: Almqvist & Wiksells Boktryckeri AB, 1965), p. 358.

31 There has been no comparable discussion among African scholars.

32 Farquhar's view appears in many of his writings, especially *The Crown of Hinduism* (London: Oxford University Press, 1920). Sharpe's book (cited above) is a study of Farquhar's understanding of "fulfillment."

33 Sharpe, *Not to Destroy but to Fulfill*, p. 339.

34 *Ibid.*, pp. 39–41.

35 *Ibid.*, p. 336.

36 Smith, *African Beliefs and Christian Faith*, pp. 18–25. See again Chapter V.

37 Hendrik Kraemer, *The Christian Message in a non-Christian World* (New York: Harper and Brothers, 1938), p. 123.

38 Sharpe, *Not to Destroy but to Fulfill*, pp. 337–338.

39 Smith, *Golden Stool*, pp. 272–273.

40 See Chapter VI.

41 Smith, "Social Anthropology and Missionary Work," p. 526. See Chapter III.

42 A. G. Hogg, " 'The Crown of Hinduism,' and Other Volumes," reviews of *The Crown of Hinduism* by J. N. Farquhar, *The Soul of India: An Introduction to the Study of Hinduism, in its Historical Setting and Development, and in its Internal and Historical Relations to Christianity* by George Howells, and *Hinduism, Ancient and Modern, Viewed in the Light of the Incarnation* by John A. Sharrock, *International Review of Missions*, III (January, 1914), pp. 172–173.

43 Hendrik Kraemer, *Religion and the Christian Faith* (Philadelphia: The Westminster Press, 1956), pp. 215–216.

44 A. G. Hogg, *The Christian Message to the Hindu* (London: S.C.M. Press, 1947), p. 30. Hogg quotes Rudolf Otto to the effect that since the religion of India and the religion of the Bible turn on different axes, it is impossible to consider one a "preparation" and the other a "fulfillment."

45 Kraemer, *Religion and Christian Faith*, p. 84.

46 See as an example Kraemer, *Christian Message in non-Christian World*, p. 111.

47 Kraemer, *Religion and Christian Faith*, p. 214.

48 *Ibid.*, p. 217.

49 *Ibid.*, p. 220.

50 *Ibid.*, p. 225.

51 *Ibid.*, p. 276.

52 *Ibid.*, pp. 358–359.

53 *Ibid.*, p. 348.

54 *Ibid.*, p. 381.

55 As proof that Smith held this view to the end of his life, see one of his last articles, "African Symbolism," written in 1952, p. 35.

56 Maurier goes well beyond Smith in seeing an opposition between Western science and the African world-view. Part of the task of the Church, as seen by Maurier, is to use science to "demythologize" the pagan African mentality. Maurier, *Religion et Développement*, pp. 88, 91.

57 For a very helpful study of the relationship of the "how" and "why" in African beliefs regarding magic and witchcraft, see Max Gluckman, *Custom and Conflict in Africa* (Oxford: Basil Blackwell, 1963), pp. 81–86. Gluckman goes on to confuse the matter, stating that "beliefs in magic and witchcraft help to distract attention from the real causes of natural misfortune" (p. 108), as if these "real causes" could be discovered by eschewing beliefs in magic and witchcraft. Admittedly the African tendency to seek immediately mystical answers prevents him from arriving at many practical solutions which would be of help to him in his daily life. Here science has an important contribution to make. Nevertheless, it is essential to recognize that, even if by scientific methods one discovers additional facts (about disease, to take an example) which are useful, scientific methods cannot answer the ultimate questions which are of most importance to the African: Why *one* suffers from the disease and the *other* does not! Why *one* responds to treatment and the *other* does not! Why *one* dies from it and the *other* does not! The Western doctor may indeed attempt an explanation, but there is a mystery beyond which he cannot go.

58 Horton makes it clear that the difference between Western and African traditional thought cannot be reduced to an empirical versus a non-empirical orientation to reality. Robin Horton, "African Traditional Thought and Western Science," *Africa*, XXXVII (January, 1967), p. 58.

59 This does not mean that the African is traditionally a "scientist." As a method, science is a product of Western thought which can be historically dated. The point at issue here is whether scientific and traditional conceptions are contradictory. As Foté's discussion of the "déterminisme scientifique" displayed in the traditional technology of iron smelting suggests, the two cannot be placed in opposition. Memel Foté, "Rapport sur la Civilisation Animiste," *Colloque sur les Religions Abidjan 5/12 Avril 1961* (Paris: Présence Africaine, 1962), pp. 46–47.

60 See J. Clyde Mitchell, "The Meaning of Misfortune for Urban Africans," *African System of Thought*, p. 196.

61 Margaret J. Field, *Religion and Medicine of the Gā People* (London: Oxford University Press, 1937), p. 134.

62 Wilson, *Communal Rituals of Nyakyusa*, p. 185.

63 B. A. Pauw, *Religion in a Tswana Chiefdom* (London: Oxford University Press, 1960), p. 40.

64 *Ibid.*, p. 39.

65 I. Schapera, "Christianity and the Tswana," *Cultures and Societies of Africa*, p. 494.

66 Messenger, *Continuity and Change in African Culture*, pp. 289–290.

67 T. T. S. Hayley, *The Anatomy of Lango Religion and Groups* (Cambridge: The University Press, 1947), p. 9.

68 Messenger, *Continuity and Change in African Culture*, pp. 293–294. Dammann also calls attention to examples of the use of the Bible as a fetish. Ernst Dammann, *Das Christentum in Africa* (München: Sibenstern Taschenbuch Verlag, 1968), p. 136.

69 Messenger, *Continuity and Change in African Culture*, p. 299.

70 E. E. Evans-Pritchard, *Witchcraft, Oracles and Magic among the Azande* (Oxford: The Clarendon Press, 1937), p. 63. See also Nadel, *Nupe Religion*, pp. 166, 201.

71 See again Chapter II.

72 Smith, *Golden Stool*, pp. 210–211.

73 Phillips seems to misunderstand African concepts of witchcraft when he states that "any appearance of sacred sanction for such things would be deplorable." He emphasizes that "the Old Testament condemns witchcraft." It is important to recognize that African culture also condemns witchcraft. The issue is not *whether* witchcraft is to be opposed but *how*. Missionaries have usually felt that the way to oppose it was to deny the existence of witches. Phillips rightly warns against such an attitude. Godfrey E. Phillips, *The Old Testament in the World Church* (London: Lutterworth Press, 1942), pp. 125–127.

74 Andersson, *Churches at Grass-Roots*, pp. 141, 210. Unlike Andersson, Debrunner does not make a personal determination of the matter. However, he testifies to the fact that missionaries have generally denied the reality of witchcraft. H. Debrunner, *Witchcraft in Ghana* (Accra: Presbyterian Book Depot, 1959), pp. 135–142.

75 Andersson, *Churches at Grass-Roots*, p. 47.

76 Wilson, *Communal Rituals among Nyakyusa*, p. 182.

77 Debrunner also accepts the possibility that witches exist: "Do witches exist? Anybody having read this study will agree with me that there is no simple answer to the question. Parapsychological phenomena may have to be investigated; the solid reality of neurosis must be dealt with and the social implications of the belief must be tackled." Debrunner, *Witchcraft in Ghana*, p. 174.

78 Smith, *Religion of Lower Races*, p. 17. Smith is not always consistent. In his book *Exploration in Africa* he calls the slave trade "the greatest of its [Africa's] old plagues." Edwin W. Smith, ed., *Exploration in Africa* (London: J. M. Dent and Sons, 1929), p. 11.

79 A much more helpful book is that of Debrunner. It may not serve as a final statement, but it is a start toward a new approach for the Church. Debrunner perceives that the success of the sects and anti-witchcraft shrines comes principally from their personal contact and personal attention toward the diseased. He calls for Christianity to heed their example. Debrunner, *Witchcraft in Ghana*, pp. 174–179.

80 In an article on "witchcraft medicine," *Inzuikizi*, written in *Africa*, in which he refuses to either affirm or deny the reality of witchcraft, Smith says: "The belief lies so deeply in them that nothing short of a reconstruction of their thought world can eradicate it." Edwin W. Smith, "*Inzuikizi*," *Africa*, VIII (October, 1935), p. 480.

81 Debrunner, *Witchcraft in Ghana*, p. 2; Andersson, *Churches at Grass-Roots*, p. 141. "Les techniques européennes n'ont pas supprimé la sorcellerie et le fétichisme." A. Doutreloux, "Prophétisme et Culture," *African Systems of Thought*, p. 236. King also affirms that witchcraft beliefs are more prevalent today than previously. Noel Q. King, *Religions in Africa* (New York: Harper & Row, 1970), p. 59.

82 Messenger, *Continuity and Change in African Culture*, p. 295.

83 Taylor, *Primal Vision*, p. 155.

84 J. H. Driberg, "The Secular Aspect of Ancestor Worship in Africa," *Supplement to the Journal of the Royal African Society*, XXXV (January, 1936), pp. 1–22.

85 See again Chapter VII.

86 The same problem of terminology is seen in the discussion of whether African Traditional Religion should be characterized as monotheism or polytheism. Once again Smith avoids sharp distinctions.

87 It may well be that Mbiti and Taylor draw this implication in their disavowal of the term "worship" as applied to the ancestors. Unfortunately they do not address themselves to the questions at issue here, and as seen earlier Taylor confuses the situation by quoting Driberg as support. Taylor, *Primal Vision*, p. 155; Mbiti, *African Religions and Philosophy*, p. 9. It is of note that Busia does not hesitate to use the expression. K. A. Busia, "Ancestor Worship," *Practical Anthropology*, VI (January-February, 1959), pp. 23–28.

88 Danquah, *Akan Doctrine of God*, pp. 183–84.

89 Sawyerr, *God: Ancestor or Creator?*, pp. 16, 56, 90.

90 Here Tempels is helpful. Tempels, *Philosophie Bantoue*, pp. 39–45.

91 For a discussion of the values of "ancestor worship" but also an affirmation that the traditional view cannot be simply taken over as is into Christianity, see Peter Beyerhaus, "The Christian Approach to Ancestor Worship," *Ministry*, VI (July, 1966), pp. 137–145.

92 In such a case the saints would include family members who have gone on before. Laroche prefers to confine the saints to those so defined by the Church. R. Laroche, "Some Traditional African Religions and Christianity," *Christianity in Tropical Africa*, p. 299. Hastings is more open on the question. Adrian Hastings, *Church and Mission in Modern Africa* (London: Burns and Oates, 1967), p. 67.

93 See again the discussion in Chapter VII.

94 Smith, *Secret of the African*, p. 139.

95 Van der Merwe, *Shona Idea of God*. p. 34.

96 *Ibid.*
97 Schapera, *Cultures and Societies of Africa*, p. 494.
98 Van der Merwe, *Shona Idea of God*, p. 35.
99 Mitchell, *African Systems of Thought*, p. 202.
100 Messenger, *Continuity and Change in African Culture*, p. 292.
101 Joseph Thiam, "Du clan tribal à la communauté chrétienne," *Des prêtres noirs s'interrogent* (Paris: Les Editions du Cerf, 1957), p. 53; E. Bolaji Idowu, *Towards an Indigenous Church* (London: Oxford University Press, 1965), p. 13; T. A. Beetham, *Christianity and the New Africa* (London: Pall Mall Press, 1967), p. 74.
102 E. Bolji Idowu, "Introduction," *Biblical Revelation and African Beliefs*, p. 9.
103 Taylor, *Growth of Church in Buganda*, pp. 214–215.
104 Taylor, *Primal Vision*, p. 88.
105 *Ibid.*, p. 89.
106 *Ibid.*, p. 90.
107 The danger is softened somewhat by the African failure to understand the missionary conception of salvation. Andersson, *Churches at Grass-Roots*, p. 149.
108 Idowu, *Towards an Indigenous Church*, pp. 44–45.
109 Christian G. Baëta, "Conflict in Mission: Historical and Separatist Churches," *The Theology of the Christian Mission*, ed. by Gerald H. Anderson (Nashville: Abingdon Press, 1961), p. 293.
110 *Ibid.*
111 *Ibid.*, pp. 294–295.
112 Christian G. Baëta, *Prophetism in Ghana* (London: S.C.M. Press, 1962).
113 Christian G. Baëta, "The Challenge of African Culture to the Church, and the Message of the Church to African Culture," *Christianity and African Culture*, pp. 51–61.
114 Baëta, *The Theology of the Christian Mission*, p. 293.
115 Busia, *Africa in Search of Democracy*, p. 9. See also Busia, *African Worlds*, p. 208; Elizabeth Isichei, "Ibo and Christian Beliefs: Some Aspects of a Theological Encounter," *African Affairs*, LXVIII (April, 1969), p. 121.
116 Idowu sees the challenge of the "independents" and yet maintains a healthy criticism of them. Idowu, *Towards an Indigenous Church*, pp. 44, 47.
117 Gerhardus C. Oosthuizen, *Post-Christianity in Africa* (London: C. Hurst and Co., 1968), p. 119.
118 Beetham says: "Whether those who will most fully respond to the challenge of traditional African religion will be found within the 'historic' or the 'independent' churches it is not possible to prophesy." Beetham, *Christianity and the New Africa*, p. 76.
119 Idowu, *Towards an Indigenous Church*.
120 One of the great values of Tempels' study is his stress on the necessity of criticizing the African world-view from within rather than from without. Tempels, *Philosophie Bantoue*, pp. 115–116.
121 Welbourn, *East African Christian*, pp. 102–103.
122 Sawyerr says: "To the ultimate question 'Whence comes evil?' there is no philosophical answer." Sawyerr, *Creative Evangelism*, p. 21.
123 Idowu, *Towards an Indigenous Church*, p. 29.
124 "At the beginning, their worship was spontaneous and joyous with an unmistakable note of assurance and victory—victory over Satan, over the forces of evil, over witchcraft; victory, in fact, over all that has been hold-

ing the soul of Nigerians in spiritual thralldom. Here for the first time Nigerians heard clearly of 'the victory which overcomes the world, our faith', and saw it demonstrated." *Ibid.*, p. 43.

125 Bengt G. M. Sundkler, *Bantu Prophets in South Africa* (2nd ed.; London: Oxford University Press, 1961), pp. 220–237.

126 Welbourn, *East African Christian*, p. 102.

127 Sundkler emphasizes the effect that the personal interest of the Zionists has on their adherents: "One must acknowledge the zeal and the energy of the Zionists, and their personal interest in those who have fallen ill. . . . The personal interest shown in the patient by prophesying and urgent prayer has a strong attraction." Sundkler, *Bantu Prophets*, p. 236.

128 "The most significant elements in these movements are that they seek to fulfill that which is lacking in the European-led churches, that is, to give Africans a form of worship which will 'satisfy' both spiritually and emotionally, and to make Christianity cover every area of human life and fulfill all human needs." Idowu, *Christianity in Tropical Africa*, pp. 434–435.

129 Andersson notes the tendency to elevate Kimbangu beyond the stature of a human teacher to one of messianic significance, resulting in a confusion of the prophet with the Trinity. Efraim Andersson, *Messianic Popular Movements in the Lower Congo* (Uppsala: Almquist-Wilkells, 1958), pp. 193–196.

130 Andersson says that in dogma and biblical orientation Kimbangu was orthodox but his ritualistic practices included pre-Christian elements. *Ibid.*, p. 60. Van Wing is much more reserved; he insists that the prophet shared the errors of his successors. J. van Wing, "Le Kibangisme vu par un témoin," *Zaïre: Belgian African Review*, XII, No. 6 (1958), p. 618.

131 Harold W. Fehderau, "Kimbanguism: Prophetic Christianity in Congo," *Practical Anthropology*, IX (July-August, 1962), p. 164. See also Andersson, *Messianic Popular Movements in the Lower Congo*, p. 56; van Wing, "Le Kibangisme vu par un témoin," p. 569.

132 Andersson, *Messianic Popular Movements in the Lower Congo*, pp. 52–56; P. H. J. Lerrigo, "The 'Prophet' Movement in Congo," *International Review of Missions*, XI (April, 1922), p. 272.

133 van Wing, "Le Kibangisme," p. 575; Fehderau, "Kimbanguism: Prophetic Christianity in Congo," p. 164; Doutreloux, *African Systems of Thought*, p. 233.

134 The main problem is the relationship of the founder to the Spirit, specifically whether Kimbangu was the incarnation of the Holy Spirit. Gilis notes that in several Kimbanguist hymns, the prophet occupies the place of the Holy Spirit. Charles A. Gilis, *Kimbangu: Fondateur d'Eglise* (Bruxelles: Editions de la Libraire Encyclopédique, 1960), p. 104. It is of significance that the "Little Catechism" of the EJCSK (Kimbanguist Church headed by J. Diangienda, third son of Simon Kimbangu) identifies the prophet with the Paraclete of John 14–16. However, the doctrinal situation is perplexing because that same "Little Catechism" expressly denies that Kimbangu is God, in spite of the fact that some of the syncretistic sects of Kimbanguism have said this. For a French translation of the "Little Catechism," see Paul Raymaekers, "L'Eglise de Jesus Christ sur la Terre par le prophète Simon Kimbangu," *Zaïre: Belgian African Review*, XIII, No. 7 (1959), pp. 737–738.

135 Gilis, *Kimbangu: Fondateur d'Eglise*, p. 82.

136 Fehderau, "Kimbanguism: Prophetic Christianity in Congo," p. 171.

137 Sawyerr, *Creative Evangelism*, p. 117.

138 Andersson perceives that the ambiguity of the African view of God as good and bad is resolved by the Christian affirmation of God's goodness: "The conclusion reached in this discussion is that both sides are represented in the nature of the Supreme God. Life and all the good things come from him; therefore he is good. But death, the incarnation of evil, comes from him too, therefore he is wicked. . . . In Christianity this contradiction in God's nature is abolished. For the Christian no doubt exists. Since Nzambi is charity, He is naturally also absolute goodness, and He demands a corresponding quality on the part of His worshippers." Andersson, *Churches at Grass-Roots*, pp. 113–114.

139 Taylor, *Primal Vision*, pp. 202–203. The meaning of the Incarnation, according to Sawyerr, is that God stands with us in the hour of suffering. Sawyerr, *Creative Evangelism*, p. 77.

140 Taylor, *Primal Vision*, p. 89.

141 Dammann rightly insists that God remain free in Africa as elsewhere. Damman, *Das Christentum in Afrika*, p. 134.

Conclusion

1 Oliver, *Missionary Factor in East Africa*, p. 291.